BRICKWORK

BRICKWORK

ARCHITECTURE AND DESIGN

ANDREW PLUMRIDGE
&
WIM MEULENKAMP

HARRY N. ABRAMS, INC., PUBLISHERS

To Gwyn Headley

Conceived and produced by Breslich & Foss, London

Project Editors: Tessa Rose, Laura Wilson, Catriona Woodburn
Editorial Consultant (Technical Section and Glossary):
David Webb, Royal Institute of British Architects
Illustrations: Richard Dixon, Royal Institute of British Architects
Designer: Roger Daniels
The additional information provided by Richard Dixon and
Philippa Lewis is gratefully acknowledged.

Library of Congress Cataloging-in-Publication Data
Plumridge, Andrew.
Brickwork: architecture and design/by Andrew Plumridge
and Wim Meulenkamp.
    p.   cm.
ISBN 0-8109-3123-0
1. Building, Brick.   2. Bricks.   I. Meulenkamp, Wim.   II. Title.
TH1301.P55   1993
693'.21—dc20   92-24191
                                                          CIP

Published in 1993 by Harry N. Abrams, Incorporated, New York
A Times Mirror Company

Printed and bound in Hong Kong

CONTENTS

INTRODUCTION

The principal building material of the world, bricks are rectangular units of clay mixed with sand and fired in a kiln or baked in the sun. The size of these units can vary widely, although, as a very general rule, if you can lift it with one hand, it is a brick, and if you have to use two, it is a block, even if it is made of clay. This is still the usual material for a brick, although concrete has become more popular in recent years. Whether it is kiln-fired or sun-dried, hand-made or machine-made, it makes no difference—it is still a brick.

Brickwork is intended for all those interested in our built environment. Our aim has been to cover all aspects of brick, presenting examples of excellent building from all over the world to demonstrate its capabilities, provide the technical principles of brickwork and, hopefully, to inspire both professional and amateur builders and architects. We hope to have written a study that is less lopsided than other books on the subject. From the late 19th century onwards, literature on brick has frequently been nationally biased, with each country presenting their own architecture as the epitome of brick building. The question of which nation was the first to use modern-type bricks was as hotly disputed as the origins of the printing press or the Gothic style.

Brick is a vast subject. The choices made in this book were sometimes guided by personal preference, but we have tried to include examples which look at brick buildings afresh, to avoid ending up with the standard fare of the architectural student. However, some buildings are, deservedly, classics and must be recognized as such. Now that the 1980s have seen concrete seriously discredited as a building material, brick architecture is being re-evaluated and once more admired for its warmth and human scale. We hope this book will go some way towards aiding this process.

A.P./W.M., November 1992

THE HISTORY
OF BRICK

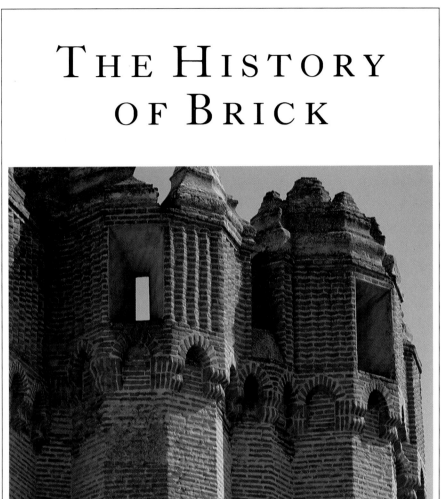

BEGINNINGS

∽

Brick has been part of man's history for several thousands of years, since prehistoric man began experimenting with dried mud and trying to solve the problems inherent in the material. The mud was slow drying, shrank dramatically when it eventually did so and cracked easily afterwards. It was discovered that these problems were lessened by mixing the mud with straw, shaping the combined materials into manageable blocks, and leaving the result to dry in the sun.

This technique of making sun-dried brick, or adobe, dates from around 5000 BC. It was known in Europe, South America, the Middle East, India, Africa and Asia, and is still used in some regions of the world, such as the remote parts of the Middle East, where wood and other materials are not available for firing bricks.

The sun-dried brick performed tolerably well as a building material in simple and primitive dwellings, despite its irregular shape and inherent unreliability. Its limitations became increasingly apparent, however, as the need arose for different and more complex structures, such as buildings for religious purposes or defensive walls. These demanded a special method or style of building—that is, architecture—and a range of different building materials. The invention of the kiln-baked, or fired brick gave these early societies a valuable new material which could help them give expression to their cultural identity.

The Mesopotamians and the Indus Valley culture in India are jointly credited with the invention of the fired brick. The earliest examples of fired bricks and kilns known to exist in the world, dating from between 2500 and 2000 BC, have been found in both areas. During its 800 years of existence (2500–1700 BC) the Indus Valley culture developed a notable brick architecture. Unusually, this was in domestic housing. The towns of Mohenjo-daro and Harappa, for example, had extensive and exceptionally fine domestic housing, most of which was in fired brick, but no temples or palaces. The technique of making fired brick was lost with the collapse of the culture in 1700 BC, and had to be re-learned many centuries later. When fired brick reappeared in Indian architecture, in the last three centuries BC, it was used not only in houses but also in pavilions, towers, shrines and temples.

In Mesopotamia, a complex brick architecture reached its fullest expression in the great ziggurats, or stepped towers, of the old Sumerian and Babylonian empires. These spectacular buildings, which were built as shrines, usually consisted of a long flight of steps leading up to a terrace which supported a tower of three or four storeys, each one smaller than the one beneath it. The shrine itself was situated in the top elevation. The height of these towers varied but is estimated at between 50 and 300 ft (15–90 m). The best-known examples are those of Babylon, the fabled Tower of Babel, and Ur. The latter was built by Ur-Nammu, the self-styled "King of the Four Quarters of the World", around 2300 BC. The remains of the tower reveal that both sun-dried and fired bricks were used in its construction, the sun-dried variety providing

the core of the building and fired brick the outer facing. Several layers of reed matting separated the two materials to reduce the danger of shrinkage.

The Mesopotamian cultures also used brick for ornamenting their sacred buildings. In the temple of the goddess Innin found at Uruk (c.1400 BC) the façade of the brick building is decorated with shapes, also in brick, including human figures set in niches. Similar reliefs have been found at Susa. Perhaps the most

spectacular example of this type of decoration is the Ishtar Gate, built in Babylon by Nebuchadnezzar II (604–562 BC). The façade of the building—part of which is now in the Vorderasiatisches Museum, Berlin—is covered in huge figures of bulls, lions and dragons modelled in relief. Each figure is composed of individually cast and brightly glazed bricks.

Nebuchadnezzar was immensely proud of his architectural achievements which included,

Above: *These steps from the ziggurat at Ur demonstrate the astonishing uniformity of shape and colour achieved by early brickmakers using primitive methods.*

impact on the Etruscans either and they continued to use stone for their burial chambers and wood, rubble and clay (sometimes baked) for their houses. However, the Etruscans furthered building techniques with terracotta and were the first to create decorative slabs for facing walls. They also used terracotta for wall reliefs. Fired brick had to wait until the emergence of the Romans for the next major phase in its development.

ROME AND BYZANTIUM

During the time of the Roman Republic sun-dried brick faced with stucco was the most popular method of building, especially for private houses. The main advantage of sun-dried brick over other materials was its low cost, a factor which ensured its popularity until the time of the Empire, despite its unreliability.

It is thought that the Romans also acquired knowledge of fired brick with their conquest of the Etruscans. The growth of the Republic into an Empire brought a corresponding aggrandizement in Rome's self-image. Emperor Augustus (69 BC–AD 27), under whose rule the Empire flourished, claimed to have found Rome a city of brick and left it a city of marble, but this statement is misleading. Marble was used to great effect, but solely as decorative cladding. Evidence of the ubiquity of brick was usually hidden from the eye by a generous layer of plaster or some other, similar, covering. Even the brickwork of the housing projects at Ostia (2nd century

Left: *Ostia, Italy, c. 3rd-century AD. A brick-built shop below a multi-storey tenement block, featuring shallow brick arches.*

Far right: The coffered interior of the dome of the Pantheon, Rome, creates spectacular effects of light and shade.

AD) was plastered over. There are a few notable exceptions to this general rule, such as the Castra Praetoria (AD 21–23), which is considered to be the first public building constructed in concrete with a fired brick facing.

The principal building materials of the Empire were fired brick and concrete, which were used in conjunction to form the core of the building. The brick was primarily used as strengthening and inserted into the concrete. The bricks used for this purpose were irregular in shape, often triangular. The Pantheon (AD 118–128), regarded as the greatest of all the surviving Roman temples, owes the success of its giant dome to a structure of concrete and brick.

Although brick was not valued by the Romans as a material for decorative purposes, their craftsmen achieved some wonderful effects with it nonetheless. Beautiful patterns in brick are to be found beneath the plaster and marble facings that have fallen away from many of the tombs along the Via Appia Antica; the intricate detailing in both terracotta and brick on the Annia Regilla tomb (c. AD 175) is a perfect example.

The Romans have left evidence of how their brickmaking enterprises were organized, both at home and in the occupied territories of the Empire. In rural areas, kilns were usually estate-owned and provided bricks as they were required, either by the villa owner or perhaps by people living in small settlements nearby. Only the larger kilns were run as commercial undertakings. In addition, there were imperial brickworks which were primarily responsible

for providing materials for public building projects and fortifications. During the reigns of the emperors Trajan and Hadrian (2nd century AD), however, there occurred a building boom which encouraged these works to expand and sell their products to private individuals at relatively low prices. This expansion lasted until the upsurge petered out during the 3rd century AD and the industry collapsed.

In most of the occupied territories of the Empire which had the materials necessary for making bricks (clay and sand) the industry flourished. Where there was an absence of these raw materials, such as Asia Minor, the Romans turned to quarried stone. Many of the occupying legions owned kilns and mass-produced bricks for public buildings as well as military installations. Brick stamps found in the Netherlands indicate that some legions both produced their own bricks and "imported" them from the kilns of other legions. In some occupied areas, such as Belgium, however, the evidence of legionary involvement in brickmaking is notable for its absence. Bricks were also exported from the Italian mainland: in Dalmatia, for example, bricks were made locally by both privately owned and imperial brickworks, yet many tiles and bricks were shipped across the Adriatic from Italy.

Many Roman bricks were stamped either with the mark of the manufacturer or the user. Accidental markings have also been found on both bricks and tiles, such as the imprints of sandals or of cattle, dogs and cats. Most interesting of all is the graffiti: obscene verse,

Above: *Roman bricks have been incorporated into the doorway of Anglo-Saxon Brixworth Church in Northamptonshire, England.*

sketches, complaints such as *Austalis dibus XIII vagatur sib cotidum* ("Austalis has been going off by himself every day for these thirteen days"), and remarks like *Satis* ("enough"), possibly indicating the end of a batch of bricks.

The 4th-century Aula Palatina, or audience hall, of the Constantinian palace at Trier is one of the last major buildings built by the Romans. Entirely faced with brick, it is a symbol of the gradual shift of power away from the declining Roman Empire to the subjugated peoples of western Europe. Several centuries would pass before these peoples came to establish their own distinctive style of architecture. In the meantime, the imperial buildings would be plundered for materials which were then recycled and used in tentative explorations towards a new architecture.

Byzantium became heir to much of the glory and wealth of Rome after the decline of the empire in the west. An architecture of arches, vaults and domes in brick was already replacing the Greek post-and-lintel style in stone before the move to Byzantium. However, a wholly new Christian style did not become established until the reign of Justinian (527–65), who was responsible for initiating some of the greatest examples of Byzantine architecture. Two of these were built during his attempt to win back the western part of the old empire: the churches of San Vitale at Ravenna (c. 526–47), a double-octagon of rather oriental appearance, and the nearby San Apollinare in Classe (c. 536–50). Both are predominantly brick, made from clay found in the nearby river delta, and both display the technique of light brick vault construction for which Byzantine architecture is noted. This expertise produced the major architectural innovation of the period, the pendentive, which enabled builders to dome over a plan of any shape. One of the most impressive examples can be seen in the church of Hagia Sophia (532–37) in Constantinople (now Istanbul). The 100 ft wide, 180 ft high (31 × 55 m) dome is built entirely of brick and owes its success to the lightness of the material.

The large building programme of the Byzantines brought a renaissance in brick decoration. Walls were thinner than previous construction techniques had allowed and could be readily pierced with openings for windows. The surrounds provided a perfect frame for decorative reliefs in brick as well as marble, mosaic and stone. Seven hundred years later, in medieval Europe, interest in Byzantine ideas would awaken an enthusiasm for lavish ornamentation on buildings.

Furthest east, in Iraq, the large palace of Ctesiphon (550) showed that the cultures of the Middle East were at least the equals of the Romans as brick builders. In particular, the blind arcading and arched vaulting would serve as models for the Persians and Turks to emulate.

THE MIDDLE AGES

A new social order was slow to emerge after the collapse of the Roman Empire in the west. The fine arts were held in a state of suspended

Below: *San Tirso, Sahagun, Spain. The blind and interlaced arcading on the apse is a characteristic feature of Romanesque architecture.*

animation for several centuries until Charlemagne's establishment of the feudal system ended the chaos and the interminable warring among petty kings. Under Charlemagne there was a revival of interest in classical culture and a resurgence of building in brick in the areas which formed the major part of the Carolingian empire, namely northern France, Germany and the Netherlands. The brick used in these areas was of the Roman type, thin and almost square in format. The early 9th-century Einhard basilica at Steinbach reveals that it was used in pillars, window and door surrounds and for strengthening masonry. Some of the brick was manufactured locally.

In England, evidence of a revival in brickmaking dates from around the 10th century, with the Saxons modelling their bricks on those found at Roman sites. The abbey-church of St Albans, built by Abbot Ealdred around 900, has Roman-type brick, as does the 11th-century Colchester castle. Large numbers of bricks were required to keep pace with the surge in ecclesiastical building in the western part of the old empire, and this led to the practice of recycling bricks and to the plundering of Roman temples and mausoleums for materials; the window and door surrounds in Brixworth church, for example, are alleged to be of genuine Roman brick.

In some parts of Europe the technique of brickmaking remained an established craft after the demise of the Romans. The Lombards, for example, had long made good use of rich deposits of river clay, developing a fine brick architecture, most notably in Milan. In Spain, Moorish architects and craftsmen had

Previous Page:
Commissioned in 1453 by Don Alonso de Fonseca, Bishop of Avila, the brick fortress of Coca Castle, northern Spain, is a superb example of Mudéjar architecture.

used Islamic brick techniques to great effect before the re-conquest. Many of these craftsmen remained in Spain and greatly influenced the architecture of their new masters. The 12th-century brick church of San Tirso at Sahagun in Spain is representative of this influence with its decoration of blind arcading, friezes and different bonds.

Who invented the modern brick and precisely when is not clear: several stories have grown up around its origins. The most unlikely concerns a Danish monk who is supposed to have hit upon the idea of using brick for the Dannewark, a defensive wall erected by King Waldemar around 1160. The Lombards and the Spaniards have also been suggested as originators, but neither claim stands close examination. The Lombards were still using the flat Roman brick when the new brick first appeared in the 12th century; and the Spanish had no knowledge of the tufa blocks on which the format of the north European brick seems to have been based. (Tufa was the commonest of the many types of building stone used by the Romans. Grey in colour, it was formed from volcanic dust.) The Germans would seem to have the best claim, for it is in northern Germany that the earliest examples of buildings in the new brick can be found, dating from around 1150. In the Netherlands building in brick started some eighty years later, according to an ancient chronicle in the province of Friesland. This states that the building of a new abbey took place in 1238, "the third year of building in brick".

The main agents responsible for bringing Christianity to northern Europe, the Cistercians and Premonstratensians, had much to do with spreading building techniques in the new brick. One important style which they introduced was the so-called Backsteingotik (brick gothic). The term "brick gothic" is perhaps something of a misnomer, because the style retained many of the characteristics of the Romanesque and later proved very adaptable, even to the frills of the late-gothic style.

The Stiftskirche at Jerichow (c. 1150) in northeastern Germany is one of the earliest examples of Backsteingotik. The decoration is very subdued and limited almost entirely to the arcature. The later Ratzeburg Minster (c. 1220) is much more decorative and has patterned infilling on its façade in addition to the characteristic arcading. The Backsteingotik style spread to the Rhineland, especially the area around Cologne, and in Denmark, in the region west of Copenhagen. The 12th-century St. Bendt church at Roskilde, begun by Waldemar the Great, the abbey-church at Sorø and Roskilde Minster, both built by Bishop Absalon around 1170, are among the most interesting Danish examples. Beautiful ornamentation in brick is also to be found in many of the village churches of Friesland and Groningen, the two northernmost provinces of the Netherlands; for example, at Ten Boer, Krewerd and Leermens (mostly late 12th and early 13th century). This type of design is repeated across the border, in German Ost-Friesland. By the 13th century, churches and abbeys in brick were beginning to appear in the coastal regions of Flanders.

In many areas of Europe natural stone

Left: *Ratzeburg Minster, north-eastern Germany. The plain plaster work on the cornice and gable has been used in conjunction with brickwork to accentuate the interlaced arcading.*

Below: *The immense gothic tower of the fortress-like St. Cecile cathedral at Albi in France is constructed entirely from the distinctive local pink brick.*

remained the primary building material because of its easy availability and low cost. The Swiss, for example, did not consider using brick until the end of the 19th century when mass production made building with the material economically viable. In France, the boom in brick building which occurred in northern Europe during the Middle Ages was virtually restricted to the north of the country bordering on Flanders and the clay-rich area around Calais. The two notable exceptions to this were Toulouse and Albi where, in the absence of natural stone, a distinctive pink brick architecture developed.

Among the first towns in northern Europe to use the new brick in buildings other than churches were the Hanseatic ports of northern Germany and the Baltic. Needless to say, it was the wealthy burghers who took the lead, eschewing the traditional wood for their houses and offices. This trend was accelerated by a revision of the town laws which attempted to make buildings less of a fire hazard by banning the use of straw for roofing and wood for supports. Brick was shown to be virtually non-combustible and its use was eventually extended to town halls, hospitals, city gates and strictly utilitarian structures such as defences and harbour installations. A remarkably high degree of sophistication was achieved in the design of city gates during the Middle Ages; Neubrandenburg and the Holsten Gate at Lübeck are especially fine examples.

It is not certain how modern brick reached Britain, a country that would later become noted for its contribution to the history of brick architecture, but it was probably as a

Left: *Bands of vitrified and plain brick give a gilded effect to the impressive Holsten gate at Lübeck, Germany.*

result of the island's newly forged trading links with the Hanseatic League. The areas around the ports that traded most heavily with the League, those on the eastern and southeastern coasts, were the first to witness extensive building in brick. Some bricks came as ballast from the Low Countries and the Baltic ports, as ships' captains quickly discovered that there was a market for brick and would routinely fill up any spare capacity with the material. Only special orders and large loads of brick had to be registered with the authorities, who then levied taxes on them, so it is difficult to obtain an accurate estimate of the extent of brick imports at this time. However, accounts at Great Yarmouth for 1393 reveal that 134,500 paving tiles or floor tiles and 13,000 bricks were imported in that year. In 1408, the authorities in Newcastle registered 6,000 floor tiles, 32,000 bricks and 35,000 unspecified tegulae.

The Continental Hanseatic towns also exported their technical knowhow to England. English town records for the period reveal names such as Michael fflemyng and Baldwin Dutchman and those of other foreign brickmakers and bricklayers, many of them Dutch and German, who found work in England. However, although the techniques in early English brick building were imported, the styles that gradually emerged were entirely home-grown.

The growth of building in brick which occurred in the Middle Ages led to a radical change in the organization of the brick manufacturing industry. This now became a speculative enterprise rather than one governed by specific requests for bricks to fulfil specific projects. Permanent brickworks were established in some towns and sold their wares to private individuals as well as to the authorities responsible for municipal building. Out of this development arose one of the major problems of the brick industry in the Middle Ages, and indeed beyond—the absence of standardization. No two brickmakers could produce the same bricks in terms of size and quality. Incredibly, this problem would not be finally eradicated until the late 19th century, despite legislation introduced in the Middle Ages.

Right: *The Cathedral of Santa Maria dell'Assunta (rebuilt 1008) at Torcello, Italy, has a Ravenna-type basilica with a monumental brick apse.*

The price of brick was gradually regulated too. In 14th-century England, for example, the price of a thousand bricks ranged from two shillings and three pence to eight shillings. By the following century the margin had narrowed to between four and six shillings per thousand. Bricklayers earned between three and five pence per day in the 14th century, four to six pence in the 15th century and up to one shilling per day in the 16th century.

THE RENAISSANCE LEGACY

Throughout much of Renaissance Italy, brick was employed as it had been since the time of the Romans for structural purposes and hidden beneath cladding of natural stone (usually marble), stucco or plaster. Brunelleschi's building projects in Rome and Florence bear testimony to this, as do the immaculate country houses and churches built by Palladio in and around Vicenza.

Northern Italy, where clay was readily available and the use of brick was as widespread as in northwestern Europe, offered greater scope for innovation. Here, a style emerged which married Renaissance-inspired design with northern building techniques. The key feature of the style was its terracotta ornamentation. In some examples—such as the 15th-century Palazzo dei Tribunale at Piacenza—brick façades are busy with friezes of images such as garlands, festoons, charioteers, heads and monsters. In others the treatment is more restrained but no less effective; examples include the rotunda church of Sta Maria della Croce at Crema, built by Giovanni Battagio in the 1490s, and churches in Modena, Ferrara and Piacenza. In the Palazzo Fava, Bologna, the terracotta ornamentation is used to emphasize the structural elements of the brick building and is a notable departure from the vogue for rusticated stone or marble facings.

In France the use of terracotta was re-established in the 16th century by Italian majolica potters who settled there. These craftsmen perfected a tin-enamelled ware and called it faience, after the Italian city of Faenza where they originated. Girolamo della Robbia (nephew of the famous Luca who was responsible for the magnificent terracotta work in the Duomo in Florence) was one of the settlers and would go on to produce what is arguably one of the best examples of French terracotta work, on Francis I's Chateau de Madrid in the Bois de Boulogne. Later, at the court of Versailles, the popularity of Italian-inspired terracotta work would encourage the aristocracy to use it on their country houses.

The spread of demand for architectural ornaments in terracotta led to the establishment of terracotta workshops outside Italy. One of the most important of these was set up in Lübeck, Germany, by Statius van Düren. The skills required to make terracotta were not always successfully passed on to native craftsmen, however. In Tudor England, for example, patrons had to employ Italians to do the work for them.

Nowhere was the assimilation of Renaissance motifs into native traditions done with greater exuberance and originality than in the

Low Countries. The so-called "Dutch Renaissance style", also called Dutch Mannerism, alternated horizontal bands of stone with rows of brick, and used strapwork and scrollwork with great effect on the gables. The books of ornamental patterns produced by the Flemish architect Hans Vredeman de Vries (1527–1606) provided the inspiration for much of the strapwork and scrollwork. The Flemish architect Lieven de Key was responsible for arguably the finest example of the Dutch Mannerist style, the Meat Hall at Haarlem (1602–3).

Other examples of the style can be found in the small but very wealthy port towns along the Dutch Zuiderzee, in Flanders and the Rhineland. Mannerist ornamentation was particularly favoured too in areas with a tradition of Backsteingotik, such as the Baltic town of Danzig (now Gdansk) in Poland which employed scores of Dutch architects and bricklayers.

The brick architecture of Denmark and Sweden also relied on the skills and ideas of Flemish, Dutch and German architects and craftsmen. Their influence is evident in churches, palaces, amenity buildings and the lesser domestic architecture; the castle of Frederiksborg (1602–20) and the Exchange (1619–25), both in Copenhagen and by the Dutch architects Hans and Laurens van Steenwinckel, are notable examples.

Ornamentation was also a key element in the distinct national styles of architecture that developed in Russia and Greece. Both styles had evolved from Byzantine beginnings. The main characteristics of the Russian vernacular were florid decoration, especially of doorways and window surrounds, and a dogged disregard for structural finesse. The style was eventually taken to an extreme bordering on parody and is seen at its most grotesque in the churches of the Trinity at Ostankino (1668), and St John the Baptist at Yaroslavl (1671–87). In mainland Greece the use of brick as exterior decoration had a long tradition: in the best examples, such as the 11th-century Hosias Lukas at Phocis, window surrounds, friezes and roof tiles all served simply to set off the quarried stone.

Below: *The Meat Hall at Haarlem in The Netherlands, by Lieven de Key (1602–1603), has a characteristically ornate brick and stone stepped gable.*

Below: *St. Basil's Cathedral, Moscow, is an elaborate fusion of eastern and western shapes, with onion-shaped domes alongside semi-circular and pointed arches.*

Right: *Layer Marney, Essex, England. This grand gatehouse was made for a house that was never built. It has a virtuoso display of black brick diapering and string courses of cut gothic leaf-work with Renaissance-style terracotta moulding on the windows.*

Far right: *Ann Boleyn's gatehouse at Hampton Court, Surrey, England, showing terracotta detailing, including Cardinal Wolsey's coat of arms and two roundels of Roman emperors. The façade is lavishly decorated with diaper work.*

Skills in brickwork developed apace in England during the Tudor period. Chimneys, in particular, presented the designer and bricklayer—often one and the same person—with an opportunity for showing off their expertise. Detailing became increasingly sophisticated and there developed a marked preference for octagonal, hexagonal and especially spiral designs over simple motifs such as squares and circles. The brick for the chimney shaft would either be cut or moulded into lozenges, zigzags, chevrons and other geometrical forms. Several different patterns were often employed in the same chimney. This technique was also applied to whole buildings; Leez Priory and the eight-storey brick Layer Marney Tower in Essex, England, are particularly fine examples.

The craftsmen required to carry out such intricate work were sometimes found in the most unlikely situations. When William Leighton, a judge at Shrewsbury Assizes, was looking for the best candidate to build his chimneys at Plaish Hall, Longville, Shropshire, he was advised that the man in question was a sheepstealer who the judge had recently sentenced to death. Without more ado the man was released from prison and put to work on the chimneys. Plaish Hall is considered an exceptional piece of brick architecture by some commentators. Unfortunately for the sheep-stealer-cum-craftsman, his workmanship did not save him from the gallows.

Domestic building was given a boost early in the 16th century by Henry VIII's decision to confiscate and subsequently redistribute land and property previously held by the Church. The wealthy men who benefited from Henry's action set about building great houses on their newly acquired estates. These houses were typically built in brick with terracotta decoration. The most striking example is Sutton Place, Surrey (1525–26) which was inspired by the elaborate terracotta enrichment of the gatehouse at Layer Marney Towers in Essex. In both houses the flamboyance of the structural decoration marks a departure from the usual restrained use of the material and gives an effect which would have been impossible to accomplish in coarse Tudor brickwork. The decoration in Henry VIII's Hampton Court is almost subdued in comparison, and only the roundels of Roman emperors, by Giovanni da Maiano, lift the work to the level of Sutton Place and Layer Marney.

Below: *Rusticated window frames and moulded pilasters at Kew Palace, London.*

The style adopted for English manor houses and palaces in the Elizabethan period was essentially Tudor with dressings of Vredeman de Vries-type strapwork. Genuine innovation in English brick architecture did not occur until the arrival of the Dutch gable. One of the first houses to incorporate curving Dutch gabling was Kew Palace (also known as "Dutch House"), built in 1631. Another important Dutch innovation at Kew was the gauged (or rubbed) brickwork, which was introduced for the pilasters and door and window openings. This encouraged the use of brick decoration for its own sake on English houses. Two examples, Cromwell House, Highgate (c. 1650) and Tyttenhanger Park, near St Albans (c. 1654), possess quite extraordinary central windows with carved window frames. Domestic brick architecture in Britain was set for a splendid 18th century.

THE AGE OF ELEGANCE

Architecture had become an increasingly demanding profession by the 18th century, with new techniques, more specialization and a voluminous literature. The status of the profession was raised by the emergence of gentlemen-architects such as Sanderson Miller and Freiherr Friedrich Wilhelm von Erdmannsdorff. The vast majority of architects, though, were drawn from the ranks of masons and bricklayers. These men were often both craftsmen and scholars. The bricklayer Venturus Mandey, for example, wrote and published several books on mathematics and also translated into English a number of Italian books and pamphlets on architecture. The age abounded with publications like *The Builder's Jewel* (1741), and the Dutch *De Aloude Metzelwerken* or *Old Masonry* (1775) which provided craftsmen with a fund of information such as tables of measurements, prices of materials and outlines of architectural styles.

Until the late 18th century brought an improvement in transport links between centres of population and outlying areas, brick was mainly reserved for use in churches, palaces, the manor and town houses of the wealthy and some commercial and public buildings. The subsequent sharp drop in transport costs allowed the material to be used in small rural houses and cottages and brick production boomed as a result.

In England the price of ordinary brick held steady at fifteen shillings per thousand, with the price of the best products ranging between twenty and fifty shillings per thousand. The wages of the labourers who produced the bricks were not high. Neve, in his *The City and Country Purchaser* (1703), quotes six pence per thousand for the moulder, four pence for the "bearer off", four pence for "he that tempers the earth" and six pence for "he that digs it". In the country it would cost five shillings per thousand bricks for "making the earth ready (after it is digged, the digging not being reckoned in the making), moulding, bearing off and burning". In London the same exercise would cost six shillings. Production had risen to between nine and ten thousand bricks per day. A bricklayer with one assistant could lay between one thousand and fifteen hundred bricks in a day. Specialist work—front walling as opposed to foundations, inner walls and barns—took longer and reduced the number of bricks laid to about five hundred per day. The daily rate for such labour ranged from between two and four shillings for the bricklayer and between one shilling nine pence and two shillings for his assistant.

Taxation was a burden everywhere in Europe. In the German states, for example, levies were put on virtually everything that crossed their frontiers, including bricks. The towns and autonomous provinces of the Dutch Republic used import duties to protect local brick manufacturers from outside competition. The 1757 duties list for the province of Holland included some forty different kinds of brick from other Dutch provinces and abroad which were subject to levies ranging from seven stiver per thousand to one guilder thirteen stiver (for British brick).

Other ways were also found to minimize unwelcome competition. In Amsterdam, for example, only goods listed in the town's statute book could be sold there. Needless to say, local manufacturers were favoured at the expense of outsiders. In 1748, a brick manufacturer from Groningen protested to the council about the unfairness of omitting his products from the list when he had gone to great lengths to ensure that his bricks were equal in quality to those produced by his rivals in the river regions around Amsterdam. His complaint fell on deaf ears, however, and his bricks remained unlisted.

In Britain the imposition of a brick tax in 1784 temporarily checked the brick boom and encouraged the labouring classes to return to traditional materials such as stone and wood. The initial levy was two shillings and six pence per thousand. By 1803 the tax had risen to five shillings per thousand. Manufacturers attempted to offset some of the effects of the tax by increasing the thickness of each brick from about two and a half inches to three inches. This move was cleverly countered by the authorities in 1803 when they doubled the tax on bricks exceeding 150 cu in (2548 cu cm).

Brick tiles, which became increasingly popular during the 18th century, were exempt from taxation. Despite being little more than a building cosmetic, they required specialist labour to erect them and this could be expensive. When professionally applied, brick tiles could look remarkably like solid brickwork; some experts have been fooled by them. One reason put forward for the development of brick tiles is that they were a relatively inexpensive way of applying a facelift to a house. The 18th century was an age in which owners were obsessed by the need for keeping abreast of the latest architectural fashion. Brick tiles could also be used to provide a weatherproof and fireproof protective covering to otherwise flammable timber structures. The tiles could be affixed by nailing them over timber battens or they could be embedded in a cement or plaster render.

The manor house received a facelift during the 18th century when simplicity and, above all, "taste" became the watch-words of a new idea in architectural style, replacing ostentation and conspicuous wealth. This enthusiasm for the natural and unfrivolous led to the promotion of plain red brick for country houses, especially in Britain and the Low Countries. The equally taste-oriented Palladians, however, objected to the colour and started a parallel fashion for pale-yellow brick. Tudor Mannerism gave way to the subdued elegance of the broad brick front, which provided ample opportunity for superb workmanship in the handling of infills, arches, window surrounds, pilasters and friezes. The versatility in the brick building of the period is especially evident in the many small manor houses of the south-east of England.

In the larger towns of the Dutch Republic, such as Amsterdam, Leiden and Utrecht, the few remaining medieval façades were changed beyond recognition in the 18th century. Gables and doorways were emphasized by stone dressing, some of them in a garish Rococo style. Most houses, though, were given simple linear and rather austere façades with brick as the main material. The medieval supporting walls were usually retained to keep down costs. Brick had long since replaced wood as the principal building material in rural areas, in farms as well as the country houses of the wealthy merchants and relatively few aristocrats. The character of these country houses would be changed out of all recognition during the course of the 19th century by the addition of plaster.

Elsewhere the fortunes of brick were mixed. In Scandinavia the influence of Dutch and German styles waned and left a void which was filled by sound yet unexceptional building in both town and country. In northern Italy

Left: *The eye-catching porch on this early 18th-century farmhouse in Norfolk, England, has a segmental pediment of brick with a stone coat of arms and Corinthian capitals.*

brick continued to be the main building material of the towns and villages along the River Po. But in Modena, Parma and Bologna the vogue for neo-Classicism ended their long tradition of building in brick. In Toulouse in France, sumptuous brick mansions were built on the Rue de la Dalbade and Rue de la Fonderie.

In Germany Backsteinbarock (brick baroque) became popular in the traditional brick building areas of the north-east and the Rhineland. The Rüschhaus (1746) in Münster, designed by J.C. Schlaun, is a particularly inspired example. It was one of the many new domestic buildings that sprang up as part of the prince-bishop's expansion of the town. The prince-bishop of Schleswig-Holstein also adopted Backsteinbarock. The architects E.G. Sonnin and Georg Greggenhofer built palaces, manor houses, town houses and farm buildings in the style for the prince-bishop's court in and around the town of Eutin. Examples of the style can also be seen in Oldenburg-in-Holstein and Lüneburg. However, by the end of the century even these bastions of Baroque had succumbed to the influence of neo-Classicism and covered their buildings with plaster. Brick did not re-emerge as a building material worthy to stand on its own, unadorned, until the early 19th century.

The revival in brick's fortunes was partly due to the influence of an ambitious scheme embarked upon by Duke Leopold Friedrich Franz of Anhalt-Dessau, who wanted to turn his small country into a "garden state". One of the architectural styles chosen by the Duke was neo-Gothic, which had developed in Britain as early as the 1720s and initially had shared the Rococo predilection for stucco and plaster. The neo-Gothicists in Britain used brick, quarried stone or wood as basic structural materials, and then stuccoed over them to produce some fanciful resemblance to the medieval style. In the neo-Gothic style adopted for the Duke's scheme, brick was employed as a major visual as well as structural element within the design. The Gothic House (1773–1813) which stands in the park of Worlitz combines Italian and English Gothic with traditional Backsteingotik: ochre and white plaster for the canal side of the building, unadorned brick for the side overlooking the park. The self-conscious imitations of medieval brick architecture which dot the vast parkland area—churches, lodges, sham castles and stables—started a vogue that soon spread to the rest of Germany.

COLONIAL STYLE

The countries most influenced by European building styles in brick building were North America, Australia and the Indian sub-continent. In other areas of the world the manner of building was usually tailored to suit the available materials. In the Cape Colony, for example, these were stone, wood and adobe with brick a comparative rarity. Whitewash or plaster covered the façades of the few brick buildings that were built there. Brick was not used with great effect either in the Spanish and Portuguese colonies in South America or in the Dutch East Indies. In semi-colonized

Left: *In its formal garden, the Rüshhaus in Munster, Germany, has an impressive façade of brick with stone detailing.*

Shanghai, marble was preferred to brick for commercial building in the 19th and 20th centuries.

NORTH AMERICA

Although the log cabin is often thought of as a typical domestic housing for the early colonists to North America, it was a relatively late arrival, introduced by Swedish immigrants at the end of the 17th century. Brick was a major building material from the start. Among the Dutch and British colonists who sailed to America in the early 17th century were brick-makers and bricklayers who brought with them bricks as well as ready-made designs for homes and fortifications. Wood was, of course, used extensively, with bricks reserved initially

for chimney stacks and official buildings. Early on in some areas, however, brick was used structurally in domestic housing, as the following 1612 description of the settlement of Henrico, Virginia, reveals: "here . . . [the brickmen] have built competent and decent houses, the first storie all of bricks . . .".

Brickmaking had become a sizeable industry in the colonies of North America by the middle of the 17th century. The New England town of Medford was one of the centres of the new industry and supplied bricks to settlements far and wide. One of the earliest surviving examples of brick building from this period is the farmhouse built by Adam Thoroughgood near Norfolk, Virginia (1636–40).

The building techniques and architectural styles applied by English, Dutch and Flemish colonists were those of their respective homelands. Professional architects were scarce—and expensive—so much of the design work was left to master-masons and carpenters whose ideas were invariably traditional and rather out of date.

The reliance on old-fashioned styles is exemplified in many brick houses; for example, Bacon's Castle, Surrey County, Virginia (c. 1655), which is a mix of the Jacobean and Tudor. The Triangular Warehouse in Boston (c. 1680, demolished 1824), built on a triangular plan with a tower at each corner and with unusually large bricks, is notable for its medieval detailing and provides another example of how craftsmen adhered to stylistic traditions that had been forgotten in their places of origin, in this case Britain.

One of the best-known examples of 17th-

Below: *Adam Thoroughgood's farmhouse in Norfolk, Virginia, USA, is built in traditional English style.*

century brick building in North America, the Dutch-style house of Peter Sergeant, a Boston merchant, was completed in the year (1679) which saw the city devastated by the first in a series of fires. By 1722, after two more fires had swept Boston and a law had been passed outlawing all materials for domestic building other than brick and stone, one thousand out of a total of three thousand houses in the city were made of brick.

Brick prices provide a useful indication of the popularity of brick. In Philadelphia in 1685, brick prices were equivalent to those in Britain. Robert Turner, a resident of Philadelphia, had this to report about brick building in his town: "Bricks are exceedingly good, and cheaper than they were, say at 16 shillings per thousand, and brick houses are now as cheap as wood. Many brave brick houses are going up with good cellars."

The Dutch settlers in and around New Amsterdam produced bricks that were smaller than the English type, and the buildings of the Dutch settlements reflected a characteristic liking for ornamental patterns. In the modest manor-house of Fort Crailo at Rensselaer, NY (1642), both the specially imported bricks and the design are Dutch in every detail.

Even after the Dutch lost their American colonies to the British, their styles continued to be influential well into the 18th century; the Leendert Bronck House at West Coxsackie, NY, built in 1738, is a case in point. However, in the absence of the stimulus of new ideas from the Netherlands itself, at least since the late 17th century, the Dutch colonial style in America became stilted and was eventually overtaken by English architectural styles that retained their zest, even though they did arrive a little late.

As the 18th century progressed, buildings in America conformed increasingly with the style concurrent in Britain. The owner-architect of Stratford Hall in Westmorland County, Virginia (c. 1725–30), chose the Palladian style for his new house, which was built on an H-plan with bricks fired on the estate. Many other brick-built mansions sprang up, from New York to Georgia, culminating in Thomas Jefferson's Virginian projects in the last quarter of the 18th century. His own house, Monticello (built, with constant alterations, between 1770 and 1809), shows the quintessentially Jeffersonian device of a brick

Overleaf: *Thomas Jefferson's influential brick façade at Monticello became a classical American prototype.*

Below: *The combination of red and grey bricks used at Stratford Hall, Virginia, USA, provides differentiation between the lower storey and the 'piano nobile'.*

Right: *The brick gable ends of the gambrel roof at Clinton Academy, Long Island, USA (1784), contrast sharply with the clapboard façade.*

main block and wings with a white portico and friezes. Monticello and other mansions built around the same time mark the point at which American architecture ceased being wholly colonial, although trends fashionable in Britain would continue to be copied throughout the 19th century. The country now had its own professional architects and no longer had to depend on imported talent. However, it would have to wait until the late 19th century before a truly authentic American style of building, the high-rise, would emerge.

AUSTRALIA

The first brick kiln in Australia was set up in 1788 by James Bloodsworth, a brickmaker, at a place subsequently named Brickfield Hill. In that same year Bloodsworth designed and built Government House in Sydney, regarded as the first Australian brick building. Despite its crude structure, this building was functioning until almost the middle of the following century. Bloodsworth, an ex-convict pardoned in 1790, was responsible for most of the earliest brick architecture in Sydney. He rose to the position of Superintendent of Buildings and on his death in 1804 was awarded a funeral with full military honours.

Production at local kilns in and around Sydney was running at well over 150,000 bricks per month within a few years of the first ships reaching Australia. Brick soon became the staple building material in Sydney and Melbourne, although at first it was reserved for government buildings and churches.

Unlike colonial America, the architecture which was practised in Australia was influenced exclusively by British styles so that it was largely an extension of English Georgian architecture. The climate in Australia, however, necessitated different approaches both in design and building practice from those current in Britain. When exposed brickwork became fashionable in the 1840s, the result was visually uninspiring because of the generally poor quality of the brick. In the middle of the century the settlers discovered a method of building that would be adopted in other countries as well: brick veneer. Brick walls were wired to a wooden frame to produce an inexpensive but superior looking house. In the areas beyond Sydney and Melbourne, where brick was the principal building material, timber and later, sheet iron, would be the mainstays.

As in Britain, polychrome brickwork began to be used in Australia in the 1860s, but it had little impact until the quality of brick improved. Several brick-manufacturing companies in Melbourne and Sydney adopted the new steam, or dry, processing technique which allowed for a greater diversity of colours. John Reed's Independent Church at Melbourne (1867–8) was an early essay in polychrome brick. Reed and John Hurbury Hunt were the major exponents of the brick revival in Australia. The latter's St. Peter's Cathedral at Armidale, New South Wales (1875) is an excellent example of the fine decorative effects achievable with brick patterning.

By the time Australia ceased to be a colony in 1901, patrons could expect to have their buildings designed by competent architects and in bricks of the highest quality.

Below: *St. Martin's garrison church, New Delhi, India (1928–1930), has a massive, ziggurat-like simplicity.*

44

INDIA

European styles of brick architecture reached India in the 18th century. Both sun-dried and fired brick had been in use for many centuries by this time, although locally available materials such as stone, in which most of the ancient temples were built, were still heavily relied upon in many areas.

The Portuguese and Dutch had been the first to partially colonize India, building forts, warehouses and houses in their national styles. The French, Danes and British soon followed suit. In time much of the early makeshift architecture was replaced by brick or stone.

Bengal was the first area to feel the effects of the enormous increase in trade with the colonial powers. The opening of the sub-continent to the Dutch, Portuguese, Danes, French and British resulted in many local businessmen becoming very rich indeed. These men showed off their wealth by building temples, usually with elaborate terracotta inscriptions recording their names, and sometimes those of the architects and bricklayers. The architectural style of most of these temples reflects native trends, especially in its incorporation of Islamic and early Hindu motifs. The enthusiasm for brick temples characterized by elaborately decorated structures and cladding reached its zenith in the 18th century. Some temples were built in European styles and of those built in brick most were whitewashed or incorporated terracotta panels which covered the brick; where the dressings have fallen away, they reveal brickwork of a very high standard.

The small Indian brick was used to build Fort William in Kalikata, Bengal and many of the European-style buildings in towns such as Lucknow. By the end of the 18th century most of the brick conformed to the English standard in terms of size and quality. Calcutta, with its large reservoir of British brickmakers and bricklayers, became the major producer of the English standard brick in India. The improvements in brick standards gradually filtered through to the domestic architecture of the indigenous population which had hitherto relied upon the sun-dried brick; the Hindi word *pukka*, was applied to buildings in fired brick—sun-dried structures were just *cutcha*. On the whole, however, the use of brick was not discernible: the material was rendered with plaster of pink, red, blue or ochre and later in white and softer hues, the preferred colours of neo-Classicism even in India.

The 19th century brought India its share of eclecticism mixed in with what the Victorians regarded as "the Indian style": brick-cored buildings faced with impressive quarried stone. In Simla, the equivalent of Matlock Bath, some of the picturesque European buildings were timber-framed with brick infills.

Brick was in vogue again at the time of the improvements to the infrastructure of many of India's large cities. In Bombay, this resulted in such splendid High Victorian buildings as the Victoria Terminus (1878–87), by Frederick William Stevens. Other buildings designed by Stevens in the same city incorporated the most exuberant architectural elements of both cultures. However, this marriage of styles did not extend to church building. The all-brick Lahore Cathedral (1883–1914), by John Oldrid Scott, looks out of place despite a more than competent design, an unhappy transplant from some corner of rural England.

In the 20th century Edwin Lutyens, the champion of brick architecture in Britain, was chosen to shape New Delhi into a fitting monument to the British Empire. He left brick to his disciples Henry Medd and Arthur Shoosmith and selected quarried stone to convey the imperial message. Shoosmith produced what must be the most singular and impressive brick building in all India: St. Martin's garrison church (1928–30). Three and a half million bricks were used in the construction of this mighty 20th-century ziggurat, a building that is neither British nor Indian in style, but purely a monument to brick.

BRICK COMES OF AGE

∞

The 19th century gave brick architecture an unparalleled opportunity for experimentation and innovation. Huge quantities of the material were required for the new factories, commercial premises, houses, railway stations, viaducts and pumping stations that industrialization demanded. In Britain, the grid of canals that from the late 18th century onwards connected most industrial towns made it possible to transport brick in far greater quantities than before, and brick production nearly doubled between 1821 and 1840, from almost one billion to 1,725,628,333 bricks (the amount of bricks on which taxes were paid in that year). The clay for the bricks was usually dug near the site of the proposed building. Leases on land containing good clay were sought after by brickmakers and, increasingly, building speculators who were keen to cash in on the boom. Brickfields sprang up all over the country, in towns and villages as well as in and around major cities. A necessary evil, they disfigured the landscape and gave off a nauseating smell. In London the demand for brick eventually outstripped the capacity of the largely unmechanized local brick industry, and supplies had to be brought in from elsewhere in the country. This pushed up costs and provided the impetus for the development of a more economical system of manufacture.

One of the first steps in the brick manufacturing process to be mechanized was moulding. William Irving's method of wire-cutting (1841) was simple and effective. The machinery was steam-powered and consisted of a large wire frame which literally sliced up large slabs of clay into brick-sized pieces.

Most of the kilns patented by mid century were, despite their inventors' claims to the contrary, either too slow or too costly to operate. It was not until 1859 that a major advance in technology allowed the development of the revolutionary Hoffmann kiln. Conventional kilns had to be shut down after each firing and then started up again for a new batch of bricks—a laborious process and costly in terms of fuel. The Hoffmann kiln was continuously fired and had twelve chambers with a total capacity of about 40,000 bricks per firing. Uniformity of colour, texture and size could also be guaranteed; the variation between bricks that appeals so strongly to the 20th-century eye was not desirable to the Victorians. With variations and improvements,

the Hoffmann kiln became the standard type for brick manufacture in the Western world and remained so until the end of World War II.

Improved digging machinery allowed the extraction of a greater number of clay types, so increasing the variety of brick colours. The bright red brick characteristic of Victorian architecture, for example, is composed of shale extracted from coal seams. Demand was high all over Europe for hard bricks and specific colours. The Belgians specially imported a whitish brick from Silesia and exported their own bricks made from the clay in the area of the River Rupel. The need to resort to imports reduced with the introduction of chemical additives which could artificially produce bricks of the required colour and texture.

Brickmaking was still a seasonal occupation in the 19th century. The Germans, especially, had a long tradition as brickmakers and provided the rest of Europe with a huge reservoir of skilled labour. Almost the entire male population of the small central German state of Lippe-Detmold would hire itself out for the duration of the brickmaking season, from April to October. These Lippians were famous as brickmakers all over Europe and could be found working as far afield as Russia. The hours were long; a 17-hour day was typical, from three in the morning until eight at night.

In Britain, where the Industrial Revolution was in full swing, there was no need for imported labour. The volume of housing in Britain doubled during the first half of the century and would virtually double again in the second half; in 1811 there were 1,849,000 houses compared with 7,550,000 one hundred

years later. Not all these houses were built wholly of brick; in Wales and the north, for example, where natural stone was relatively cheap and easily available, brick was often restricted to "party" walls. Most of the new dwellings were artisans' cottages and back-to-back houses, built for the growing industrial workforce by cost-conscious employers. Some of the most dispiriting examples of working-class housing are to be found in northern France and southern Belgium, especially in and around Liège and in Mons and Char-leroi where the iron foundries and mines

attracted large numbers of people. The miners' settlement of Bois-du-Luc (1838–47) at La Louvière, near Mons, is a travesty of neo-Classicism. The tiny terraced houses are stripped down to the bare essentials of interlinking brick walls, a few arched windows, a bit of white stone dressing and minimal roof space. The contrast with the late-Classical elegance of the industrial complex of Le Grand Hornu (built 1820–36 by Bruno Renard), also near Mons, could not be more marked.

A different type of workers' housing can be found in the industrialized regions of the

Above: *The brick structure of Le Grand Hornu near Mons has been plastered over and painted yellow. Rusticated bases to the pillars strengthen the overall design.*

southern Netherlands and in the German Ruhr valley. Built at the end of the century, the workers' houses found here are in the neo-Renaissance style favoured by the colliery owners for their own villas. Most of the houses are semi-detached with brickwork in several colours and are set amidst flower gardens or tiny allotments. In concept these settlements were similar to the British garden cities, although cynics attributed the wide streets and simple layout to an imperative for the company's police force to be able to reach trouble spots in double-quick time rather than a genuine desire to create a pleasant environment for the workforce.

The phenomenon of "jerry-building" emerged during the 19th century and was fiercely debated until steps were taken to stamp out its worst excesses. Jerry-building was not unknown on the Continent, but the evidence suggests that building malpractice was more widespread in Britain than elsewhere. This is hardly surprising, given the pace, intensity and essentially laissez-faire nature of British industrialization. Typically, a small builder would invest his own money and labour in the construction of a few cottages or tenements. The greater the economies in building materials, the greater the profit, and with walls half-a-brick thick, or only consisting of plaster and lath on stud, it is little wonder that many jerry-built houses collapsed after only a few years. The practice flourished in the absence of effective government controls and attracted investment from all quarters. The influence of philanthropic bodies such as the Peabody Trust, dedicated to providing better housing

for working people, together with the implementation of the Public Health Act of 1875, helped curb the worst excesses of jerry-building without entirely eradicating it. The last back-to-back houses were built, illegally, in Leeds in 1937.

In the second quarter of the 19th century a major revival in brick architecture took place in Germany, notably in Berlin, where the architect Carl Friedrich Schinkel (1781–1841) created a happy fusion of opposites, most successfully of neo-Gothicism with Classicism. Schinkel's style demanded bricks of very high quality and he set up his own special kilns to ensure that he got them. Two of Schinkel's finest achievements in unfaced brick are the military barracks on Lindenstrasse (1817–18, destroyed during World War II) and the Friedrich-Werdersche Kirche (1824–30).

Schinkel also made terracotta a fashionable building material once again and used it with great effect in his neo-Classical design for the Academy of Architecture (1832–6, also destroyed during World War II). The extensive array of terracotta panels was the building's most striking feature.

Like all great figures, Schinkel had his disciples. One of the most interesting of these was Friedrich Ludwig Persius (1803–45), who was inspired to build a series of pumping stations in the oriental style in and around Berlin. The pumping station in Potsdam (1841–3), his best work, looks like a small mosque with its polychrome tiles and painted brick. Two other followers, A.D. Schadow and F.A. Stüler, built a perfect little Russian

Below: *The delicacy of the
pierced terracotta
balustrading contrasts with
the massive overall form of
the Town Hall in Berlin,
Germany.*

church of SS Peter and Paul (1834–7) at
Nikolskoe, on the outskirts of Berlin.

After the mid century railway stations,
industrial buildings and churches were built in
a style based on Romanesque and early
Renaissance architecture. The definitive piece
of brick architecture from this period is without
doubt the much-maligned Berlin town hall
(1861–9), built by the little-known architect
Hermann Friedrich Waesemann. The structure of the building is simple enough: a
rectangular block with a tower at its centre.
The superb terracotta detailing of the façade
ensures the town hall a place in the vanguard
of European architecture. This building
marked the end of the brick revival which
Schinkel had inaugurated. The neo-
Renaissance style became more florid with
facings in natural stone preferred to plain
brick. Innovation in brick architecture now
shifted from Germany to Britain.

Colour is the key element in much of the
new brick architecture that emerged from
Britain during the second half of the 19th
century. The fashion for colours in brick
architecture is often ascribed to the influence of
John Ruskin and especially to his works *Seven
Lamps of Architecture* (1849) and *The Stones of
Venice* (1851–3). The explanation for it given
by the architect Halsey Ricardo in 1897 is
probably more accurate: ". . . red buildings
arose more, I think, as a protest against the
monotony and colourlessness of our streets.
Now that we have tasted blood—so to speak—
we want more, and we want it permanent."

The Gothic-Revivalist William Butterfield
(1814–1900) was the acknowledged master of

polychrome brickwork, with All Saints' church (1850–9) in St Margaret Street, London, being one of the best examples. The exterior is mainly red brickwork set off by diapering in black brick and detailing in Bath stone. The interior is a riot of coloured tiles, bricks, terracotta and stone.

An interesting sub-style to emerge from the Gothic Revival was the Vernacular, pioneered by G.E. Street and expounded in his book *Brick and Marble in the Middle Ages* (1855). Street put his ideas into practice at Boyne Hill, where he built virtually an entire village consisting of a church, vicarage, almshouses and a school, all in red brick banded with darker coloured brick.

On the Continent the neo-Gothic style was adapted to suit the requirements of the building materials available, and the use of brick was not central to its success. In France, for example, Viollet-le-Duc abhorred the use of brick in ecclesiastical architecture and built most of his churches in quarried stone. The Dutch architect Cuypers, on the other hand, chose brick for his buildings, despite being an ardent follower of Viollet-le-Duc. Cuypers' best works include several neo-Gothic churches and, in Amsterdam, two masterpieces in the neo-Renaissance style, the Rijksmuseum and the Central railway station.

Polychrome brick was a major element in the exotic architectural style popular all over Europe later in the century. This style was to be found in villas on the western and southern coasts of France, in the bull-fighting arenas of Barcelona and Lisbon and, perhaps most fittingly, in the building which housed the

Above: *The exterior of All Saints' Church, London, incorporating red and black bricks and Bath stone.*

Right: *The multi-textured polychrome interior of All Saints' Church, seen here through a metal screen.*

Below: *Cuypers' poly-chrome Rijksmuseum, Amsterdam (1877–1885). This detail shows a sculpture of the architect peering round the corner.*

Turkish Baths in London. Many commercial and industrial buildings sported tiled domes and minarets. Among the most remarkable surviving examples of these are the Zacherl Insecticide Emporium (1892–3, by Kurt and Julius Mayreder) in Vienna, St Paul's House (1878, by Thomas Ambler) in Leeds and, a late example, the Yenidze cigarette factory (1907–9, by Martin Hammitzsch) in Dresden. More Italianate than Moorish but nevertheless part of this style are two commercial buildings in Glasgow: Templeton's Carpet Factory (1889, by William Leiper), and the present ICI warehouse (1900, by W.F. McGibbon), inspired by the Bargello in Florence. The idea for Archibald Ponton and W.V. Gough's Granary building (1871–3) in Bristol also has its origins in medieval Italian brick architecture.

The Italianate style was employed with great effect in an unlikely cause, to improve the looks of what was often a stone-clad brick monstrosity – the factory chimney. In Britain many chimneys were improved as part of the rebuilding programme necessitated by the Smoke Abatement Act (1870). One striking example is the shaft of the Western Pumping Station at Pimlico (1875) which is in uniform yellow brick right up to the top portion where it ends with an Italianate flourish. Many examples of decoration imaginatively applied to chimneys can be found all over Europe. Brickworks were often special in this respect, their chimneys serving as giant showcases for the range of products offered by the factory.

Minor domestic architecture gained in status during the 19th century to a point

Left: *Elaborate polychrome diaper patterns are used at every opportunity on the ornate façade of Amsterdam Central Station (1881–1889), also by Cuypers.*

Far right: *Ponton and Gough's restored Granary building in Bristol, England.*

Below right: *Victorian chapel at Cerne Abbas, Dorset, England.*

Below left: *Edwin Lutyens' romantic, picturesque Folly Farm in Berkshire, England.*

previously reserved for public and ecclesiastical buildings. The two styles which helped to bring this about in Britain were the Queen Anne Revival and the Vernacular. Both reflected the ethos of William Morris's Arts and Crafts Movement in their commitment to simplicity in design and in the handling of materials. Philip Webb's Red House (1859–60), built at Bexleyheath for William Morris, exemplifies the Vernacular. Simple yet picturesque, its design depends on only two elements: bricks for the walls and tiles for the roof. The Queen Anne style, championed by William Nesfield and Norman Shaw, looked

back to the brick architecture of early 18th-century England and Holland.

The influence of the Arts and Crafts Movement was felt until the end of the Edwardian era. Experimentation with natural stone, timber, even concrete and unusual materials such as pebble was encouraged. Brick was still the primary material but, as so often in the past, the extent of its contribution was often concealed; in the many country houses built by Voysey, for example, behind a covering of rough stucco.

In the next century the brick neo-styles developed in Europe and usually exported to

North America went out of fashion. American ideas in architecture began to make their mark, overturning the established pattern of influence.

FLUCTUATIONS: THE 20TH CENTURY

∾

Throughout its long history brick has proved remarkably resilient to competition from other materials. It has met its greatest challenge in a century which has seen architecture become increasingly indebted to engineering for its success. The invention of the steel girder frame in Chicago in the mid-1880s revolutionized high-rise building and signalled the end of brick's role as a structural mainstay. Concrete, steel and glass have come to be regarded as the principal materials of modernist architecture—the international style that did away with "useless", non-structural elements of decoration, and regarded itself as purely functional. Yet brick has featured with great effect in several of the major styles to emerge during the 20th century: the Prairie School in the United States, the Amsterdam School and European expressionism, as well as the particularly British Vernacular style of Edwin Lutyens and the Thirties' London Transport Style. Now it plays a new role in Postmodernism, which welcomes ornamentation and looks to styles and periods other than Modernism for its inspiration. Any building material can pall on the imagination and even architects firmly rooted in the modernist tradition have periodically turned to

brick as an antidote to functionalism; Le Corbusier and Mies van der Rohe, for example.

The technological advances which allowed a new age in building to develop were first put into practice in Chicago. The rebuilding programme embarked upon after fire devastated the city in 1871, stimulated both builders and architects to come up with innovations that would meet the stringent new safety standards demanded by the city authorities. The most important of these was skeleton construction, which was made possible by the development of the steel frame in the mid 1880s. Until its introduction, brick and traditional methods of construction continued to be used.

By the late 19th century the United States was beginning to throw off its cultural dependence on Europe and shape an identity of its own. In the field of architecture the break with European tradition was very definite, and resulted in the emergence of a new architectural language that placed function and utility above the old concept of beauty for its own sake. The so-called Chicago School of architects were in the vanguard of this new thinking, which developed out of the re-building of Chicago. The architectural style envisaged by the entrepreneur Peter Brooks for his Montauk Building (1881–2, demolished in 1902) owed little to European ideas. In his commissioning letter to the architects Burnham and Root, he wrote: "I prefer to have a plain structure of face brick, eight stories and also a basement, with a flat roof to be as massive as the architect chooses and well braced with iron rods if needed. The building throughout is to

Below: *Thin bricks help to emphasize the horizontality of the Robie House, Chicago, USA, by Frank Lloyd Wright.*

be for use and not for ornament. Its beauty will be in its all-adaption to its use."

The beauty of one of the early skyscrapers, Louis Sullivan's ten-storey Wainwright Building (1890–1), derives mainly from the use of red brick for the building's vertical elements. Brick did remain the most popular material for domestic building in the United States; at the turn of the century, the yearly output of one of America's brick manufacturers, albeit the largest—the Hydraulic Press Brick Company of St Louis—totalled 300,000,000 bricks.

Bricks were also the prime material used in the first truly innovative style in domestic architecture to emerge from the States. This was developed by Frank Lloyd Wright, in a series of villas which he built from the 1890s onwards in the cities along the Great Lakes and the leafy suburbs of Chicago and Buffalo. Wright's designs became quite popular in Europe once they were published in 1910–11. Architects there married them to their own expressionistic designs, producing a style that survived well into the 1950s. Wright's solutions look simple enough (for example the Heath House, 1905, and the Martin House, 1906, both in Buffalo, N.Y., and the Robie House, Chicago, built in 1908): a sprawling house with low roofs, but the result was a building which emphasized its horizontality and, though devoid of ornamentation, produced a pleasing effect in the interplay of interior and exterior space.

Frank Lloyd Wright's houses were instrumental in the naming of the new style: the Prairie School. Not only did the flat, horizontal buildings by Wright suggest the expanse of

Left: *Brick architecture in Manhattan. The Chrysler building by William Van Alen (1930), is constructed from brick, stainless-steel and glass.*

Above: *The brick General Electric building is ornamented with a lightening bolt and flame forms.*

Above right: *Raymond Hood's American Radiator Building (1923), now the American Standard Building, has eight storeys of black brick on top of a four-storey base of polished granite.*

the Midwestern prairies, but this was also the area where most of them were built. Almost all of the architects who were connected with this style were pupils of either Sullivan or Wright (the latter had started as a draftsman at Sullivan's office).

Perhaps the best pieces of brick architecture in American architectural history were erected in small towns in the vast Midwestern plains, and they were all banks. Most important is Sullivan's National Farmers Bank at Owatonna, Minnesota (1906–8), primarily a big strongbox of a building, but immensely enlivened by Sullivan-type Art Nouveau terracotta. This building spawned a whole series of repeat performances, most of them masterful improvisation set by the Owatonna building: the Merchants' National Bank, Grinnell, Iowa (1917–18); and the Farmers' Union Bank at Columbus, Wisconsin (1919). Several were designed by other architects, for example the Merchants' Bank of Winona, Minnesota (1911–12), by the partnership of Purcell, Feick and Elmslie, or the Interstate National Bank at Hegewisch, Chicago (1917–18), now demolished, by Parker N. Berry, and there were many more. All that hard-earned Midwestern money encased in beautiful brick vaults, built like jewel caskets, and waiting for the Great Depression, certainly provides a powerful symbolic image. But the bank buildings proved a dead end in architecture, although nowadays they might provide some pointers for postmodern architects.

The true strength of the Prairie School lay in domestic architecture along the lines of Frank Lloyd Wright's houses, and the European expressionism of the 1910s and 1920s never really became popular in the States. But what few outstanding examples there are of the expressionist style in America, were all built by architects strongly influenced by Wright. Francis Barry Byrne's St. Patrick's Church at Racine, Wisconsin (1923) and, much in the same vein, but even bolder, the Church of Christ the King, Tulsa, Oklahoma (1926), show a departure from the horizontality of Prairie School designs, with pinnacles piercing the air. But even here, the large wall spaces prove that Sullivan and Wright were not forgotten. The other example is Bruce Goff's Page Warehouse of 1927, also in Tulsa, his hometown. It is a five-storey building in which the pattern of the brick and concrete corbelling seems not to be able to decide between horizontality and verticality. However, by that time, mainstream commercial architecture in America had firmly opted for the skyscraper.

In contrast to the experiments in high-rise building taking place in America, much of Europe's avant-garde architecture continued to rely on brick for its shape, texture and effect. In the years immediately before and after the First World War, architects in Germany, the Netherlands and Scandinavia chose brick for a range of ultra-modernist building projects. Arguably the most important contribution to the development of brick architecture in the 20th century was made by the Amsterdam School. The movement's godfather was H.P. Berlage (1856–1934) who used both brick and tiles in a rather linear Dutch Art Nouveau style of building. His most influential work,

Below: *The vertical, angular ornamentation of the Shipping Society Building in Amsterdam gives the building a cubist look.*

the Amsterdam Exchange building (1897–1903), prepared the way for the School's first commission, J.M. van der Mey's bizarre building for the Shipping Society in Amsterdam, the Scheepvaarthuis (1913–16). The huge building projects like the bow of a ship—a visual statement on the type of business it houses.

Van der Mey, de Klerk and Kramer were the chief exponents of the style developed by the Amsterdam School. Most of the architects involved with the School were committed to translating socialist ideals into architecture, aided by the patronage of Amsterdam's socialist council. The Eigen Haard housing estate (1913–21) is undoubtedly the School's most successful attempt at creating a "communal" art in which architecture, the highest art form, incorporates sculpture and other decorative arts as well. Better housing and building were to be achieved through the use of "natural" materials, especially brick, in an individual style of true expressionism (a term first applied to architecture in a Dutch publication of 1919). These aspirations were met in the Dageraad housing estate (1918–23), a design which included curves, wave patterns, small design effects in brick and round or square towerettes. In a typical Amsterdam School housing estate, no two houses looked alike but nevertheless the overall effect was one of unity and cohesion. Brick, wood (for windows and doors) and roof tiles were cleverly deployed to enhance each other. Expanses of brick were broken by small, strategically placed windows made even smaller visually by sub-dividing them with extremely small panes. Stunning

effects were produced by switching from one brick pattern or colour to another, with roof tiles often extending downwards along the walls.

Robust and detailed ornamentation for the large wall areas was another important characteristic of the Amsterdam School, and brick was usually used to achieve these decorative effects. A light stone was favoured for most of the sculpture, although Hildo Krop, the municipal sculptor, also often worked in brick.

The style became so popular that eventually every Dutch provincial town could boast its Amsterdam School town hall, post office, police station or church. Utrecht, for example, has two very interesting buildings in the style: the huge main post office (1917–24, by J. Crouwel) and the Tolsteegbrug police station (1925, by the local public works department). The style was also used for small country houses and villas, most notably in the village of Bergen, with wood and thatch as the main materials and brick used solely to provide a solid framework. This picturesqueness and constant reliance on traditional materials identify the style as essentially romantic, despite its modernist credentials. The movement lost much of its impetus in the late 1920s and by the 30s it had deteriorated into a formula. Even so, some of its ideas would continue to crop up in later Dutch domestic architecture.

The major Dutch architect to emerge from the shadow of the Amsterdam School was W.M. Dudok. His best known building is Hilversum Town Hall (1928–30). Dudok's work pointed forwards to De Stijl and func-

tionalism, but with brick being preferred to steel, glass and concrete. The "natural" materials used by the Amsterdam School and Dudok have given their buildings a durability which is altogether absent from the De Stijl designs. In comparison, many of these now look shoddy and not at all functional.

In Germany one of the most influential architects of the new century was Peter Behrens (1868–1940). In his factory buildings for the German industrial giant AEG (1907 onwards), Behrens used steel and glass as infills to all-brick walls. Later in his career Behrens was greatly influenced by expressionism: the colours used for the brickwork of the administration building of the Hoechst Dyeworks, Frankfurt (1920–5), range from orange and yellow to blue, shades reminiscent of the colours favoured by expressionist painters.

Brick was given a role too in a number of other important expressionist buildings. That architectural epitome of German expressionism, Erich Mendelsohn's Einstein Tower in Potsdam (1920–1), has a brick core faced in cement. Hans Poelzig's design for a chemical factory in Luban, Poland (1911–12) depended solely on brick for its effects. The gables and windows of this building appear as expressionist travesties of the kind found in medieval Baltic warehouses, and the design of the main structure owes much to Ledoux's neo-Classical work of the late 18th century as well as Schinkel's Berlin projects of the 1830s and 40s. Brick and glass were used for the façade of Fritz Höger's Chilehaus in Hamburg (1923). The building's stiletto corner mimics

Left: *Hilversum Town Hall in The Netherlands, is executed in uniform cream brick, with some horizontals subtly emphasized by one-course bands of black bricks.*

the Amsterdam Scheepvaarthuis and would not look out of place on the set of Robert Wiene's film *Das Kabinett des Dr Caligari* (1919). However, it could be argued that the expressionist credentials of this building have been overplayed at the expense of other features, such as the broad frontage and the wavy horizontal roofing of the projecting upper storeys, which serve to neutralize the verticality of the design.

Höger's all-brick Sprinkenhof, also in Hamburg, looked forward to the "völkische" architecture with its patterns reminiscent of half-timbered nogging found on Friesian

Left: *The Chilehaus by Fritz Höger in Hamburg, Germany, makes an exciting visual statement with its accentuated use of a corner site.*

Below: *The Grundtvig Minderkirche, Copen-hagen, Denmark: a radical re-working of a gothic cathedral shape.*

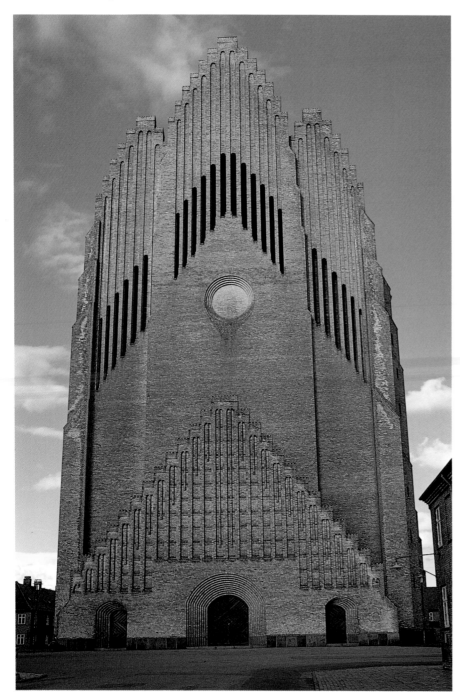

farmhouses. Brick was used to good effect in the rebuilding programme for the Böttcher-strasse, in Bremen (1923–31), the phantasma-goric juxtaposition of restored 14th-century town houses with weird and wonderful designs for the new houses serving to highlight the romantic aspect inherent in north German expressionism. The highly expressionistic Paula-Becker-Modersohn House and Atlantis House were by the Fascist architect Bernard Hötger. Hitler, however, never liked the Bremen project and although certain factions in the Nazi Party defended expressionism, it, together with the modernism it represented, did not find favour among the hierarchy as a vehicle for their ideology. The Führer's imperial aspirations were best represented in public buildings which looked to the past for their models. Marble was often the preferred material and brickwork disappeared under layers of rendering. The influence of modern-ism lived on, though, in the designs chosen for private houses built during the Nazi period.

Scandinavia's exploration of the expres-sionist possibilities of brick was limited. In both Denmark and Sweden the familiar was generally preferred to the avant-garde. The one great exception to this conservatism is P. V. J. Klint's Grundtvig Mindekirche in Copenhagen. The original design won a com-petition in 1913 but work only started on the building in 1921 and took almost twenty years to complete. The brick façade of the church is steeply gabled with a stepped organ-pipe design. Stockholm town hall (1909–23), built by Ragnar Östberg, is another unusual brick building of the period, mixing traditional

Left: *Brick provides a unifying link between several disparate elements in the restored Böttcherstrasse in Bremen, Germany.*

forms with the slightly exotic and a dash of expressionism.

From a Continental perspective, 20th-century British architecture might be viewed as one long retreat into a continuous series of revival styles. In the light of recent developments one might also look upon them as one long rehearsal for post-Modernism. It was largely due to Edwin Lutyens (1869–1944) that brick kept its place in British domestic architecture for so long. Lutyens initially drew on ideas from both the neo-Renaissance style and the Arts and Crafts movement before developing the Vernacular style that would make his name. His many country houses in brick include Folly Farm in Berkshire (1905–12). The handling of the brick in this example is typical Lutyens. He used different bonds and different sized bricks (mainly 2 and 3 inch bricks), as well as dissimilar hues of colour. Where necessary, for example in the canting buttresses, Lutyens inserted tiles between the bricks, thereby denying the cubic character of the materials. Lutyens became a target for modernists who labelled his architecture provincial. Now that modernism is no longer avant-garde, and has itself been relegated to the provinces, Lutyens' work is once again appreciated on its own terms and valued for its human scale.

Lutyens-style brickwork, much of it uninspired and derivative, saw British architecture peacefully through the first half of the century. It was a far cry from the situation on the Continent where, expressionism finally dispensed with, concrete, steel and glass took over. The one distinctive style to emerge in

Britain during the Thirties came from an unlikely source. Called the London Transport Style, it developed out of a new building programme for the London Underground. The man in charge of the programme, Frank Pick (1878–1941), had already demonstrated his design flair by commissioning posters for the Underground which would put Britain at the forefront of modern poster art. Charles Holden, Pick's principal architect, set to work on the design for the first batch of stations, choosing a pale natural stone and concrete as his main materials. The idea of introducing brick into the scheme was fostered by a tour of Scandinavia, north Germany and the Netherlands undertaken by Pick and Holden in 1930. It was decided to use brick as the main material, with bands of concrete to provide accentuations, for the new stations on the "Piccadilly" Underground Line. The stations themselves have been designed as architectural vignettes, individual statements on the interplay between basic shapes.

By the beginning of World War II brick was out of favour so far as the modern architecture of the developed world was concerned. In Third World countries the progress of brick was mixed. In India, where styles imitated Western architecture, brick was used increasingly. They had also, as we have seen, acquired the knowledge of producing brick to high standards. In many other areas, though, there was no real need for large-scale brick manufacturing, nor could it compete in cost with traditional methods. A case in point is the Oaxaca Valley, south of Mexico City. Until an earthquake hit the valley in 1931, sun-dried brick was the main building material, even in the towns, and fired brick was only used for decoration. The use of fired brick increased after the disaster, leaving adobe for only the poorest households. The next logical step was to mechanize production but this proved uneconomic because of the static nature of society in the region. There was a living to be made by individual brickmakers because their output (roughly 400 bricks per day) and costs matched the low level of demand in the local economy. This is still the situation in many Third World countries, even those, like Mexico, with a highly industrialized neighbour.

Brick seemed to have little future in the immediate post-war period in Europe. More modern materials were preferred for the massive rebuilding programmes, even for housing. The building industry had virtually ground to a halt during the war and the extent of the devastation—80 per cent of building stock in some German cities, for example—caused an acute housing shortage by the time hostilities ended. The pressure was on to provide housing quickly, cheaply and efficiently. Concrete fulfilled all these requirements and became the major building material for industrial and commercial architecture as well as housing. The quality of the building, though, was generally very poor. Some Fifties housing was little better than the jerry-building prevalent in the previous century, the ill-fitting prefabricated slabs guaranteeing only a steady supply of cold running water down the inside walls. For the window frames quality hardwood was passed over in favour of the most inexpensive kind or, worse

Below: *Red brick quoins and string course at Folly Farm, Berkshire, England.*

still, strips of plastic coating. Such practices met the minimum standards required by law, and builders were obliged to do no more. Cost-conscious and opportunistic investors and town councils justified their building of drab, low quality, off-the-peg frame houses and office blocks by pointing to the virtue of functionalism. Architects increasingly orientated themselves to the thinking of their direct client, the investor. Those architects who kept faith with brick were regarded as exponents of a retrograde architecture at best, or incurable provincialists at worst. Britain became perilously close to forgetting its garden city ideals which were now only realized in small neo-Georgian developments for the upper middle class. In Amsterdam the Social-Democrat descendents of the city council that had backed the Amsterdam School now proposed putting their citizens in tiny high-rise apartments calculated to the last square inch. In accepting modernity, the wider public neglected to demand quality in return. The result was identical high-rise slums across Europe, from Leipzig and Amsterdam to Paris and London, to mark the true triumph of the International Style.

The turning point came in 1968 with the spectacular collapse of the Ronan Point block of flats in London. Dissatisfaction with high-rise building and the obliteration of the old town centres had been growing, even among architects, and the Ronan Point tragedy finally concentrated minds on the need for a different, more human, kind of architecture. Brick would be fundamental to this new approach, but several problems had to be overcome as

brick made its first, tentative comeback. Much of the knowhow of building with brick had disappeared, especially on the Continent, where the modernism had been embraced more wholeheartedly than in Britain. In the 1970s the new demands were met by facing concrete frames with brick and setting this off with brightly painted wood. This style evolved in the Netherlands and was adopted in several of the new towns that sprang up around the cities in the west of the country, such as Almere and Maarssenbroek. The results were not at all encouraging. The brick facings looked what they were, cosmetic, and at odds with the design of the building. The result was a rather unhappy case of Le Corbusier meeting Hansel and Gretel.

The genuine revival of brick in architecture was concomitant with the saner forms of postmodernism. Architecture as an art, or even as a craft, was virtually re-invented as practitioners looked with new eyes at old styles and formerly fringe activities such as "spontaneous" architecture or "architecture without architects". Brick returned as itself, a wholesome, natural product, and not an industrialized artefact. For those architects critical of the straitjacket of conformity to which technological progress had subjected brick, there was an increasing supply of handmade brick types.

Among the most remarkable and indeed amusing pieces of brick architecture to emerge in the latter part of this century are the American SITE-group's designs for several shops in the Best chain. Each of these incorporates a joke. The brick-faced wall of the Peeling Showroom (1972) in Richmond,

Far left: *The American SITE-group's whimsical Forest Showroom in Richmond, Virginia, USA.*

Right: *The 'jigsaw' of different colours on the Byker Wall, Newcastle, England, emphasizes the nature of brickwork.*

Virginia, for example, literally looks as though it is peeling away from the main structure. The Forest Showroom in Richmond, Virginia (1978–80), appears to be a ruined building in a forest.

Elsewhere brick was being used with serious intent rather than as a Pop Art joke. In Britain, the Byker redevelopment area in Newcastle, built in the early 1970s by Ralph Erskine, is a major advertisement for the brick revival. The so-called Byker Wall is composed of bricks of different colours inserted at strategic points in its long curving façade. Concrete, wood and asbestos feature elsewhere in the scheme. Another example of brick revival is the Intellekt bookshop in Ghent in Belgium (1980), by Van Impe, which has strong overtones of Art Nouveau and incorporates many round and oval windows within a vertical multi-storey structure. The various shades of brick are emphasized by white bands of stone.

In the Netherlands postmodernism has tended to follow the style proposed by Rudolf Steiner. Dornach in Switzerland, where Steiner based his anthroposophical movement in the 1920s, is the showcase of this style. The major difference between the two approaches is in the materials used, the Dutch preferring

Below: *The design for
The Cascades in London's
Docklands places emphasis
on shifting planes rather
than changing colours.*

brick to concrete (and timber), which were Steiner's principal building materials. The main building of the NMB Bank in Amsterdam-Bijlmermeer (1987) by A. Alberts, is a re-statement of an idea used by the architect in an earlier project, a villa built among houses of standard design in the residential area of Rijnsweerd in Utrecht. The villa, which was completed in 1980, is a bricklayer's dream come true, virtually alive with brick and bristling with outcrops and mini towers in the material. Except for the tiles on the roof, no other material is in evidence. The most notable feature of both the villa and the NMB Bank building is the skill evident in the brickwork. They are exuberant celebrations of brick, acknowledgements of the material's status as a major building material.

Nowhere has the influence of modernism met stronger resistance than in Britain, where a long history of vernacular architecture and a liking for traditional materials have combined to save brick from complete usurpation by modern rivals. It is not surprising, therefore, to find British architects chief among the experimenters with brick or to note a consciousness of its heritage in their work. John Outram's Pumping Station on the Isle of Dogs (1989) in the Docklands area of London displays an almost Victorian attention to detail and seriousness in the treatment of the material. It is arguably the finest brick building of the decade.

Another development in Docklands is a variation on a theme first explored by Erskine in the Byker Wall in Newcastle, although this time the setting is an upmarket apartment

BRICK DESIGN

Far right: *New meets old in Manhattan*.

Despite inheriting the knowledge and technology for making perfect bricks of every shape and colour, the 20th-century construction industry has frequently tried to turn its back on brick, encouraging complicated "Modern" solutions to age-old design problems. However, some designers and craftsmen have resisted the lure of materials like steel, glass and concrete, and continued the brick tradition.

The 20th-century decline in the use of brick really began with the emergence of the Modern movement at the end of World War I. Led by architects such as Walter Gropius in Germany and Louis Sullivan in America, it was characterized by the use of machine-made components and simplicity of design, and its devotees tended to regard brick as a material which symbolized the beliefs—and mistakes—of the previous generation. Paul Sheerbart, a German writer, wrote in his *Glasarchitektur* treatise of 1914 that brick architecture was the undesirable product of industrialization, stating that "it was the steam railway that produced the brick metropolis culture of today from which we all suffer". However, despite the general rejection of brick, a few of the movement's protagonists did employ it within their buildings, although it was normally hidden. Only a few of the important structures, such as Ludwig Mies van der Rohe's Memorial to Karl Liebknecht and Rosa Luxemburg in Berlin (1926) openly exploited brickwork.

New Modernist buildings were erected in steel, glass and concrete—comparatively untested materials which were sometimes used in unsuitable situations, and the results, while often spectacular, were not always completely successful on a practical level. Concrete buildings, for example, soon become stained by rain and soot, and turn a depressingly dull shade of grey, and similar effects can be seen on metal cladding, which looks fine until it rusts or oxidizes. Such problems do not exist with brick architecture. The character of brickwork is such that its charm derives from the effects of ageing, irregularity, and even imperfections.

There is an increasing awareness of the need to conserve our existing buildings, and restoration, once so frowned upon by Modernists, is beginning to take place. This is certainly helpful in stimulating the public's interest in architecture generally – old buildings which have been cleaned often reveal details of colour and craftmanship which have long gone unnoticed.

Public awareness of architecture is important, as a climate of informed opinion can go a long way towards encouraging good architecture, and thereby working towards the creation of a more attractive and varied built environment. Far more important than the details of the protracted debate on shape and form—Modernism versus Classicism—is the need for good quality, durable buildings, whatever their material and style. This is where brick comes into its own.

Innovations in the use of brick during the past 25 years have rarely had the glamour of the more avant-garde building projects. However, the introduction of modern techniques such as steel reinforcement have greatly

Far right: *Fell's Point, Virginia, USA: two different textures on a single building. The machine-finished look of the facings on the front façade of this house provide an interesting contrast to the re-pointed original bricks of the side wall. These bricks are laid in American bond (English garden-wall bond), which was not followed when the non-structural facing bricks were applied.*

enhanced brick's structural potential, enabling it to be used for ever larger and more complex structures. Most importantly, brick remains one of the most versatile, reliable and widely used building materials of all.

BRICK SELECTION

Choosing the right brick is an important and time-consuming task for architects. While it is possible to choose bricks solely for their colour and texture, there are other factors to be considered: a weak facing brick, for example, is not an ideal candidate for heavy engineering

Right: *Brick and tile works in Suffolk, England.*

work. No standard classification system has been devised, but ideally the architect needs to take into account the brick's method of manufacture, normal use and arrangement of voids, as well as its colour and surface texture.

TEXTURE AND APPEARANCE

Most bricks are manufactured from clay, although popular alternatives now include calcium silicate and concrete. Clay bricks are sub-divided, and named after their place of origin or clay strata; for example, Bengal clay (India), Lombardy clay (Italy) and Oxford clay (Britain). They are suitable for most types of building work, but their counterparts have certain limitations.

The three manufacturing processes—pressed, wirecut and soft mud—influence the texture and appearance of the finished brick (see pages 165/6). Most bricks are produced by the pressed process which gives a smooth, unblemished look and always leaves one or more "frogs" on the bedface. Wire-cut bricks, which account for nearly one third of the world's brick production, are easily distinguished by the drag marks caused by the cutting wires pulling pieces of grit over the bed face, and by the absence of "frogs". They are also dense and uniform in shape, and have hard and sharp arrises. The soft mud process, involving the hand or machine pressing of soft clay into a stock mould, produces bricks with a creased face and slightly irregular shape. Of the two types, hand-pressed bricks are invariably more attractive.

Bricks generally come in four main types: solid, perforated, cellular and keyed (see

page 164). Solid bricks are the easiest to form and are manufactured using the wirecut method. In most cases, they have no holes, cavities or depressions, although some countries permit the inclusion of small holes to aid handling. Perforated bricks are also produced using the wirecut method, and these incorporate a series of small holes which pass through the brick. The presence of perforations means that the quantity of clay and overall weight of the brick are reduced. Unless the perforations are very large, there is no significant loss of strength. Consequently, holes are generally limited to 25% of the brick's volume and 10% of the face area. Larger holes are permitted in Mediterranean and Alpine countries and are set in different directions: bricks used in Mediterranean areas are perforated horizontally to encourage air movement and therefore cool the structure, while Alpine countries prefer vertical perforations to improve thermal insulation. Cellular bricks contain the largest proportion of void to solid and can be produced by either of the two pressed methods. Cavities may exceed 20% of the gross volume and are always closed at one end so that, by laying bricks with the cells pointing downwards, the cavities are protected against filling with mortar. Keyed bricks are pressed bricks with rectangular or dovetail recesses on their faces to provide a key for rendering.

Surface texture is traditionally determined by the type of material, means of manufacture and surface application. Commonly available finishes include smooth, semi-vitreous, course-dragged, stippled, combed and creased. Bricks made with clay have naturally occurring pits,

Far left top: *Roman tile bricks laid in a herringbone pattern, acting as a lacing course to a flint wall.*

Far left bottom: *Header bond using vitrified purple brick headers with red brick quoins to the windows and doorways. In some places, the vitrified surface has been chipped, exposing the red brick beneath.*

Left top: *An example of stretcher bond using common brick, on an early 20th-century cavity wall.*

Left bottom: *A 17th-century example of English bond.*

stones and fossils which are absent from their concrete counterparts. Concrete and calcium-silicate bricks have a uniform appearance and there is little variation in colour, shape and texture. Bricks produced using the soft mud process invariably have a sand-face finish as a result of the sand used in the process adhering to the damp clay. Hand-moulded bricks can be prohibitively expensive, and pressed bricks with mechanically applied surfaces and artificial textures provide a cheaper alternative. Wavy striations and creases are lightly inscribed, or pressed, onto the face of the green (unfired) brick to give a natural and weathered appearance.

Although in theory any brick can be used for any building type, design philosophy and tradition often restrict the choice. It is difficult to deny, for example, that smooth-faced bricks are more appropriate to high-tech city buildings than to thatched cottages.

SHAPES AND SIZES

The standard brick is regular in shape. A few exceptions can be found, but these tend to be proprietary bricks, belonging to individual companies. Attempts have been made to develop bricks that are larger than the standard size, in the belief that they will be quicker and more efficient to lay. Unfortunately, large bricks are often difficult to raise with one hand, and a bricklayer may have to lay down his trowel and position the unit with both hands. The additional action results in little, if any, time saving. It also highlights the best definition of the difference between bricks and blocks: a brick can be picked up and laid down with one hand, while a block requires two. Standard bricks, however, vary slightly—British bricks tend to be slightly larger than those used in Central Europe and America, but considerably smaller than those used in the Alpine and Mediterranean countries. On the whole, African and Indian bricks are the same size as those in Northern Europe, because of the influences of colonization.

Proprietary bricks come in all shapes and sizes. Some attempts have been made at modernizing traditional bricks to fit in with the current construction techniques—usually by changing the dimensions. A good example of this is the "modular" brick, which was considered by many builders and architects to be the logical development of the standard brick unit. The aim was to provide a means by which buildings could be designed on a regular grid of round numbers, ie, multiples of 100 mm (4 in). However, this would have necessitated the re-design of all other building products and the modular brick has consequently failed to sustain even a modest share of the market.

The design of the "V" brick was a further attempt to produce a large, labour-saving unit. It was developed as a means of creating a cavity wall using single bricks made from perforated clay. Although it performed as well as a regular cavity wall, and included vertical perforations which made it possible to lift with one hand, it needed very careful laying to prevent mortar from filling up the perforations, which made it inefficient to use.

The current concern for the appearance of our built environment has encouraged a

Below: *Irregular bonding, with bricks in header courses laid on edge.*

revival of interest in traditional detailing, in sharp contrast to the 1950s and 1960s. The prevailing design philosophy of these decades dictated that brickwork be used in simple, flat and unadorned planes and panels, with any special shapes employed (such as copings and cappings) achieved by cutting regular bricks rather than using bricks specially formed for the purpose. Good cutting demands considerable skill, and many attempts have proved unsuccessful. Cut bricks are also more susceptible to frost damage, and concern over unstable cut bricks has led to the re-evaluation of specially formed bricks for specific applications.

In an attempt to formalize the production of these special bricks, some countries publish standards describing the various configurations and sizes available. Some of the standards are extensive—for example the new *British Standard*, which includes a range with 320 variants on 70 basic shapes—and provides a wonderful kit of parts from which an architect may create limitless decorative features in brickwork. Confusingly, however, special bricks come in two forms: "Standard specials", and "Special specials". Standard specials are those bricks which are listed in the published standards and asked for regularly. "Special specials" are those bricks which are designed for one particular purpose on one particular building, and have to be produced to order (see page 171).

Both standard and special specials are generally categorized as either bonding or decoration units. The bonding bricks are used to complete a recognized pattern or brick bond, avoiding vertical joints through two or more

Below: *Brick courses swept up to form a raking buttress in a variation of tumbled-in brickwork.*

courses. Typical examples of these bricks are "closers", which are bricks used to start and end a stretch of bonding, and "bats" which are half or three-quarter bricks. Decorative bricks are those shaped bricks which combine practical and decorative purposes and are classified according to their shape or function. They include capping and coping bricks, radial bricks and bullnose bricks, to name but a few.

Many of these non-uniform bricks are requested by architects for the restoration of historic buildings; bricks from an earlier period are often of a different size from those available today. Others are required to fulfil a particular design intention. The English architect Sir Edwin Lutyens had a particular liking for thin bricks and used them regularly for his country houses. The opposite was true of the American architects who designed the auditorium at Berkeley High School in Michigan using bricks with a face dimension of 8 in × 8 in (200 × 200 mm).

COLOUR

Modern bricks come in an astonishingly large variety of colours. Credit for this is largely due to scientific research into the effects of heat on clay and the reaction of the chemicals in the raw material during the firing process. Colour can be either integral, resulting from the reaction of natural chemicals present in the clay, or superficially applied—by adding sand or oxide pigments to the surface of the brick faces before firing. These are fired with a thin laminate which can be easily chipped or damaged, revealing the colour of the underbody.

Left: *Tiles laid on end form a striking coping on this brick garden feature.*

Right: This Flemish bond wall, made with multi-coloured bricks, has tuck pointing on the horizontal joints.

Despite the fact that manufacturers of clay bricks try to maintain uniform colour by adding mineral oxides during the process, it remains impossible to impose complete uniformity on bricks—even the length of a stretcher shows differences of colour between individual bricks. Uniformity is better achieved with calcium silicate and concrete bricks.

Close inspection of almost any single brick will reveal a multitude of subtle tonal variations never duplicated exactly in any other brick. Bricks which include noticeable variations in face colour are popularly known as "multis" and named according to their base colour; for example, multi-reds.

ARCHITECTURAL FEATURES

Many contemporary architects complain of being tied by the economic dictates of patrons who require justification for any variation from basic stretching bond brickwork—even the introduction of simple soldier-course brick arches is sometimes denied on cost grounds. However, some enlightened patrons do realize that the character of our built environment can be enhanced by architectural features, especially the use of wall decoration. The majority of these modern embellishments reflect established 19th-century forms, particularly the use of polychromatic brick arrangements and the re-employment of plinths and cornices. Major decorative features like arches and corbels can even be cosmetically applied to a precast concrete backing which, although purists tend to regard it as a dishonest use of brick, is similar to the Roman veneering technique developed under Julius Caesar two thousand years ago.

ARCHES

The earliest known arches are Babylonian, and date from around 4000 BC. Like any new building technique, it was regarded with a mixture of fascination and apprehension and was quickly relegated to the lowly function of drain construction. Apart from its use in the entrances to the early palaces, the arch was rarely employed as an exposed feature until rationalisation by the Romans, under whom its utilitarian and decorative values were finally realized.

The Romans' refinement of arch-based

architecture liberated builders from the limitations of the simple lintel-based building style and started a revolution in architecture and engineering. The Romans employed the brick arch in both residential buildings and in the Empire's great secular monuments, such as the Colosseum in Rome (AD 72–80), and the aqueducts. Unfortunately, as the Roman Empire collapsed, the supplanting peoples plundered Roman edifices for second-hand building materials and very few examples of the Roman brick arch survived—the exceptions are usually found on ancient city gates and early churches.

Relying almost entirely on the mass of structure above it for solidity and support, the early brick arch had a corpulent and heavy appearance. Despite significant slimlining by Roman architects and engineers, the arch failed to achieve its full potential until the 4th century AD, when it was perfected by the Byzantines.

The modern brick arch has benefited from nearly two millenia of continuous engineering and technological improvement—both to "working" arches and to "veneer" or non-structural arches. The purpose of a working arch is to resist an imposed load or force, transferring it to an adequate support such as a column or pillar. A veneer arch is added to a building for purely aesthetic reasons. The development of concrete and steel frame construction, cladding support systems and pre-assembled panels has meant that non-structural arches may be applied to the face of a building like a thin veneer.

The product of two thousand years of

Left: *The façade of St. Bartholomew's church (1902) by Stanford White, in Manhattan. Very thin bricks are randomly coursed and bonded in a mosaic-type pattern, with a variety of stones of different colours and textures inserted for decoration. The three curved swords featured in the roundel are the symbol of the saint's martyrdom.*

Right: *Gifford's Hall, Stoke-by-Nayland, Suffolk, England. This arched Tudor gateway features moulded brickwork, including a label mould, with diapering and carved brickwork on the wall above.*

Left: *Circular archway at Lullingstone, Kent, England. The wall is built in English garden-wall bond, with a rough brick arch. This is a good example of how it is the wedge-shaped joints of a rough arch, rather than the bricks themselves, which are responsible for the shape.*

reform and changing fashion is a group of arches following three principal shapes; flat, curved, and pointed (see page 194). The simplest form of arch is the rough arch, which is formed using ordinary uncut bricks laid in a heading bond arrangement with tapering mortar joints. Stretchers are usually only used as outer supports or "skewbacks" for distributing the thrust of the arch onto the abutments, or as a lacing course if the arch is several courses thick. Because of their construction, rough arches often have wide, tapering mortar joints, which give them an unattractive appearance. They are usually used in places where they will be largely hidden, such as relieving arches over lintels.

The ugly appearance of tapering joints can be largely overcome by tapering the bricks instead. At their best, with rubbed brickwork, tapering brick arches can look charming, but in their crudest form, that of the axed arch, they are rough and visually unappealing. Axed arches are formed by using ordinary bricks, hewn with a bolster and hammer by the bricklayer into wedge-shaped voussoirs and finished off with a bricklayer's axe or "scutch". The principal problem with axed arches is that their success depends entirely on the cutting skill of the bricklayer, and crude scutching makes for irregularly shaped bricks with untidy mortar joints between them. Masterful cutting, however, can result in a beautiful arch, matching the precision of a cut and rubbed, or gauged arch.

Gauged arches were very popular during the 18th century, dominating the architecture

Above: *This estate cottage in Berkshire, England, was built in 1800 to house farm labourers. The gabled porch has a semi-circular brick arch with stone copings and imposts.*

Far right: *The arched ceiling of Crouwel's post office building in Utrecht, The Netherlands.*

of that period. Elegant and genteel, the gauged arch reflects the consummate care and attention to detail which was characteristic of the best 18th-century building. Unfortunately, few modern builders and developers are prepared to finance the time-consuming art of cutting and finely rubbing soft bricks on carborundum stone to achieve a precise shape, or the preparation of the small quantities of lime putty necessary for jointing, especially if the remainder of the wall is in cement mortar. Purists tend to object to gauged arches in regular brick walls because of the variation in texture and joint thicknesses between fine, rubbed brickwork and ordinary rougher bricks. While this is valid to some extent—the difference is like comparing cashmere with tweed—most people do not notice the change, being far more likely to notice the colour difference, as rubbing bricks are chiefly soft pink, red and orange coloured.

Popular types of flat arch are the soldier arch and the camber arch, also called the Georgian arch because it is found on many buildings of that period. Flat arches are so-called because of their virtually horizontal extrados (outside curves), but most have a slightly cambered intrados to counteract the optical illusion of sagging caused by radiating joints above a level opening.

Most flat arches, except rough and Soldier arches, are built with special shaped bricks. Soldier arches, immensely popular in modern architecture, are very easy to construct: regular bricks are stood upright (at right angles to the normal brick coursing) above a standard lintel. With a completely horizontal intrados, the soldier arch is popular with modern builders because it requires no expensive special bricks and is quick to construct. So popular has it become that it is barely recognized as an arch at all, and is more often simply known as a soldier course. Sadly, soldier arches have little, if any, aesthetic appeal, and cannot begin to compare with the curved elegance of their more refined counterparts.

The ubiquity of the curved arch on both ancient and modern buildings has led many people to believe that it is the only arch shape. Like most flat arches, curved arches are formed using special or tapered bricks, although an arch with a large radius can be constructed from a series of uncut bricks set in tapering joints like the rough arch. Small brick arches above a window or door opening are common enough sights, but it is the larger examples which can be truly stunning, such as the monumental parabolic arches spanning the great hall of the superb Hoofdpostkantoor (Post Office) in Utrecht (1917–24) by the Amsterdam School architect J. Crouwel. With their typically Dutch use of thin bricks and wide joints, these are remarkable not only for their size, but for their elegance. Another breathtaking collection of powerful arches are the buttresses to the Parroquia del Pertetuo Socorro (Parish Church of Perpetual Help) at Ciudad Hidalgo, Michoacán, Mexico (1969–83), by Carlos Mijares. Each massive arch is an architectural entity in itself, but they gracefully intertwine with each other to make a coherent whole. The ingenious use of rat-trap bond reduces the scale of the structures, although the effect is still awesome.

No drawings were produced by the architect, and the building is a testament to his ingenuity, as well as that of his untrained workforce.

Pointed arches are formed in the same way as curved arches, but with an obvious pointed crown. The pointed arch is generally associated with the great Gothic cathedrals. One of the most impressive recent examples of the pointed arch is in America, on the Calvary Undenominational Church at Grand Rapids, Michigan. It is a straightened version of a Tudor arch (see page 195), and acts like a magnet, commanding attention and drawing visitors into the building. Its architect, Tom Roode, chose brick because it was "essential in creating the desired atmosphere of the sanctuary—a sense of tradition, warmth and longevity." The interior of a church is also a suitable place for large brick arches, such as those in the new Church of Holy Angels at Altrincham in Cheshire, England. The setting of powerful arches over a large space or void certainly appears to have a calming effect on our mood and behaviour, so it is especially appropriate for a church.

The history of the development of the arch paralleled refinements in vault construction (see page 197), and it is difficult to regard the two as separate. In fact, the simplest type of vault, the barrel or tunnel vault, is little more than a very deep arch. On the whole, brick vaulting is restricted to the less sophisticated types of vault, such as barrel vaults and groin vaults. This is because the small brick is not suitable for the dual functions of ornate shaping and structural performance—cut away too much of the brick, and insufficient body

remains to do the physical work. For this reason, the magnificent fan vault of scholastic and ecclesiastical architecture of the 15th century were built in stone. However, the brick vault, while not spectacularly beautiful, certainly had its uses. During the Industrial Revolution in 19th-century England, engineers discovered that the traditional timber floors of factories, mills and warehouses were unable to support the new, heavier machinery. Using a series of long and low brick-arched vaults set between the cast iron structural frames, they could increase a floor's structural performance and make the building more fire-resistant at the same time.

Brick vaults are not difficult to construct. Like arches, they can be easily formed by using tapered voussoirs set over a temporary timber support called centering. In the construction of a barrel vault, bricks are staggered so that they bond with neighbouring bricks. Groin or cross vaults (formed by the intersection of two identical barrel vaults meeting at a right-angle) are a little more awkward, as the bricks have to be shaped in two directions. Like basic arches, vaults depend on mass for stability and support, and they therefore need very thick walls and spandrels, which, if they are formed entirely of brick, are very expensive. To reduce the cost of both labour and materials, traditional vaults have interlocking brick linings with the intervening space filled by a cheaper packing material such as concrete or brick rubble.

Their frequent underground location means that less notice is taken of the vault than of the arch, although examples in cathedrals and

Left: *Opened in 1990, the converted vaults in the Royal Society of Arts, London, add valuable space to the 1774 Adam building.*

churches are the exception to this. One of the most important and earliest vaulting achievements can be seen over the banqueting hall of the palace of King Chosroes at Ctesiphon (c. AD 550) in Iraq. It is a massive elliptical vault which rises 120 ft (37 m) and its fusion with an array of attached columns, arcades and string courses on adjacent walls gives the palace a distinctly Roman character.

Although brick vaulting has been used in the construction of cellars, bridges and tunnels, vault construction has virtually disappeared from modern architecture, especially now that many contemporary builders use the cheaper and more flexible alternative of reinforced concrete. However, the acute shortage of space in the inner cities has meant that many vaults are being opened up to provide additional floor space at minimal cost, and the revealed charm of the old brickwork can create a pleasant environment for a workplace, dining area or exhibition space, such as the newly converted vaults in the Royal Society of Arts in London.

DOMES

Brick domes are the natural development of the brick vault (see page 198). Most of the early domes, particularly those created by the Romans, were usually formed in concrete and lined with a finer material such as stone or lead. Brick was often used to form the ribs which supported the dome structure, and connected at intervals by bonding tiles to form compartments for filling with concrete. It was also used as reinforcement and ballast, and many of the bricks were produced in a tri-angular or wedge shape. This was true of the dome over the Pantheon (AD 118–28) in Rome, and the massive dome of the Hagia Sophia (AD 532–7) in Constantinople.

There are some notable examples of brick domes in the Samarkand region of Russia. Samarkand was originally part of the vast Mogul empire, and the Shrine of the Living King (Shah-i-Zinda) and other tombs in the vicinity were rebuilt in the 14th and 15th centuries with richly decorated domes in sumptuous moulded, carved and glazed bricks. The nearby Temple Vestibule at Samarkand demonstrates a more sedate use of brick for the dome lining. This is very similar to the way brick was used in the building of 18th-century ice-houses. Many of these contain brick domes and two of the most notable examples are the Dutch "ijskelders" at the Huis te Linschoten, near Utrecht (restored in 1980) and the Huis de Rijp, near Haarlem (restored in 1976–7).

With these few exceptions, no brick domes of real significance have been constructed in the past three centuries. Domes are far more likely to be constructed in concrete than in brick, although the contemporary use of stainless steel fixings makes it possible to utilize brick as a dome lining.

PIERS, PILLARS AND COLUMNS

Piers, pillars and columns are basically vertical, free-standing members, usually load-bearing. These three terms are largely interchangeable although only 'pier' (from the Latin *petra* meaning rock) can refer to the section of wall between a door and a window—

Left: *Brunelleschi's Duomo in Florence, Italy. The stone facing is missing at the base of the dome, revealing structural brickwork including corbelled supports.*

confusingly, this is referred to as a pillar in Gothic architecture. When it is a projection from a wall it is usually referred to as an "attached pier"—an integral part of a building, providing structural stability to a vertical surface, such as a wall. Most piers are rectangular in shape because they are easy to construct, although any shape is possible (see page 183).

Piers are found on many modern brick buildings, and not just for structural reasons. Used on the outside of a building, they provide an arrangement of recurring vertical features which project beyond the wall face and create a series of shadows, adding depth and softening the overall appearance of the building. Piers can also reduce the perceived scale of a building which would otherwise be monolithic. A good example of this is the Norwich Union Building in Croydon, England, which has been designed with a series of brick piers which project from first floor level with semicircular corbels. These have no structural function but bestow a major visual feature on what would otherwise have been just another dull, flat-faced office building. Countless examples of this type of use for piers can be found in almost every major town and city throughout the world. The narrow, elongated building with an internal frame system has become synonymous with modern commercial architecture. Although it provides scope for long horizontal windows to ensure plenty of daylight within the building, this also has the effect of making each floor appear to be independent of the floor below, which weakens the overall design concept. The application of piers to the face of such a building can reverse

this effect by physically "connecting" each floor and giving the building unity. Double piers can provide the architect with a neat and simple solution to the problem of ugly rainwater pipes and thick black expansion joints. These unsightly features can be hidden in the convenient recess made by a pair of piers set close together. However, mixing single and double piers on a façade is not a good idea, as an isolated thicker pier can be as visually intrusive as the pipes and joints themselves.

There is no technical difference between a pillar and a column, although some architectural purists insist that a pillar, unlike a column, need not be cylindrical or conform to any of the classical orders. These features form only a small part of a building, but they can still have a significant effect on the overall design.

Brick columns are sometimes non-loadbearing elements providing a decorative veneer around unattractive structural steel or concrete shafts. As most engineers design these shafts to be as thin as possible, they can often appear weak in contrast to a sturdier brick façade. Brick cladding gives these supports a more solid and stable appearance which integrates them with the rest of the building. For example, in the recently restored Registry of Deeds and Probate Court building at East Cambridge, Massachusetts, a rough-built brick dressing surrounds the steel columns which are the structural core. Internal columns which perform little, if any, structural purpose, can be built entirely of brick. This gives opportunities for unusual effects such as spirals to be created, using special shaped bricks.

A decorative colonnade appearance can be

Left: *Columns from a plantation house near Mississippi, USA, burnt during the American Civil War. The worn rendering has exposed radial brickwork beneath.*

Far right: *The Royal Scottish Academy of Music and Drama, Glasgow. The tiled capping to the angled plinth and soffit is colour-matched to the surrounding colonnade.*

achieved by linking brick pillars. Although these are rarely of practical benefit to a building, they can create a very powerful visual image. Two of the most successful examples of this can be seen at the Catholic Order of Foresters Headquarters in Naperville, Illinois, and the Royal Scottish Academy of Music and Drama in Glasgow, Scotland. The Royal Scottish Academy was designed with brick pillars supporting a projecting roof in the traditional manner. Set in front of the actual building face, the colonnading gives the building a light and spacious feeling. Although the colonnade on the Naperville building is not typical like the one on the Scottish building the effect it produces is similar. This one is free-standing, away from the fabric of the actual building, forming a combination of light and shade, with the warm-toned solid masonry pillars against the light, cool curtain-walled building behind, producing an exciting contrast.

CORBELLING

The term corbel derives from the French "*corbeau*" meaning raven, and, in architectural terms, it means a beak-like projection. Traditionally, the term corbel refers to a projecting block which supports a horizontal feature such as a beam, but modern convention allows the term to encompass a number of horizontal brackets which project beyond the face of a wall as cantilevers (see page 185).

The earliest known corbels were made by the Aegeans in the 15th century BC. They developed the technique in order to help them make wider openings in structural walls—until that time, the width of an opening was restricted by the limitations of an unsupported section of lintel. By projecting short sections of a building material in a series of steps, the Aegeans found a way to make the lintel span a greater distance and so increase the width of the opening. By expanding this simple, but effective, technique so that a series of tapered brick or stone units projected beyond the one below, they were able to use corbelling to support simple arches and vaults, and, within a relatively short time, they had refined the vault system and used it to great effect on a host of major buildings, including King Agamemnon's Tomb (c. 1325 BC). However, most of these early corbels were built in stone—the Aegeans were not adept bricklayers, and many of their brick constructions were crude.

The modern corbel has evolved from Turkish and Islamic architecture, where this technique was a critical part of the construction of the predominant features—pointed arches, vaulting and triangular decorative forms. An abundance of early monuments such as the ebullient tomb of Ismail Samanid at Bokhara (902 BC) and the 167 ft (51 m) high tomb-tower of Sultan Qabus (1007 BC) still survives, demonstrating a wealthy architectural vocabulary which includes brick corbelling, carving and sculpting. It was these rich details which were so greatly admired by travelling Europeans, who copied them when they returned to their own countries.

Almost any rigid material with a regular shape and size can be used to assemble a corbel. The unit size of the material is of little

Right: *This turn-of-the-century church on the Isle of Wight has a corbelled facade, with recessed panels to the corner towers, a crow stepped gable and a pointed arch.*

Far right: *Corbels supporting 'stacks' of projecting polychrome bricks.*

consequence, although smaller blocks are easier to manoeuvre into position than larger ones and give a softer overall appearance. Brick is an ideal medium for corbels with enormous structural possibilities. There is, however, a maximum corbel distance which must be adhered to unless additional reinforcement is included. This maximum distance is known as the one-third rule—a single block should not project more than one-third of the unit's bed length, and the maximum distance corbelled by a series of blocks should not exceed one-third of the wall's width. Without the support of the mass of the remaining two-thirds, the corbelling bricks could break off and fall.

Although the majority of simple brick corbelling is used for traditional load-bearing purposes, in recent years architects have used it solely for decoration, usually with good results. After the glut of flat-faced buildings which dominated world architecture between 1950 and 1960, ornamental corbels, giving the effect of light and shadow on an otherwise flat brick plane, are a welcome change. The possibilities for non-structural corbelling in brick are greater than for structural corbelling, because purely ornamental corbels do not have to obey the one-third rule, being supported by steel fixings tied or cast to a separate structural member (in concrete or steel) hidden within the corbelling.

Corbelling is also popular because of its versatility. Even small areas of it can significantly affect the onlooker's perception of a building. Corbelling applied to the corners of a very large structure, for example, can reduce

the building's apparent mass. A good example of this is the office building at 1718 Connecticut Avenue, Virginia, where small areas of corbelling give a delicate, chamfered appearance, and make the building considerably less monolithic.

Decorative corbelling can also be used to help integrate a building into an environment where the existing architecture dates from a past age, such as the Arrowcroft shop development in Chester, England, where bold corbels have been employed as a modern interpretation of the timber-framed style of the neighbouring medieval buildings.

In response to the demand for quick and easy corbelling, some manufacturers have developed special brick corbels for use on both corbel and batter details. Some of these are little more than inverted plinth bricks and corners, while others are rhomboid shaped— generally speaking, these bricks have little, if any, structural function, and often require complex fixing techniques with intricate arrangements of stainless steel ties and brackets. Nevertheless, corbels are an important embellishment which provides an architect with an excellent remedy for flat-planed architecture, a means of reducing perceived structural mass and a way of articulating an otherwise dull wall with light and shadow.

PLINTHS
One description of a pyramid is that it is an extravagant series of plinths supporting a tablet of stone. Although the description is incorrect, it nevertheless provides a simple mental image of what a plinth is and what it is

Left: *An oriel window supported by corbelling from a central pier at the Red House (1859–1860), Bexleyheath, England, by Philip Webb.*

Right: *Battered brick plinths below a string course of moulded stone at Castello Estense (late 14th-century–16th-century), Ferrara, Italy.*

expected to do. Basically, a plinth is a projection at the base of a wall (see page 182).

The first plinths were the Greek *crepidum*, or stepped bases found beneath the Classical Greek temples. These were formed in stone, rather than brick, and gave the structures a balanced, harmonious look. Like their ancient counterparts, modern plinths have no structural function—their main purpose is to provide an attractive solution to a number of design problems, including that of visually reducing the mass of a building and "anchoring" it to the ground, and raising a structure above a flood plain.

It is interesting to look at the psychology of plinth design. Plinths which incorporate a large and steeply pitched face tend to perform an anti-social function by dissuading the passer-by from getting too close to the building. The subliminal statement of the need for

privacy makes them ideal for commercial premises where an alternative boundary wall or fence would be undesirable. In contrast, low-level plinths with a flat-top or shallow pitch encourage the reverse. They are often used as informal seats on public buildings, such as art centres, where the requirement is for a relaxed ambience with structures performing an unobtrusively functional role.

The shape of the plinth is of little consequence, although all plinths should include an angled cap to allow for the drainage of rainwater and reduce the possibility of staining and frost damage. Many examples from the 16th and 17th centuries project only a short distance and typically include a moulded crown formed from special shaped bricks or terracotta blocks. Although they were included on some of Europe's brick manor houses, such as Sutton Place near Guildford, England (1523)

Left: *Chamfered plinths on a massive structure at the Cathedral of St. Cecile in Albi, France.*

Below: *Elaborate chimney stacks at Hampton Court in Surrey, England, with spiral, lozenge and chevron designs.*

and Kasteel Gemert at Gemert in the Netherlands (1740), moulded brick plinths have not stood the test of time. Chamfered plinths, such as the ones on the extraordinary cathedral of St. Cecile in Albi, France (1282–1512), have fared better. The plinths on the French cathedral project as far as 6 ft (2 m) from the face of the wall, but modern plinths tend to be less extreme. Modern builders favour chamfered plinths largely because they can be formed with standard bricks, or, for a little extra cost, with cant bricks which feature splayed corners, rather than the more expensive terracotta and special shaped bricks. Another plinth shape which is occasionally seen is the concave or swept plinth.

CHIMNEYS

Historically, architects and builders have chosen to embellish brick chimney stacks far more than any other structural component of their buildings. The reasons for this are unclear, as chimneys, more often than not, are placed either out of sight or at a point where lavish decoration cannot really be enjoyed by the onlooker from the ground. However, the sheer exuberance with which these extremities have sometimes been highlighted prompted Sir Alec Clifton-Taylor to comment that "it was here that a builder enjoyed himself most . . .". Certainly, chimneys represent some of the finest and most elaborate examples of brick ornamentation that have ever been created. The finest examples of brick chimney ornamentation can be seen on the great houses of Tudor England. This was a flamboyant time, when new innovations were eagerly

Left: *These chimneys at Bacon's Castle, Surrey County, Virginia, USA (c. 1655), are 'diamond set' at an angle of 45 degrees to the wall.*

adopted by a wealthy nation who employed the greatest architects and builders of the age. Many of these were imported from Europe, chiefly from Italy, France and the Netherlands, and they took the opportunity to demonstrate their skills to a new and appreciative audience. Octagonal, hexagonal, circular and spiral shapes began to appear on chimneys, adorned with moulded and carved brick relief. Although moulding and carving brickwork were relatively new arts in the mid-16th century, the bricklayers—many of whom were local craftsmen of limited training—were able to execute patterned brick relief from the range of embellishments popular during the period, such as lozenge, quatrefoil, Tudor rose, fleurs de lis, and other heraldic devices.

The brick chimneys of the Tudor period were also notable for the way in which individual stacks were assembled to form one large shaft. Most were clustered in groups of two or four but occasionally larger concentrations emerged. One of the earliest examples is the group of ten chimneys at East Barsham Manor in Norfolk, England, where the stubby terracotta shafts are arranged in two rows of five. While very impressive in themselves, these large concentrations of chimneys can appear too heavy for the main structure, and detract from the grace and balance of the rest of the building. This can also be true of single chimneys if no thought is given to their collective impact on the skyline. Much more effective are the collections of two, three or four shafts, strategically placed along a ridgeline, very common on European buildings of the medieval and Tudor periods.

These large stack combinations were to re-emerge as a dominant feature during the 19th-century Arts and Crafts Movement. Philip Webb, one of the main theorists of the movement, went to extraordinary lengths to streamline his chimney flues with easy curves, often involving cut bricks to avoid thick linings, which were set in "well made fresh cow-dung mortar". In contrast, Sir Edwin Lutyens, who designed some of the masterpieces of Arts and Crafts architecture, preferred muscular-looking brick chimneys and included them on his designs to add visual mass and solidity. Many of Lutyen's chimneys were plain and undecorated but their size and form exercise a magnetic attraction nonetheless.

Chimneys did not become a regular feature on small houses and cottages until the end of the 17th century, after a series of catastrophic fires, such as the great fire of London in 1666, had destroyed many European towns and cities. The chimney was regarded as a way of protecting the many timber-framed buildings from the spread of fire, and brick was the ideal material because it was cheaper, and more flame-resistant, than any of the available alternatives, including stone. However, while the owners of the great houses could afford to have the finest fired bricks laid in sophisticated arrangements, poorer people had to make do with simple structures in unfired clay. Brick's natural heat-resistance also made it a popular choice for fire-surrounds and hearths. Like the chimney shafts, hearths and fire-surrounds in large houses were often embellished in moulded brick, but even a humble cottager was able

Above: *Gaudi chimney pots made with thin bricks in stacks comprising projecting tiers of bricks alternately turned through 45 degrees and supported from diagonally-set corner corbels.*

Right: *This decorative chimney stack, on an otherwise modest 'cottage orné', incorporates a variety of decorative devices including a dentil course supporting a stone coping.*

to achieve an ornamental fireplace by arranging bricks in a simple herringbone pattern. Ever since the 16th century, these two techniques continue to be employed in building fireplaces.

When the exuberant Tudor style made way for more sober Classical successors, the design of the chimney matched it brick for brick. The fashion for large, classically styled houses required a simple, almost serene, appearance, and the new chimney designs were similarly refined, with a straight and uncluttered profile. Any added decoration was of a sober nature, with no more than a simple recessed panel or course of moulded bricks added as a kind of visual punctuation. Unusually, it was the chimneys of the smaller houses of the period which fostered a more decorative look, with tumbling and hound's tooth motifs being regularly employed. In many examples additional effects were achieved by angling the shaft on its brick base so that the design could be enhanced by heavy shoulders which gave an interplay of light and shadow. The change from tall to short chimneys came about because of the adoption of fire-proof clay roof tiling for all types of buildings. Tall chimneys were no longer necessary, and with the area available for decoration diminished, the decline of the magnificently ornamented chimney was under way. Its re-emergence was due largely to the 19th-century Industrial Revolution. In the drive to mechanize industrial processes, tall chimneys became essential—they needed to achieve a sufficient draught to draw the exhaust gases from the boilers, and also to expel smoke at a high altitude, so that it could disperse easily. Unless a particularly affluent industrialist wanted to display his success with something especially dynamic, the designs were kept simple, although they always incorporated brickwork of the highest quality. In many, the decorative effect was achieved solely with strong brick bonds (typically English and Flemish in two- and three-brick thick wall linings), which supported the large (usually 200 ft or 60 m high) structure. At their best, their simple elegance makes them as eloquent as their highly decorative predecessors. Regrettably, even the use of elegant bonding has disappeared from most new chimneys, and the stretcher bond arrangements which typify most modern constructions of this type possess none of the character of the earlier examples.

The burning of smoke-producing fuels, such as coal, introduced two important developments in chimney design; kinked flues and chimney pots. In the vast majority of houses, the flue, which prevents downdraughts from extinguishing the fire or blowing the exhaust smoke back into the room, is hidden from view. However, the exposed bend, normally on a flank wall, can add an attractive external feature. A common means of constructing the bend is by the gradual raking of bricks from the wide base to the thickness of the chimney shaft. The visual effect, dignified and graceful, fits equally well on crooked cottages and formal houses.

The chimney pot, formed for much the same purpose as the bent flue, reduces the size of the flue aperture and encourages the wind to strike against the pot edge and therefore draw

Left: *China kiln chimney from Ironbridge, Shropshire, England, set in English garden-wall bond.*

smoke from the shaft. The crude but effective ancestor of the chimney pot was a stack of stones tilted to form a pyramidal crown over the flue opening. Whilst this simple formula was suitable for rural cottages, the method was far too crude for more ornate formal houses, and it was for these that the preformed chimney pot was developed. Early chimney pots were sculpted from clay, but the ideal material is terracotta, whose hardy nature is excellent for withstanding the constant onslaught of rain and frost.

The ease with which terracotta may be sculpted seems to have encouraged chimney pot makers to develop decorative forms and motifs, in particular, the circle, hexagon, octagon and spiral. Many of these forms were adorned with richly sculpted patterns like heraldry, lozenges and the ever-popular fleurs-de-lis.

Whilst chimney pots may be regarded as an attractive extension of the flue, some people consider them as blotchy additions to the roofscape. There is sometimes good cause for this criticism, especially today, where the argument may be extended to include the chimney stacks themselves. In our continued attempts to produce cheap buildings, we accept mundane chimneys which have none of the character of their forebears and are a distracting element in what would otherwise be a pleasant roofscape.

The modern preoccupation with saving heat energy and the ban on smoke-producing fuels have led to many home-owners blocking or removing their chimneys in the post-war years. However, there is a growing trend towards open fires, with many existing blocked flues being re-opened and new houses being built with fireplaces and chimney flues. Cost cutting tends to mean that chimneys are characterless shafts of rectangular bond stretcher brickwork, rather than exciting, ornate structures.

PAVING

Much of the modern demand for brick paving stems from the backlash against the functionalism and uniform appearance of black and grey tarmac. The demand for a more personalized streetscape has led to increased interest in the colourful versatility of brick paving. The reasons for its popularity are not difficult to identify: it is a natural material with a warm character and a rich assortment of colours and textures, which provides a human scale, particularly if it is covering large paved areas which would be formidable in a poured substance such as tarmac or concrete. However, it must be handled with care—a sea of uniform brick paving can be just as unappealing as many of the monotone substitutes.

Brick paving is not a new development. It was regularly used by the Romans, and by the 16th century it had become popular for flooring material in small cottages, and in the utility rooms and out-buildings in great houses. Most of the existing examples are in private houses, but a notable exception is the floor in the Utrecht Centraal Museum, in the Netherlands. External brick paving was also used at this time, especially in Belgium, Germany, the Netherlands and Scandinavia, where it is still a common feature. Elsewhere

Left: *Brick chimney interior from Casey's Farm, Rhode Island, USA.*

115

in Europe, like France and Great Britain, brick was considerably less popular than cobbles or granite setts, and few examples survive.

Brick may seem a strange choice for a road material, but it is fairly widespread. It is popular in Northern Europe—the first time visitor to Amsterdam in The Netherlands or Lübeck in Germany may well remember the cities just as much for their brick infrastructure as for their canals or marzipan.

In recent years, brick roads have become synonymous with the *woonerf*—an urban street system which controls the movement of vehicles, giving priority to pedestrians. The system was developed in The Netherlands and relies on the careful deployment of shaped and coloured surfaces to define which areas are for vehicles, and which are for the exclusive use of pedestrians. Besides being quieter than conventional metalled road surfaces, brick is thought to have a psychological impact on drivers, encouraging them to slow down and drive with greater care. So far, the system has proved enormously successful.

Paving bricks need to be hard and well-burnt to withstand constant wear and tear from feet and wheels. Being unprotected, they also require low porosity and good resistance against frost. The best paving bricks are traditional Dutch and adamantine clinkers. Dutch clinkers are small clay bricks, kiln-burnt at a high temperature, with an attractive semi-vitrified and warped appearance. Adamantine clinkers look similar but are harder, denser and heavier, with a smooth surface and chamfered edges which make them ideal for

kerbs and channels. The naturally rough texture of bricks gives them a firm, non-slip surface. Additional safety can be achieved by using bricks with a serrated or embossed finish, although this tends to make them uncomfortable to walk on—they tend to be used only at places like road crossing points.

There are two basic methods of paving: rigid and flexible. Rigid paving involves the bedding of paving bricks onto a thin layer of dry cement or lime mortar set over a concrete base, with the vertical brick joints grouted with mortar. It is particularly suitable for steps, ramps and slopes, and for "hard landscaping" features such as retaining walls and planters; because the joints are rigid, the stability of the paving is increased, allowing a greater freedom for decorative bond arrangements. Flexible paving involves the setting of brick paviors onto a bed of dry sand. They are laid with thin gaps between them, which are then pointed up using sand and compacted with a mechanical vibrator. Stability is achieved through the friction with adjacent paviors (known as "interlock"). Flexible paving is ideal for both road and pedestrian areas and is preferable to the rigid method because the sand allows natural drainage, and the bricks may be easily lifted and replaced during any maintenance work. One problem which is common to both is that bricks may vary in length, leaving a variety of gaps which must be filled with mortar or sand. The decorative potential of both methods is enormous. Designs can vary from the simple arrangements of changing bonds and colours to very elaborate ones, such as the ingenious

Left: *The restored Tudor rose motif in the courtyard of Kentwell Hall, Suffolk, England.*

Tudor rose motif in the courtyard of 16th-century Kentwell Hall in Suffolk, England. In theory, there are as many paving bonds as there are brick wall bonds, but in practice, they tend to break down into four basic types: Stretcher or Running bond, Herringbone bond, Basket-weave bond and Stack bond (see page 181).

Stretcher bond, where each stretcher is placed centrally over the vertical joint between

Right: Well worn brick paving, laid in an informal herringbone pattern in Gertrude Jekyll's restored herb garden at Knebworth, Hertfordshire, England.

the two bricks in the previous row, is probably the cheapest. Popular during the last two centuries, it is now unfashionable as a paving arrangement. However, it is ideally suited to areas where traffic is mostly pedestrian, such as shopping arcades and footpaths. Usually, bricks are set so that the long sides are parallel to the main traffic flow, giving the paving a strong directional emphasis. This is also true of Stack bond, which has a two-directional emphasis. Stack bond, a continuous series of brick lines running in the same direction, is often said to have little character of its own, so English Stack bond, with alternate brick lines at right angles, is often preferred.

The two best-known ornamental arrangements are Basket-weave bond and Herringbone bond. Basket-weave is made by setting squared brick groups—two bricks if bed-up, three if face-up—in alternating directions, giving a grid-like appearance. It is suitable for large expanses of paving, particularly pedestrian precincts. Herringbone bond, with the bricks set at right-angles to one another, is more appropriate for vehicles. It can also be useful in small spaces, because it tends to visually enlarge the area where it is laid. Most herringbone patterns are orientated at 45 degrees to the general direction of flow, which is better for reducing "wandering" effects in the mortar joints than the alternative 90 degree orientation. Most brick manufacturers develop their own special shaped paviors, such as the interlocking brick. These are brick units with a similar shape to the letter "I". Some manufacturers also make functional "accessory" bricks, which fall into five basic

Left: *The garden at Folly Farm, Berkshire, England. Formal herringbone brick paving set in areas of stone.*

Below: *Waveland State Historic Site in Lexington, Kentucky, USA (1847): American bond (English garden-wall bond) and herringbone paving.*

would not have been achieved if concrete or tarmac had been used instead of brick.

Public reaction against monotonous and single-surfaced materials has brought with it an awareness of environmental quality. The demand that paved areas should be designed to the highest visual, as well as functional, standards, can be regarded as one of the major aesthetic revolutions of the 20th century.

RADIAL BRICKWORK

Despite its enormous decorative potential, radial brickwork—curved or circular brickwork using special shaped bricks—is an under-used architectural feature. This is partly due to the difficulty of constructing a true curved shape and partly because radial-shaped buildings are not, generally speaking, an efficient use of space. The most effective use of radial brickwork is as a means of continuing a wall around an acute corner, or softening harsh rectangular building forms, through the introduction of circular staircases and curved wall reveals.

The Romans built some of the first round buildings utilizing radial brickwork including the theatre of Marcellus (23–13 BC), the Pantheon (AD 118–128), and the Mausoleum of Hadrian (AD 135), but they usually used brick as the structural framework and clad their monuments with other materials such as concrete. This can be seen on the Colosseum (AD 72–80) where the effects of decay and pillaging reveal the brickwork to good effect. Radial brickwork is also evident on the religious edifices of early Islamic architecture. Two particularly impressive structures are the 100 ft (30 m) high spiralling al-Malwiya minaret at Samarra (AD 836–852) and the 200 ft (60 m) high decorated minaret of Cham in Afghanistan (12th century AD). The modern demand for tall buildings is for offices and apartments rather than minarets and towers, and developers are aware that circular plans are less space-efficient than square or rectangular ones. For this reason, the radial brick structures of the last century tended to be

Above: *This extraordinary residential building in the Spaarndammer buurt in Amsterdam incorporates a three-storey oriel window, built in headers.*

Right: *This early 19th-century London house features segmental bays with blind windows in between, made of ordinary London stock bricks.*

Right: *University of Virginia, USA. This crinkle-crankle wall with saddleback coping is made from standard bricks in stretcher bond. These walls may be built in a half-brick thickness, because the curving shape gives the structure added strength.*

fairylandish water-towers and chimneys, and, in this century, very few radial brick buildings of any kind have been erected. Radial brick-work is not particularly difficult to construct nowadays, because of the availability of special bricks which help to overcome the difficulty of achieving a perfect curve. These bricks have an arced face, and, like other specials, they are more expensive than standard bricks. A cheaper alternative is to use the traditional system of setting standard flat-faced bricks with tapering joints, but the result is rarely aesthetically pleasing, mainly because it is impossible to achieve a really smooth curve.

The soft, elegant look of radial brickwork is deceptive—the gently curving façade disguises a self-buttressing wall which is stronger than its flat-planed counterpart. This strength makes it ideal for retaining walls, such as the "crinkle-crankle" or serpentine wall, which follows a continuous, snaking curve. One of the best modern examples of radial brickwork used for this purpose is the wall built in 1989 at the entrance to the Hampton Oaks residential development in Stafford County, Virginia. An even stranger variant of the crinkle-crankle wall is the wavy wall, which has oscillating brick courses and an undulating cap as well as a snaking plan form. This presents additional constructional difficulties requiring bricks of varying shapes and lengths, and the talents of a very skilled bricklayer, on whom its success entirely depends, as the complexity makes detailed architect's drawings superfluous.

Unsurprisingly, there are few examples of wavy walls, although there is one successful example at the Nene Housing Society development in Peterborough, England. It is a delightfully flamboyant gesture in an exciting housing development.

PRE-ASSEMBLED PANELS

As the name suggests, these panels are manufactured away from the building site, and, once *in situ*, they are hoisted into position with a crane and bolted to the structural steel frame. Panels are created by setting bricks face down onto a timber frame and casting a reinforced concrete backing behind. Normally, cut perforated bricks are used, with the semi-circular perforations providing a "key" to the concrete, so that the two bond together. In situations where perforated bricks are not suitable (a specific finish may be necessary, or a detail needs extra support) the facing bricks can be fixed to the concrete backing with stainless steel cramps or wall ties. The brick joints are usually filled by the concrete, but they can also be pointed in coloured mortar to match a particular finish.

The main advantage of these panels is that they can be made under controlled conditions which can never be equalled on site—especially important when a complex detail is required. Cheap to construct, they can be manufactured and fixed during winter conditions, which is useful in areas which suffer from heavy frosts or long periods of sub-zero temperatures. They are quick to fix once the structural form has been erected, and help to reduce the need for scaffolding, which is especially useful in areas where scaffolding would obstruct pedestrians or traffic.

A basic requirement of modern architecture is that brick buildings need to possess both the structural integrity of reinforced concrete as well as the aesthetic qualities of brickwork. Pre-assembled panels provide both. Almost any design of panel is possible—the main design concern is the fixing of panels to the frame. The majority of pre-cast work is found on new buildings, but the system can work equally well for the refurbishment of existing structures, such as the Wills Tobacco Company's building in Bristol, England where pre-assembled brick details were used successfully during restoration work in 1987. A good example of pre-assembled panels on a new building can be found on the supermarket next door to the Wills Tobacco Company's building. It was found that the expenses incurred in making the store fit in with the architectural character of the adjacent Edwardian building would be greatly reduced if precast panels were used.

Precast panels are not only suitable for intricate shapes like the arches on the Bristol supermarket. The panelled walls of the enormous Target store in Irving, Texas, used large expanses of plain flat and curved panels to great effect. The architects used a stack bond technique—impossible on a "real" brick wall because of its lack of bonding strength. In many situations, pre-assembled panels can provide a quick and cost-effective solution to a design problem, and their added bonuses of precision and flexibility have opened up new possibilities for design which are increasingly being exploited by architects.

DECORATION AND EPHEMERALISM

Decorative brickwork has existed almost since the creation of bricks themselves, with notable early examples dating back to 3rd-millennium BC Mesopotamia, where facing bricks carried distinctive stamps, sculptures and inscriptions. The interest in decorative brickwork had largely disappeared by the 4th century BC and did not re-emerge with any degree of prominence until nine centuries later. During the intervening period it was mainly overlooked by the Greeks and Romans, although it enjoyed a brief revival under Julius Caesar as ornamental veneering over concrete walls.

The renaissance of brick in general—and consequently brick decoration—began in the early 6th century AD with the large building programmes of the Byzantine Empire. The Byzantine buildings appear to conform to a single structural pattern of light timber roofs with clay tiles over walls which were thinner than previous techniques had allowed and which could be easily pierced with window openings. The expanses of plain wall surrounding these windows provided a perfect space for decorative reliefs, and brickwork soon found its place alongside marble, mosaic and stone. Byzantine architecture had a great influence on medieval Europe, where interest in decorating buildings still remains with us.

ASSORTED FINISHES

Introducing bricks of one colour into a wall of another looks simple; the casual onlooker rarely appreciates the expertise necessary to achieve the overall effect. Coloured brick patterns come in a wide variety of forms, from the simple band or bands of a single colour which crop up in a number of 1980s buildings to the complexity of a full polychromatic arrangement. Between these two are scores of assorted patterns, including the popular diaper and chequer devices, which convert a normally flat brick wall into an exciting and delicate lace-like structure.

The art of applying coloured patterns to a wall is thought to have originated in mid-15th century France. Some of the early French examples, such as the ornate dovecot at Boos Manor near Rouen, are similar to those found in the Islamic world, and may have come into the French vernacular via the Moorish influences of Spanish architecture. Knowledge of this technique was soon disseminated throughout Europe, the extent and effect of the patterning depending on local brick manufacturing skills. The early builders always had a readily available choice of colours simply because the bricks rarely emerged from the kiln burnt evenly. The principal requirement, then as now, was for the headers to be different in tone from the remaining wall, with greys, blues, purples and, if possible, black being the most popular colours.

Many of the first attempts at coloured patterning were tentative and visually weak, although some examples from the 15th and early 16th centuries—such as St. John's College, Cambridge, England (1511)—do demonstrate the bold effect of diaperwork, which started a fashion that was to dominate the architectural style of the English Tudor

Below: *This 19th-century stone house has decorative, tumbled-in brick gables.*

period. By the end of the 1550s, very few important brick buildings failed to incorporate a section of coloured patterning. The 17th and 18th centuries saw the introduction of a new Classical architectural ideology which required greater finesse in decorative details, and although many of the techniques used in the Middle Ages were retained, they were regularized in a way which tended to lessen their visual impact. The trend was helped by the spread of Flemish bonding which maintained stronger horizontal emphasis and also incorporated a regular header arrangement, making it easy to introduce an all-over pattern. Some of the most spectacular examples of this technique can be seen in the village of Cranbrook in Kent, England, where almost every Georgian building has an area of blue headers diapered on soft pink stretchers.

Diapering appeared regularly throughout the 19th century, although its regularity and consistent colour is uncomfortable when compared with the fragmented and worn appearance of its predecessors. An interesting comparison of the diapering technique of the Middle Ages and the 19th century can be seen in the courtyard of Fulham Palace in London, where the fatigued Tudor diapers are still infinitely more engaging than their technically superior but monotonous Victorian counterparts. At about the same time as Victorian diapering was introduced at Fulham Palace, the French architect Jules Saulnier was creating a stunning arrangement on his Menier Chocolate Factory (c. 1871) at Noisiel-sur-Marne on the outskirts of Paris, France. This outstanding example of the *brique-et-fer* style of building employed brilliantly coloured infill panels of red, yellow, yellow-ochre and black bricks set in a diaper pattern with additional tiles and medallions in ceramic tiles.

The term diapering is commonly applied to the regular arrangement of any small coloured pattern over a wall. Ordered regularity is the key to its success, and it requires experience of the effects of brickwork and design; too much colour, or the use of conflicting or inappropriate colours, can impose the wrong emphasis on a wall. There is also the additional problem of linking the pattern with the brick bond. Most diaper work is formed by laying contrasting headers to form a lozenge pattern and requires a considerably greater number of headers than are normally provided by either English or Flemish bonds. Consequently, the pattern can generate a large number of headers and create a peculiar bond arrangement.

A popular alternative to the lozenge pattern in diapering is the chequer motif. Chequer patterns can be achieved by replacing the headers of Flemish bond brickwork with darker coloured bricks. The arrangement in English bonding is less simple, and may require the introduction of headers within the stretcher course. The visual impact of chequering depends largely on the choice of colours used: darker headers appear to provide mass and reduce the perceived height of the building, while the use of lighter colours has the opposite effect. Compatible colours achieve the best results: the popular mixture of blue and grey, or blue and red bricks gives the building a dignified appearance, while the stark contrast of black and white bricks may

Below: *The magnificent
Menier chocolate factory,
by Jules Saulnier, situated
on the outskirts of Paris.*

Far right: *Glazed brickwork at its best.*

Below: *Yellow headers and red brick stretchers — the reverse of the usual colour-scheme.*

give an uncomfortable "chess-board" look. Chequer patterning also occurs through the naturally occurring colour variations of headers and stretchers on the same brick. This can often be more attractive than those examples where the different coloured bricks have been deliberately selected. Two examples of the natural chequering effect are the Protestant Episcopal Church of Old Trinity, Church Creek, Maryland, USA (1674) where the chequering and overall design is more reminiscent of a rustic cottage than a church, and the Dutch-looking Governor's Palace at Williamsburg, Virginia, USA (c. 1720, rebuilt after 1781).

The practice of galleting (sometimes referred to as garreting or garnetting) provides an unusual decorative effect. The term derives from the French *galet* (meaning pebble), and the technique itself involves the introduction of objects and materials into the mortar joint while it is still pliant. In most cases, the introduced materials are sharp pieces of flint, stones or coloured pebbles, although any substance can be used; sometimes glass bullseyes or bottle ends are used to replace a header. The practice seems to have been initially used as a means of reinforcing and reducing the area of the mortar joints, but it offers wonderful opportunities for decorative effects. Galleting can introduce both colour and sparkle to a wall, and one of its main attractions is that it allows the use of locally available materials.

Polychromatic brickwork—the deliberate arrangement of several colours of bricks into an ordered pattern—is the most exciting and controversial form of brick patterning.

Some observers consider it fairylandish, while others believe that it is architecture at its most vigorous and virile. Successful "constructional polychromy", to give it its true name, demands a highly developed design skill as well as an innate understanding of colour. Some of the best examples of polychromy were produced in the 19th century, when the fashion for highly decorated buildings enjoyed a revival.

The British architects William Butterfield and Samuel Sanders Teulon were among the best exponents of polychromy. While Teulon's work was more technically innovative, Butterfield's achievements are probably the more memorable with their vibrant use of multi-coloured brick stripes and geometrical forms. The interior of All Saints Church in Margaret Street, London (1850–9), perhaps Butterfield's greatest achievement, is remarkable. The walls erupt into a profusion of geometrical arrangements with several materials and colours. Red, black and off-white bricks and tiles combine with green, grey and yellow glazed tiles, and black and red mastic joints set into pale stone and terracotta. Butterfield also used coloured brick in his designs for Keeble College, Oxford (1867–75), breaking away from the usual collegiate stone vernacular. His lively employment of red, yellow and blue stripes, chequers and helix configurations, which he blended with sandstone dressings, is regarded as a highpoint in brick elaboration. However, it was not popular with the Oxford establishment of the day, who were so disgusted by what they termed his "streaky-bacon" design that they formed a society to steal bricks in a futile attempt to bankrupt the foundation. By comparison, Teulon's work is generally less colourful than Butterfield's but more refined in its quality of detail. He sometimes displayed a taste for the bizarre; his design for Elvetham Hall, Hampshire (1859–62) used a combination of red and blue stripes and prickly floral patterns.

Across the Channel, the French architects like Viollet-le-Duc and Lacroux were furthering the cause of polychromy during Napoleon III's rebuilding of central Paris. Haussmann, the ruthless Prefect of the Seine Department, had been appointed by the Emperor to oversee the task, and had directed that all buildings lining the new boulevards should be dressed with stone façades. However, his edict was not applied to either commercial or private buildings, and the designers of these enjoyed greater freedom to indulge themselves in *brique et fer* architecture using polychromatic brickwork.

This prolific rebuilding stimulated a demand for pattern books showing standard designs. Numerous lavishly illustrated books were produced including Viollet-le-Duc's *Habitations modernes* (1875), Lacroux's *La brique ordinaire* (1878) and Pierre Chabat's *La brique et la terre cuite* (1881). These illustrated a collection of standard building designs, employing a spectrum of details and features which were to make up the new architectural vocabulary. The most interesting aspect of these architectural atlases is not the designs for the domestic villas and commercial premises themselves, but the profusion of polychromatic brick-bonding patterns and details for windows, door and chimneys utilized in them.

Left: *The polychrome chapel at Keeble College, Oxford, England, by William Butterfield.*

Lacroux's passion for constructional poly-chromy was amply demonstrated in his book, which shows the wealth of regular brick patterns and decorative motifs popular in the late-19th century, with pictures of many examples of banding, chequering and diaper work as well as extremely fine arrangements and colour matching. More importantly, it shows a range of decorative patterns, such as diagonal stripes, waves, zigzags, rows of crosses and tartan effects. These can easily be achieved within the main brick bonds and can also be used in friezes and on plain walls, as well as for more elaborate projecting copings, cornices and gables.

A close study of Teulon's St James's Church at Leckhampstead, Berkshire, England, reveals a trait which cannot fail to disappoint polychromy lovers. The church (1858–60) is rightly regarded as a fine example of English polychromatic brickwork and incorporates all that is to be normally expected of a 19th-century polychromy—bands of buff, red and black brick with similarly coloured diapering and arch voussoirs. However, a close look reveals that the church is actually constructed of red bricks, some of which were painted to resemble buff coloured bricks and others coated with a thick layer of soot to give the appearance of black bricks. This faking is not an isolated example—it was often done in areas where coloured bricks were hard to obtain.

Nowadays, true polychromatic brickwork is very rare, remaining largely a feature of the visually enlightened and affluent past. In its place, the term polychromatic brickwork is used to cover minor decorative features such as coloured brick bands on external walls to signify floor levels and to dress window and door openings, sills and lintel courses. This use of the term weakens its otherwise vibrant association with the work of Butterfield, Viollet-le-Duc and others, and is really just a grand title for some rather uninspiring ornamental brickwork.

One exception to this is the Isle of Dogs Storm Water Pumping Station (1989) which prevents London from flooding during the rare high water levels of the River Thames. Its architect John Outram used polychrome brickwork with brightly painted pre-cast concrete and stylized Classical details to enliven a

Below: John Outram's exuberant Storm Water Pumping Station on the Isle of Dogs, London.

Below: *Bricks provide a good surface for mural painters. This advertisement is on 34th Street and Eighth Avenue, New York.*

strictly utilitarian structure. The building is an example of stripy brickwork at its very best, with a varying mixture of blue, red and yellow bricks combined in a symmetrical but irregular pattern. These stripes are arranged in three thick bands. The top layer, (normally in shadow from the overhanging roof) is set in dark blue brick and reduces the perceived height of the building. The central band is made up of buff coloured bricks and this sits upon a darker plinth-like base in blue brick. All three bands are interrupted by thinner stripes of red and buff bricks, which lighten the overall mass of the building.

The fiery character of polychromatic brickwork can occasionally be seen in brick murals, perhaps the only contemporary art form which comes close to observing the principles of true polychromy. Interest in brick murals has grown considerably during recent years, thanks to some remarkably effective works which have succeeded in raising the status of the art and its practitioners. Indeed, the overall effect is similar to the *Pointillism* method of painting practised by French Impressionists such as Georges Seurat, except that they applied coloured dots of paint on a canvas, while muralists use coloured rectagular bricks in a wall.

The quality of a mural depends wholly upon the creative expertise of its artist and his understanding of brickwork and colour. Generally, large murals tend to be more effective than small ones because the rectangular brick shapes are less recognizable and the design image is softer and clearer. When the rectangular brick shapes are noticeable, as in small murals, they

Below: *A touch of local colour – Paul Watlington's steel worker mural in Sheffield, England.*

present a blurred and fuzzy appearance which distorts the intended design and only disappears when seen from a distance. One of the best brick murals is the portrait of a steelworker in Sheffield, designed by Paul Watlington in 1984. It stands over 36 ft (11 m) tall, a remarkably life-like portrait in an array of blue, grey, brown, red buff and white bricks.

Nowadays, given the extensive range of bricks and brick colours available from manufacturers, the possibilities for creating any polychromatic effect are virtually unlimited.

RAISED AND PROJECTING BRICKWORK

Interest in raised brick decoration reached its peak during the 18th century, after a concerted effort by bricklayers in the previous century to lift the status of their craft to that enjoyed by stonemasons. Some bricklayers even boasted that they could complete a house without the need to employ expensive masons for ornamental work such as aprons below windows, recessed or projecting panels and projecting parapet features.

Projecting brickwork involves the simple protrusion of part of one brick over another to form, for example, a drip—a projecting cornice for preventing rainwater from running down the face of a wall.

The most popular use of projecting brickwork is as dentilation below a string course or cornice. Dentilation mainly occurs in a course of headers and is a simple enough motif created by projecting every other header beyond the face of a wall. An interesting alternative occurs

Left: *Ornamental brick from Torcello, Italy, featuring a dog's-tooth label course and a moulded terracotta cornice.*

Above: *Blind window detail with a raised pattern of moulded bricks.*

in Flemish bond brickwork where every header is projected forward, although the slightly irregular appearance is less effective. A different effect can be created by setting each header in a diagonal arrangement so that it creates a serrated appearance. The device is popularly known as dog's tooth, or, in America, hound's tooth. Both dentilation and dog's tooth are particularly effective and are regularly used in the upper courses of walls and under eaves. They can be produced using ordinary rectangu-

lar bricks or, if a particular effect is desired, special shaped bricks.

Strapwork, another projecting brick pattern, normally involves a highly complex arrangement of projecting rectangular bricks forming a combination of circular, oval, squared, lozenge and other shaped patterns. The best examples of strapwork are to be seen in buildings dating from the late-17th century, when the device was at the height of its popularity.

Rustication is usually associated with stone rather than brick but examples of rusticated brick can occasionally be found. The idea is to give a rich and bold texture to an exterior wall by emphasizing large masonary blocks with deep joints, but, as a rule, brick's essentially *petit* character does not make it suitable for the effects of scale required, so the technique was never widely employed in the way it was intended. Most examples are seen on brick quoins at the corners of buildings, when rustication takes the form of chamfering the edges of the brick. A very rare exception is seen on The Old House at Blandford in Dorset, England, where the entire external walling has been rusticated in brick. Despite the fine quality of the workmanship at Blandford, the overall effect achieved with small units masquerading as large blocks is uncomfortable, producing a visual peculiarity.

PERFORATED BRICKWORK
One of the simplest ways of achieving a decorative effect is by puncturing the face of a brick wall with holes, thus creating a delicate pattern of shadows. The most effective results

are obtained when the holes are at regular intervals or create a formal pattern. This occurs in honeycomb walling, in which bricks are omitted at regular intervals along the length of a brick course, and alternately in each rising course. Honeycombing is popular for two reasons: its economic use of bricks, and its ability to provide good ventilation and the free circulation of air. However, the technique has limited usage, especially in countries with cool climates, and most examples are found in agricultural buildings such as barns and dove-cotes. Many western domestic buildings utilise honeycomb walls as sleeper walls below timber floors, because they support the floor and allow the free movement of air around the timbers, helping to prevent rotting. In tropical climates, the simple honeycomb wall can provide protection from direct sunlight through its solid sections, whilst the open voids allow a cooling breeze to ventilate the shaded area.

A slight variation of honeycombing can be

Above: *A Victorian barn in Worcester, England, with honeycomb wall detailing.*

produced by neglecting to fill the putlog holes in a brick wall. (Putlogs are short horizontal sections of scaffolding that have one end built into the wall for structural stability and are normally plugged with brick or mortar when the scaffold is removed.) The variation needs only to be taken one stage further to turn it into a highly attractive feature suitable for both residential and commercial buildings—this is achieved by filling the putlog holes with bricks which project beyond the face of the wall, throwing soft shadows on the surface. However, its nickname "burglar bond" highlights its obvious disadvantage.

Below: *Victorian decoration: a moulded-brick ornamental frieze detail from an 1892 London house.*

SHAPED BRICKWORK

Despite its suitability for most applications, the rectangular brick is often restrictive for designers who want to achieve a particular visual effect. Some of those restrictions can be eliminated by using alternative configurations or special shaped bricks which have been purpose-moulded to the desired shape. Before shaped bricks became widely available, the bricklayer had to shape the bricks himself on site by sawing, cutting or rubbing them. Features such as copings, labels, mullions, transoms and architraves, string-courses, pilasters and cornices depended for their success on the skill of the bricklayer.

The moulding technique has changed very little over the centuries, and modern manufacturers still use the traditional method of throwing wet clay into a timber or steel mould. Moulding is a flexible solution for creating simple or intricate ornamental profiles. Bricks formed in this fashion are known as "purpose-moulded". This is the cheapest means of producing special shaped bricks, particularly if a quantity of identical specials is required. There are, however, occasions when the ornamentation is so intricate that it is not practical to mould the brick, and the alternative carving or gauged work is more suitable.

Gauged brickwork evolved in the Netherlands during the 16th century, and many of the early examples show a remarkable degree of finesse. This type of decorative work is nowadays generally restricted to gauged arches over doors and windows. The process of creating gauged brickwork begins with saw-cutting the hard brick roughly into shape and then rubbing the edges smooth on a piece of hard stone. Much care is necessary, particularly during the first stage, as burnt clay is quite brittle and easily fractures when struck with force. Hard bricks, chosen because of their durability, rarely give more than simple, bold forms and soft bricks called rubbers are necessary for the most sophisticated and intricate gauged work.

Even before the appearance of soft brick rubbers, it was not beyond the skills of early bricklayers to achieve elaborate designs. The most notable examples are English, and found in houses built during the reign of King Henry VIII. Buildings like Giffords Hall in Suffolk, and East Barsham Manor and Oxburgh Hall in Norfolk include corbelled bands of moulded cusped trefoils and quatrefoils, pinnacles with moulded crockets carved in various leaf shapes, and carved finials. The gatehouse of East Barsham Manor also included a complete coat-of-arms in brickwork carved *in situ*, using special large bricks standing several courses high. The effect is impressive but aesthetically uncomfortable, as is often the case when large bricks are used for special features.

Carved brickwork is a natural progression

Left: *Late 19th-century moulded brick cornice using the popular egg-and-dart motif.*

Below: *Chelsea Embankment, London. A late Victorian carved and rubbed panel with tapering pilasters and a design of lilies.*

from gauged work and is used for elaborate details such as capitals. The brick is first cut to approximate shape, usually *in situ*, with a hammer and bolster, or, in the case of fine work, by wire-saws, files and copper strips before being brought to the desired shape with a soft rubbing brick. Brick carving is considered an art rather than a craft, and few of its modern practitioners have a background in the bricklaying trades. This situation is a far cry from the Middle Ages when the bricklayer's expertise encompassed the creation of delicate brick detailing such as window aprons and heads, scrolls, Ionic capitals and egg and dart moulding.

Today carved, gauged and rubbed brickwork is rarely seen on anything but specific restoration work and one-off commissions. The cheaper contemporary alternative of employing special shaped bricks is far more common, but no matter how expertly executed, it almost always appears crude in comparison. The restoration at Hampton Court Palace, after a disastrous fire in 1986, is perhaps the closest one can get to the masterly brickwork of the past. Much of the restoration involves reproducing the ornate and intricate rubbed brickwork of the Tudor original. This is achieved by piecing together the remains of two or more original bricks and copying them. A "soft" brick is then roughly cut, using this template, and the approximately shaped unit is finished with carborundum stones and coarse paper. The new work is then pieced into the original brickwork. Apart from being cleaner, the reproduced brick is not discernibly different from the original.

After their heyday in the 19th century shaped bricks gradually declined in popularity reaching the nadir in their fortunes in the 1950s and 60s. For the rare occasion when special shapes were employed perhaps for copings and cappings, regular bricks were usually cut to the required shape in preference to using bricks specially formed for the purpose. This approach demanded considerable skill and in many cases the result was unsatisfactory with cut bricks proving unstable and susceptible to frost damage. Concern over these disadvantages has led to the re-adoption of manufactured pre-formed specials. The demand for special shaped bricks increased during the 1970s as design attitudes began to change. The greater interest in decorating buildings with brick has led to a renaissance in 19th-century architectural detailing, increasingly through the use of special shaped bricks.

In addition to special shaped bricks, an architect may very occasionally need regular shaped bricks of an unusual size. Many of these non-uniform bricks (categorized as special specials) are used by conservation architects in the restoration of historic buildings, because bricks from earlier periods are generally of a different size from those available today. Others may be required to fulfil a particular design intention.

Special bricks are simply accessories used to refine or articulate brickwork through changes in surface alignment, such as the use of curves and angles, or for capping walls and ramps. They add a degree of finesse and it requires extra care and attention to incorporate them successfully into a building and provide a sure finishing touch. The detail may be a novel design or a simple course of cant bricks providing a coping to a wall. Specials are expensive, but the added cost is almost always compensated for by the visual richness which they can provide.

BRICK COCKTAILS

The combination of brick with other materials is a simple technique and it can be highly successful, provided that the choice of the second material is sound. This was not always the case in the past, when builders and architects were limited to whatever material was available locally; today, the ease with which material can be transported from place to place means that almost any substance can be obtained. The best results are almost always achieved by introducing a material with a diametrically opposing colour and texture to the chosen brick, although the finished effect also depends on the extent of the mixture, and how and where the combination is used. The most popular blend of materials has historically been a cocktail of brick with knapped flint, chalk, tiles, ashlared stone or concrete rendering.

The intermingling of brick and flint is popular. Flint, like chalk, is readily available but relies upon other, larger size materials to enhance its structural potential; organizing the brick into a regular lacing course arrangement provides a bond between the facing and rubble-built core. Combined in a regular pattern brick and flint are seldom visually pleasing, but where a piece of flint is substituted for small areas of brickwork, such as

Above: *Early 17th-century brickwork. Brick headers with knapped and dressed flints laid in a chequer pattern, with crude flint galleting and brick quoins.*

Far right: *Casa Vicens, Barcelona, Spain. An exciting mixture of stone and glazed tiles, with projecting brick fins corbelled out from the walls.*

dark brick headers, the result can be excellent. Knapped flints are particularly suitable for this, although chalk may be used as a cheaper alternative.

The amalgamation of brick and stone is another popular and effective combination which is widely seen throughout the world. The best effects are usually achieved by combining brick with ashlared limestone and sandstone, although, technically, any stone type can be used. One of the clearest examples of this is the exuberant fret mixture of bright red brick and stone on the Latin American Baroque Sanctuary (begun c. 1745) at Ocotlan, Mexico. Another unusual combination occurs at Wallington Hall, Norfolk, England, where red brickwork is interspersed in a chequer pattern with rough, unashlared brown carstone. Unfortunately, this combination is not successful and the overall effect is tawdry.

Nowadays, Western architects rarely use stone with brick because it requires the use of specialist labour and is therefore very expensive. Where materials are mixed, the modern preference is for a combination of brick and cement rendering. Render is a perfect modern material for a brick cocktail because it emphasizes the opposing colour and texture characteristics of the two materials. As a result, it can be seen on a large number of buildings. A particularly outstanding example is the water tower at Mönchengladbach in Germany (1908–9), where eight vertical pillars and six horizontal bands of red-brown brick combine spectacularly with the large yellow ochre rendered panels.

The combination of brick and tiles is nor-mally restricted to internal fittings, but it was regularly used in Moorish architecture. The Spanish architect Antoni Gaudi (1852–1926)—arguably the world's greatest exponent of polychromatic architecture—drew heavily on Moorish influences, blending them with his own ideas. His unique style and use of colour sprang from his fascination with nature, and he is often quoted as saying "nature is not monochromatic". When someone complemented the sandy brown colour of his stone masterpiece, the unfinished Sagrada Familia in Barcelona, Spain, he tersely replied "it's going to be painted over". But unlike other exponents of polychromatic architecture such as Viollet-le-Duc and Butterfield, Gaudi rarely used coloured bricks for his polychromatic façades. Works such as the Casa Vicens (1883–8) and the Casa El Capricho (1883–5) achieved their dynamism through the use of sober brickwork for the backdrop, onto which were planted an extensive range of highly decorative ceramic tiles and stamped bricks.

ANGLED BRICKWORK

There are many examples where the combination of materials is reversed so that brick is introduced as the substitute. Most examples of this, such as flint and chalk, use brick as a horizontal lacing course to reinforce a wall constructed of an otherwise awkwardly shaped material with little bonding ability of its own. The other major use is in the form of brick nogging, especially in timber-framed structures.

Nogging is the name given to any brickwork which is used to fill the spaces between

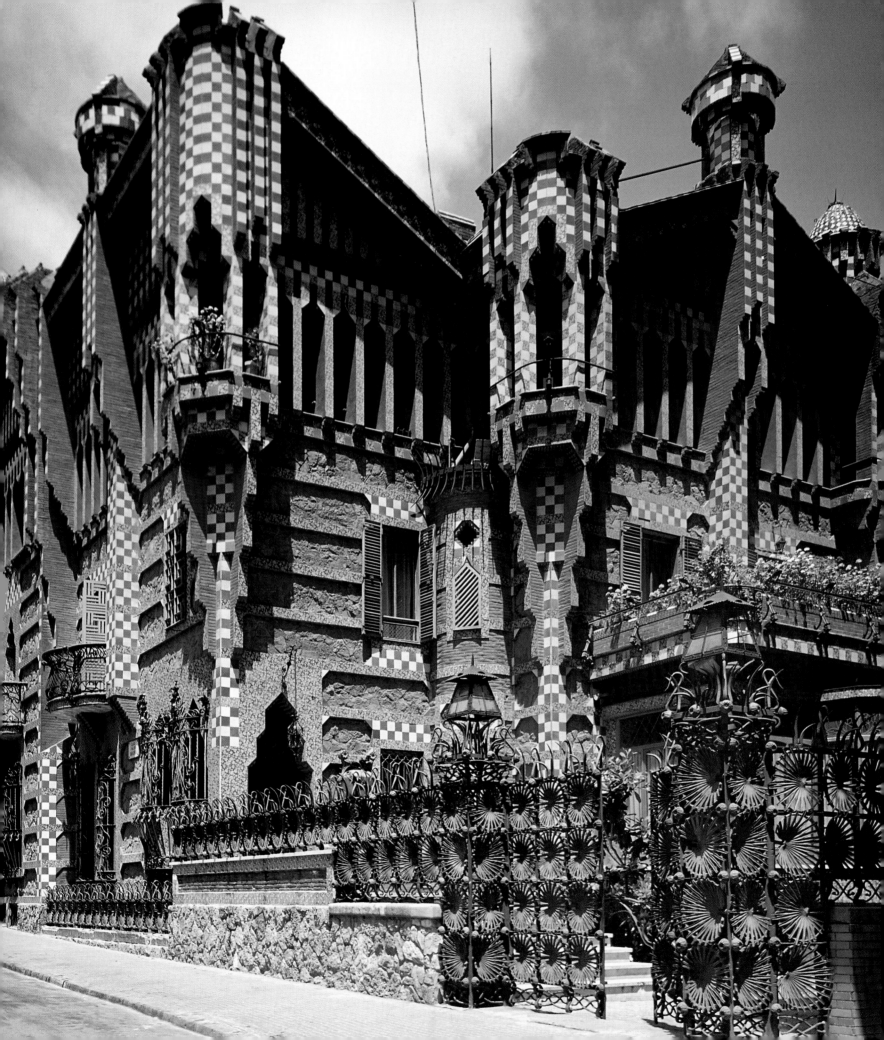

timbers in a timber-framed building. It has its origins in 16th-century Europe, when builders were experimenting with a variety of materials as substitutes for the wattle-and-daub filling between the members of the oak frame in order to find a more durable and fire-resistant material. Brick was the obvious choice, and much used for this purpose. However, contrary to popular opinion, brick nogging did little to improve the comfort of a building. In fact, it frequently made matters worse, as the nogging was often heavier than the wattle-and-daub it replaced and caused structural distortions. It also tended to project beyond the face of the framework, providing many ledges where trapped rainwater would penetrate the soft bricks and saturate the walls of the building. However, nogging did have one considerable advantage over other materials—it was fire-resistant. Another important consideration was the fact that bricklayers were cheaper to employ than the specialist daubers needed to apply the alternative wattle-and-daub filling.

Brick nogging can be arranged in many forms, and, because it is often set in short panels and tied to the timbers by metal nails between mortar joints, little attention need be paid to good bonding principles. The simplest arrangement is to set the bricks in stretching bond or to lay the brick on edge; countless examples can be seen throughout Northern Europe. A common alternative, and one which is certainly more decorative is the chevron or herringbone pattern.

Herringbone brickwork involves setting bricks in an oblique formation of opposite directions in order to make them self-supporting, the resulting zig-zag pattern being not unlike the fish skeleton from which it takes its name. The object of the herringbone formation is to maximize the number of whole bricks used, although the arrangement does necessitate a large number of small triangular brick sections around the junctions with the vertical and horizontal timbering. Not only are these triangles difficult to cut, they are also the weakest points in the panel.

Angled brickwork also occurs in the form of tumbling. Brick tumbling is the term used to describe areas of bricks set diagonally to the main brick coursing but at right-angles to the roof slope, gable or chimney breast where it is most commonly seen. It is unlikely that tumbling was designed for ornamental purposes rather than for the practical reason of avoiding cut faces exposed to the weather, but it is nonetheless decorative.

BRICK TILES

The world of architecture has few deceits: in most cases, what you see is what you get. A curious exception to this is fake brick, developed in the 18th century and commonly known as mathematical or brick tiling. Its function was to deceive the observer into believing that a wall was made from real bricks, when its true material was something else entirely. To be successful, brick tiling requires a kit which includes headers, stretchers and corner units so the user is able to copy brick bonds, together with a range of gauged and rubbed bricks for any decorative work. The results can be highly authentic.

Left: *This Medieval house in Sussex, England, has traditional herringbone brick nogging laid in a timber frame.*

Below: *These mathematical tiles are laid in Flemish bond. The timber moulding used in the window surround serves to conceal the edges of the tiles.*

The reason why brick tiles were developed remains unclear. Certainly, 18th-century owners were preoccupied with remodelling their properties to demonstrate the architectural fashion of the day, and brick tiles were a way of applying a "face-lift", especially to buildings constructed of less durable materials. They were also a means of weatherproofing and fire-proofing vulnerable timber structures. However, brick tiles were not cheap; the considerable care required for their manufacture and the specialist labour needed to erect them made them an expensive addition to a house.

Brick tiles were usually formed in thin "tick-shaped" units of clay—regional variations, where they exist, are slight. They had a flat vertical face on their lower portion which provided the brick appearance, and an angled upper portion over which the next tile was placed to provide a hidden fixing to the wall (see page 171). The modern equivalent of the brick tile is the brick slip. Slips are simple rectangular brick shaped clay units—thicker than tiles, but considerably thinner than standard bricks. They are mainly used to create a brick veneer for structural concrete, and occasionally for internal decoration such as fire-place linings, internal wall surfaces and sometimes for external walls where old brickwork has begun to deteriorate. Most are manufactured by sawing off the face of a normal brick, although shaped units such as dog-leg and gauged brick slips are still made as specials. Cutting provides two main advantages: firstly, colours can be matched to standard brickwork, and secondly, it can achieve different thicknesses without the need for special manufacture. Many brickmakers produce pre-cut brick slips as stock items, although it is possible for them to be made on site with careful cutting. Unlike brick tiles, brick slips need to be glued to a rigid backing. Cement and mortar rarely achieve an adequate bond, so glues such as styrene butadiene rubber (SBR), epoxy resins, cement and rubber latex based adhesives need to be employed.

GLAZED AND ENAMELLED BRICKS

"Glazed brickwork" includes any brick with a ceramic face—in practice, this includes both glazed and enamelled bricks. The traditional method of glazing is to introduce a vitreous base, such as lead glass, onto the face of the brick before firing. The vitreous material liquifies in the heat of the kiln and bonds to the brick face as the two cool together. Modern brickmakers generally use safer substances such as potassium, sodium, tin or zinc —the choice of material depends on the tint required. The alternative method is the "salt-glaze" method, for which salt is introduced into the kiln during the firing of ordinary bricks. The sodium vapour produced by the heat combines with the silica in the brick earth to form glass, which solidifies and unifies with the face of the brick during cooling.

Enamelled bricks are produced differently from their glazed counterparts. The face of the unfired brick is coated with enamel before it is placed in the kiln, and it vitrifies in the heat, bonding to the surface of the brick and producing a glossy finish. Colours are created by mixing pigments into the enamel. Most enamelled bricks are created by this one-process system, although it is possible, if not always desirable, to apply enamel to an already fired brick. However, as bricks fired more than once are liable to crack, they do not prove as durable as regularly made ones.

Glazed bricks can be used externally as well as internally, although traditional uses have been in areas where cleanliness was important, such as lavatories and dairies. When used externally in an urban setting they have one enormous advantage—besides being reasonably self-cleaning in the rain, they are also resistant to grafitti, which can be easily removed. The earliest glazed bricks were developed in ancient Babylon, and they can still be seen on the Ishtar Gate (604–562 BC) which is now in the Vorderasiatishes Museum in Berlin. The Babylonians' manufacturing processes were very similar to those used today, except that the mud bricks were sun-baked instead of being kiln-fired.

Glazed brickwork was very popular during the 19th and early 20th centuries, and most urban examples date from this time. It is often hard to differentiate between glazed bricks and the equally favoured ceramic tiles, so many fine examples have probably been overlooked. After a break of about seventy years, glazed brickwork is beginning to re-emerge as a structural building material. Two important modern examples are the Phico building in Pennsylvania and the "Circle Development" in the docklands of London. The Phico Group's headquarters was built in Mechanicsburg, Pennsylvania, in 1985, and its design emulates the Pennsylvania Dutch Barn which is a feature of the countryside in this state. Many of its traditional motifs were copied using polychromatic arrangements of glazed tiles, and the result is a visually stimulating building with an attractive array of tiles in red, grey and white. In contrast, the bolder Circle Development (1990) in London includes a seven-storey-high circular piazza in monotone cobalt blue glazed brick, which was chosen as a means of breaking from the yellow-brown

Below: *A rare modern example of the external use of glazed tiles: CZWG's Circle Development (1990).*

coloured canyon-like streets in the surrounding area. The blue glazed bricks are bright, shiny and confident—in this case, colour makes an important difference: constructed in white glazed bricks, the development would have looked more like a giant *pissoir* than a housing development.

Sadly, this building does show up one of the difficulties of using glazed brick in a temperate climate: the bricks have effloresced, and the resulting white stains are much too noticeable to be ignored. However, the glazed finish does prevent the efflorescent salts from being absorbed into the bricks themselves, and the staining emerges through mortar joints, where it can easily be wiped away.

Another potential hazard of glazed bricks is that, being an eighth of an inch deeper than standard bricks, they require thinner mortar joints if regular coursing is to be maintained, and any slight variation in the glaze colour is noticeable, particularly on a large expanse of wall. Most importantly for the developer, glazed bricks are, on average, ten times the price of ordinary ones. It is probably for this reason that the vast majority of them are used for restoration work. One such example is the Templeton Carpet Factory (1889) in the centre of Glasgow in Scotland. Designed by the architect William Leiper, its intricate, polychromatic brickwork is set in a diamond and "carpet-weave" pattern. During restoration work, replicas of the various shades of blue, brown, green, orange and white glazed bricks were made to replace the damaged ones on parapets and turrets. It was worth doing—it is difficult to think of a richer or more

Left: *Templeton's Carpet Factory in Glasgow, Scotland has now been restored.*

Above: *Sculptured brickwork from the Prasat Kravan temple in Angkor, Cambodia, (AD 921).*

Right: *The final panel of Walter Ritche's "Creation".*

delightful example of glazed brick architecture.

Landscape architects have used glazed bricks for many years; the contrast between the smooth, man-made surface and the rougher natural textures of plants is particularly popular, and many urban gardens have glazed capping bricks on planters and retaining walls. They can also be used for ornamental features and footpaths, particularly around fountains, where they provide a "wet look".

Glazed brickwork is also known to appear in the most unlikely of situations. One such case was a consignment for the ocean liner, *Queen Mary*, where glazed bricks were used for the lining of the swimming pool.

SCULPTURED BRICKWORK

The idea of using sculptured brick is far from new. Anaglyphtic facing bricks from third millennium BC Mesopotamia have been discovered and similar impressed and moulded bricks are also known to have been produced by the Chinese Han Dynasty (202 BC–AD 221). However, the sculptured bricks of the late 19th century are more akin to the carved and gauged brickwork of the 17th and early 18th centuries than the inscribed bricks of China and Mesopotamia.

Like decorated brick, sculptured brick was adopted with enthusiasm by architects in the late 19th century who were constantly searching for new ways to beautify their buildings. Improvement in industrial manufacturing processes meant that ornamental bricks could be produced en masse and with different types of patterning. Bold, low-relief type patterns such as geometric shapes or flowers could be pro-

duced by machine-pressing semi-dry powdered clay over a carved die. Larger, more ornate patterns with higher relief were made possible by employing the alternative production method; this involved pressing wet clay into a plaster of Paris mould which absorbed moisture from the clay, allowing it to contract and separate from the mould for firing. One-off products such as ornamental sculptured panels were produced by this method.

High production costs have significantly reduced the demand for sculptured bricks. However, a limited range is still available from a few manufacturers. The most likely designs are standards such as rose and fleur-de-lis motifs.

Brick sculptures are the modern equivalent of the 19th-century ornamental sculptured panel and they demand special skills which make them the province of the sculptor rather than the brickmaker. The attraction of brick for sculptors is that it offers them an opportunity of producing a range of textures within one work; they can choose a variety of textures, from the rough and pitted natural surface to an almost satin-smooth finish. This is particularly well demonstrated in the work of Walter Ritchie, especially his human figures such as his five panelled "Creation" at the Eye Hospital in Bristol, England where the natural surface of brick suits the texture of cloth while a rubbed, smooth finish perfectly reflects the delicacy of skin.

Most sculptors work to their own preferred system, but generally an initial design is produced as a small sketch. It is then re-drawn at full size before being copied onto the surface of

the brick. The redrawing is particularly important, as it allows the sculptor the opportunity of refining both the detail and proportions of the work.

The type of brick chosen will, of course, depend on where the sculpture is to stand and whether it will need to withstand frost and other weather conditions. Also, some bricks are better to carve than others, or they offer a wider range of effects. The sculptor has the choice of either modelling unfired bricks or carving fired bricks, such as a finished wall. Unfired bricks allow the sculptor the option of emphasizing

Right: *Goldsboro, North Carolina, USA. Brick bird mural by Patricia Turlington and Jane Westbrook.*

details by applying slips and coloured glazes; the one drawback is their susceptibility to distortion during the firing process. Ultimately, the choice depends on the design and the effects that the sculptor wants to achieve.

Brick sculpture as ornamentation for buildings is invariably on a large scale. One of the largest is Mara Smith's 18 × 61 ft (5.5 × 19 m) long "Reflections" (1982) on the American Bank's computer centre in Reading, Pennsylvania. The sculpture was created by arranging unfired bricks on the floor of the artist's studio. After carving, the bricks were numbered before being dismantled for drying and firing, and then reassembled and erected on the building. The same technique can also be employed for smaller carved walls, such as the one at Home Farm, near Milton Heights in Oxfordshire, England, where, in 1987, thirty-three mentally handicapped children worked with the sculptor Ruth Bader Gilbert to carve a wall containing 400 bricks with designs depicting the activities at Home Farm. Brick has been favoured by many modern sculptors, including Eric Gill, whose work includes the crocodile on the Cavendish Library in Cambridge, England (1933).

If a finished panel of brickwork is to be carved, the brick arrangement should be in heading bond, to ensure sufficient strength. Carving tools are selected to suit the type of cutting required and the composition of the brick. Typical tools are a "pitcher", or broad chisel and "punch" and "point" tools. Finer detail is worked with smaller chisels and finished with abrasives such as carborundum and silicon carbide for smoothing the surface.

Below: *Moulded terracotta detailing around the archway of Watts' Mortuary Chapel, Surrey, England.*

Lettering in architecture has often been regarded as a secondary embellishment, but it can serve as a visual complement to a building. Letters sculpted in brick are less likely to spoil the overall visual balance of a building, in a way that large metal or plastic signs often do. The same techniques as those given above may be used to prepare lettering panels, although many craftsmen prefer to carve *in situ* on a finished wall using a hammer and tungsten chisel. Cosmetic dyes are often used to highlight the lettering.

TERRACOTTA

Terracotta (from the Latin *terra cocta* or "cooked earth") is one of the oldest building materials known to man. It is manufactured, by moulding and firing fine grained clays, which are specially selected and prepared so that impurities are eliminated (see page 162). Its method of manufacture has led to difficulties in determining where exactly brick ends and terracotta begins, and for this reason it has been included as a separate section.

The popularity of terracotta has been sporadic, with long periods of neglect by architects and builders. Although its history dates back to around 1400 BC, only in the 19th century was terracotta given its proper recognition as a structural material which could be both functional and elegant. Terracotta had much to recommend it to the 19th-century architect; it was cheap, came in an attractive range of colours from cream to dark red, it was easy to mould and, above all, durable.

Above: *The Bank Tower, Cardiff, Wales. Elaborate terracotta ornamentation including a balcony, arcading and two splendid gargoyles.*

However, its great reputation as a cheap and durable product was irreparably damaged in the late 19th century by a decline in the production standard, and the sale of carelessly fired material. Architects became wary of using a material that was liable to deteriorate rapidly, and by the end of the Second World War the popularity of terracotta had plummeted. Few companies produce terracotta nowadays because it is very labour intensive, and the chief demand for terracotta is for the restoring of existing terracotta work.

Terracotta's principal advantage is its flexibility: equally suitable for flat cladding slabs and intricate ornamental work. The simplest form of terracotta is the flat cladding panels first used by the Romans to create decorative slabs for facing walls. Roman panels were typically about 18 × 9–12 in (460 × 230–300 mm) in size and included holes through which they could be nailed to the timbers of the house.

For economic reasons, the slabs used by modern architects are generally much larger. They are attached by hidden metal fixings behind the slab which are bolted to the structure. Terracotta panels work in the same way as any precast cladding, are easily erected and, provided they are of a regular size and form, reasonably inexpensive. Terracotta is preferable to concrete or stone because of its durability, the non-absorbent surface which makes it easy to clean, and above all, its wealth of rich colours.

One of the world's finest examples of terracotta building and ornamentation, Alfred Waterhouse's Natural History Museum in London, (1880–95) is faced entirely in terracotta. The cladding panels are creamy yellow and bluish-grey in colour and their variations of tone, together with the material's semi-glaze, look like marble from a distance. Waterhouse's choice of terracotta was a shrewd one. The material's longevity has saved the museum from high maintenance costs, while the marble-like façade presents, at a fraction of the price, the appearance of wealth and stability.

It is the fine consistency of terracotta and its manufacturing process which makes it suitable for use as high quality ornamentation. The material is made by mixing fine grained clays which are moulded and left to stand for two to three days before firing. During this standing time the semi-dry terracotta has a natural strength which allows it to be sculptured to almost any shape without collapsing. Remarkable finesse can be achieved before it is fired to secure the finished form. Terracotta can be either glazed or un-glazed, and today it is generally accepted that *'faience'* is the term used for glazed terracotta. It can be covered with a clear glaze or an opaque colour.

The ideal use of ornamental terracotta is in conjunction with other materials, and the most suitable is brick. Introducing small richly moulded and sculptured units of different colours and texture to a building with brick and diaper patterning can give it an exquisite delicacy.

The natural colour of terracotta is pink although stronger and darker shades can be achieved by increasing the amount of iron oxide present in the clay. Most terracotta is

Left: *The main entrance of Waterhouse's National History Museum, London, with an intricate terracotta frieze and semicircular stilted arches, supported on clustered columns with highly decorated capitals.*

Below: *Manhattan's
23-storey Flatiron building
by Daniel Burnham
(1903) is clad in
decorative terracotta.*

therefore red, brown, biscuit or creamy-white, but modern production techniques can achieve any shade by the adding of chemicals to the clay. Age and exposure to the environment will soften the colour into a rich variety of hues: red, brown, russet, chocolate, orange, salmon and straw. Some manufacturers have developed techniques whereby more than one colour can be produced on the same item, although the technique is complicated and the results can often be disappointing. The success of terracotta as a building material depends chiefly on its finish. It is capable of giving a warm or cold appearance, and hard or soft texture. Soft, warm finishes and colours engender a cosy, almost sensual effect which is a pleasure to touch. Hard, bright cold finishes can be ideal in areas where the aim is for an efficient or clinical appearance. In northern hemispheres the colour can often appear soapy and lacking in definition, whereas in hotter climates the impression is of a shiny, polished surface. The material does tend to work best in countries where the light is bright and the atmosphere dry, but the quieter and gentler effects yielded in environments where the light is soft and the atmosphere damp and hazy can still be amazing.

While some modern architects and designers are familiar with the benefits of terracotta and continue to use it, there are others who point to the expense and difficulty in construction as their justification for ignoring it. The tide is beginning to turn, however, as more and more people awaken to its beauty and versatility—terracotta appears to be starting its next renaissance.

Left: *Michelin House,
London (1905–1911),
has an eye-catching faience
exterior, with a dentilled
cornice surmounting a
chequered frieze.*

BRICK TYPES

∞

The individual properties of the many raw materials available for brickmaking contribute to the wide variety of brick types. Different materials require different manufacturing techniques to produce brick types which vary in terms of strength, durability, weight, texture and colour. Clay, calcium silicate (sand-lime and flint lime) and concrete are the most commonly used basic materials.

Calcium silicate and concrete are relatively consistent materials and their manufacture can be controlled to produce a standard product. The raw materials for producing clay bricks, however, vary widely. These variations are primarily determined by geological differences which include the mix and proportion of components and the formation and depth of the deposit. They contribute to the regional characteristics and the range of colours, textures and finishes in the final product.

Historically, and currently in the US and the UK, the majority of bricks are made from clay, and any study of brickwork will mainly be concerned with them. However, a brief description is given of the materials and manufacture of other types of brick before giving a fuller account of clay brick manufacture.

CALCIUM SILICATE BRICKS

Calcium silicate bricks evolved from German experiments in making stone at the end of the 19th century. They are made from pressing a mixture of hydrated lime, water, and either silica sand (sandlime) or crushed flint (flint-lime) into the required shape, hardening the shapes in a sealed autoclave and then pressure-steaming them for between eight and twelve hours. The heat of the pressure-steaming promotes a reaction between the sand and lime to produce a strong homogeneous brick. This 'curing' process improves the strength and hardness of the brick, and by varying its duration the performance characteristics can be adjusted.

Calcium silicate bricks are normally a dull white colour. Metallic oxide pigments may be added to give a pale colour of pink, grey, yellow or brown. In addition, the facing surface can be mechanically textured if required. The resulting product is of a uniform shape and size with sharp arrises which will chip if handled carelessly. The precise, regular and hard-edged shape has, however, restricted the appeal of the calcium silicate brick for facings. The increased popularity of the type in recent years is almost entirely due to its wide availability and low cost.

Calcium silicate bricks may suffer deterioration if they are impregnated with strong salt solutions and then subjected to freezing. Their use should be avoided in coastal areas prone to salt water spray.

CONCRETE BRICKS

Concrete bricks are composed of a mixture of cement, sand and an aggregate such as crushed stone. They are moulded in a similar fashion to calcium silicate bricks and undergo curing, either through natural weathering or in an autoclave. Most concrete bricks are harder, chip and damage more easily, and are less pleasant to handle than clay or calcium silicate bricks. They are mainly used as 'common' bricks in districts which have little or no clay.

SLAG BRICKS

Used principally for paving, slag bricks were made in the 19th century by running molten slag (the mineral waste produced from iron smelting) with lime into iron moulds. The cast bricks were removed when the outer crust was hard and the interior still molten, and annealed (heated and then cooled) in ovens. They are no longer made.

TERRACOTTA AND FAIENCE

Both terracotta and faience are made from a variety of fine, pure clays with a nucleus of silica and alumina and small quantities of alkaline matter which create the surface vitrification necessary for durability. The material is of a similar quality to that used for tiles or pottery, and is fired to a temperature in excess of 1000°C to achieve a high degree of vitrification (fusion of the geological components).

The description 'terracotta' covers large moulded blocks which can be filled with concrete if required and anchored with metal cramps to the main wall of a building to form a cornice, string course or other functional or decorative feature.

The term 'faience' is used to describe large flat slabs or tiles; an average size would be 12 × 16 in (30 × 40 cms). They often have ribbed backs and are set on a concrete bed to form a facing to a building.

Both products can be glazed or unglazed, but in popular usage the term 'terracotta' refers to both a moulded block and a flat slab with a matt finish in the colour of the clay—often a dusty red—from which it was made; whereas 'faience' is often used to describe glazed units.

Both unglazed and glazed terracotta are prepared using the 'wet clay' process: the clay is carefully ground, mixed with water and strained, mixed again (pugged) and kneaded. The mixture is then packed into dry plaster moulds smeared with soft soap to prevent adhesion, and left for two to three days. During this time the plaster absorbs moisture from the clay, causing it to shrink and loosen in the mould. On removal the clay is tooled to a finish before being fired once. This single firing reduces the risk of crazing but also limits the range of colours achieved naturally. By applying a slip glaze and firing a second time, a much greater depth and variety of colour can be achieved.

Faience can be prepared using either the 'wet clay' or 'dust pressed' method. The dust pressed method involves the blending of fine, sieved clay, which has a maximum moisture content of 12 per cent. The mixture is compressed under great pressure before firing. The choice of method depends largely on the eventual exposure of the finished faience: slabs produced by the dry pressed method are more accurate than those produced by the wet clay method, but they are also less durable and more porous. For these reasons, dry pressed faience is best used for interior work, while faience produced by the wet clay method can be used internally and externally.

Terracotta and faience come in a variety of colours, about twenty, those occurring naturally (i.e., without a glaze being applied) ranging between buff and red. The 'natural' colour can be varied by applying a wash of a different watery clay called a 'slip'. Glazing was used to provide a variety of colours and in the United States and Australia was sometimes used to imitate stone finishes.

The durability of terracotta and faience in their unglazed form is in the hard, thin, vitreous unglazed skin called a 'fire skin'. The breakdown of this 'fire skin' or, in the case of other finishes, the 'slip' or the glazing, will lead to the deterioration and break down of the clay body which is not durable.

CLAY BRICK MANUFACTURE
∽

RAW MATERIALS
—

GEOLOGICAL BACKGROUND

Clay is a mixture of fine rock particles derived from the prehistoric weathering of other rocks. The particles sometimes remained at the source of their formation, often at considerable depth. Such clays—which are not mixed with any other rock particles—are known as primary clays.

More often the particles were distributed in various ways: by water, to be deposited as silt at the bottom of lagoons, sheltered estuaries or the sea bed, where an accumulation of organic matter might also develop; by glaciers and ice sheets producing an unstratified mixture of stones, sand, chalk and other minerals with the finer clay particles; and as wind-blown dust during the last ice age, when water levels receded, exposing particles of silt.

The varied origins of the particles, types of dispersal and their deposition have determined that the term 'clay' embraces substances which have very different compositions. Provided that they are in an accessible location, many of them are suited for making bricks.

CLAY DEPOSITS

Deposits of clay suitable for brickmaking can be classified as:

Superficial: The clay is found just under the topsoil in many low lying areas, particularly in southern England. It is easily dug by hand, and until the industrial revolution and the development of mechanical excavators, it was the main source of clay. Its variety contributes to the regional differences in colour and texture of bricks from local brickworks.

Shales: Compressed laminations of hard clay with a flaky consistency. They are frequently found in proximity to coal seams.

Deep Clay: Deposits of clay to depths, sometimes as much as 80 ft in thick seams, which justify the cost of excavating. They are generally lake bed or oceanic deposits with a high proportion of organic matter and a natural moisture content which can mean that they may be used with very little preparation and be fired with a substantial fuel saving over other clays.

Clay for brickmaking is sometimes referred to as 'Brick-Earth'. Strictly, this term describes the superficial, thin deposits of silty clays from the Pleistocene epoch (the last ice age: 1.8m–10,000 years ago). Such deposits were easily dug and therefore widely used for bricklaying in ancient times, but the term became commonly applied to any clay from which bricks are made.

No clays can be used in their raw state without preparation. The main types of clay suitable for brick laying are classified as strong (plastic) clays, loamy (mild) clays, and marly clays.

Strong or Plastic Clays: These are often called 'pure clays' and contain hydrous silicates and alumina (in infinitesimally small particles), in roughly equal quantities, together with small quantities of lime, magnesium and sodium. They are usually maintained in a plastic state with a natural moisture content. Their plasticity means that they are an essential ingredient for bricks that require hand moulding, although, in their pure form, they distort and shrink when fired. The introduction of additional sand will reduce this tendency. They may also require the addition of lime before successful brickmaking can be achieved.

Loamy or Mild Clays: These contain a high proportion of silica and are popularly known as 'sandy clays'. They produce bricks which are less susceptible to warping and shrinkage than those produced from strong clays.

Marly or Calcareous Clays: These contain a high proportion of lime and usually make good bricks. Finished marl bricks vary in colour from light pink to dark red, with a rough, sandy finish which has made them popular for facings.

The chemical properties of the clay, its

preparation, and the different degrees of burning, determine the quality of the finished brick. Good clay is composed of approximately three-fifths silica, one-fifth alumina with oxides of calcium, iron, manganese, magnesium, potassium, sodium and sulphur forming the remainder. The precise quantity of oxides helps to determine the brick's colour. Iron oxide, for example, will turn the brick from a bright red to what appears to be a dark purple, almost blue.

Clay often contains salts which render it unfit for brickmaking. Magnesium and calcium sulphates, for example, act as a flux during firing, causing the brick to warp and twist, and also contribute to efflorescence in use. Clays are often weathered before processing to reduce the salt content, or they can be neutralized by the addition of small quantities of barium carbonate to the clay.

Clay Shale: This is compacted clay formed from fine-grained sedimentary rock. It contains mica flakes and often a high proportion of carbonaceous matter, as considerable quantities of the clay shale used for brickmaking are extracted from coal workings. The bricks produced from this material are hard and durable and suitable as facings. They are usually smooth-faced, dull buff-grey, brown or red in colour and of a uniform shape.

Fireclay: This is similar to clay shale in that it is mainly excavated during mining operations to reach coal seams. It contains large amounts of silica, alumina and oxide of iron and is primarily used for the manufacture of firebricks, capable of resisting high temperatures. The bricks are rough textured and yellow in colour.

SHAPING THE BRICKS

—

The basic process of brick making is simple. Clay is dug from a superficial deposit, mixed with water to make it plastic, moulded either with hands alone or by pressing it into a mould, followed by either baking it in the sun or slowly drying and then firing it in a kiln. Even today, bricks are made in this fashion in many countries. Mechanization, specialized equipment and cheap transportation have increased the quantity of bricks produced, and chemical analysis and adjustment of clay composition, together with precise control of the firing process has enabled manufacturers to produce a product of consistent quality. But it is still, nevertheless, recognizably the same product.

The brick making process described in the following sections deals principally with methods found in the developed countries and, where appropriate, reference is made to differing practices in other parts of the world.

SOURCES OF CLAY, AND TRANSPORTATION

Before the development of transportation and mechanical methods of excavation, clay was dug by hand, usually close to where the

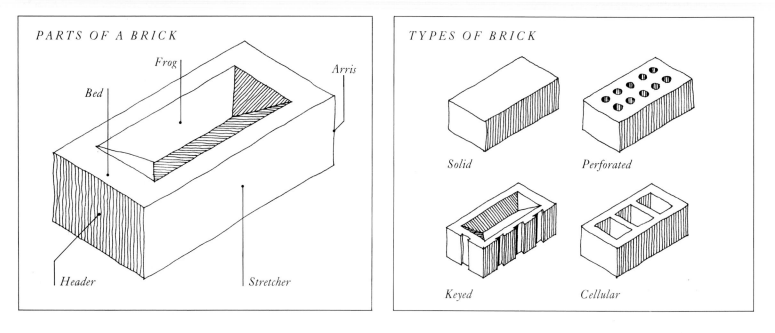

PARTS OF A BRICK

Frog

Bed

Arris

Header

Stretcher

TYPES OF BRICK

Solid

Perforated

Keyed

Cellular

finished bricks were required. It was not possible to extract clay from any depth and so superficial deposits were exploited, after the 'callow', which is the layer of vegetation and soil immediately above the usable clay, had been cleared. Such deposits are still used today—although worked by modern methods.

Some sites were accessible by river, but not until the development of canals and, by the mid–19th century, railways, was the transportation of bricks in large quantities possible. The advent of the steam shovel at the end of the 19th century and the dragline excavator in the 1930s enabled the deep seams of older underlying clays and clay shares to be worked.

Today, road transport and vehicles with hydraulic cranes ensure that no destination is out of reach, but at the same time these, together with the vast scale of operations, have contributed to the closure of many of the smaller brickworks and the loss of regional identity.

PREPARING THE CLAY

The traditional method of preparing brick clays involved digging up the clays in autumn and leaving them in heaps to weather until spring, when they were turned and tempered with water before being kneaded by barefooted workmen. Some clays contained the right proportions of materials for good brickmaking, but more often, adjustments had to be made. This could be the addition of sand or finely ground ash to the pile. One of the advantages of tempering with bare feet was that stones could be easily identified and thrown out.

The pugmill is a horse-powered mechanical device for tempering the clay, which was probably invented by the Dutch in the late 17th century. It consists of a tub, with a vertical shaft from which projects a spiral of horizontal knives. Clay and other ingredients are placed in the top, kneaded by the knives, and extruded at the bottom in a form ready for moulding.

Nowadays all clays are dug mechanically and stockpiled before being taken to be crushed in a mill. Rectangular box-feeders, with compartments for each material, are connected by conveyor belt to the grinding mill which consists of two large rollers revolving in a circular pan with a perforated base. There are dry pans for hard clays and semi-dry pressing, and wet pans for hand-moulding and soft-mud processes.

MOULDING THE CLAY

Handmade Bricks

The first bricks were formed with the hands alone. Bricks of sun-dried mud from 8000 BC have been excavated at Jericho. They resemble a long loaf of bread with thumb marks on top

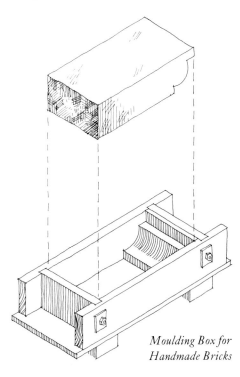

Moulding Box for Handmade Bricks

– possibly to provide a key for the mortar. Another ancient method was to divide the clay into similar sized lumps and form it into rectangular shapes with flat pieces of wood like butter pats.

The Romans made thin bricks partly because they took less fuel to fire. They sometimes formed the bricks by treading or banging the tempered clay into a flat sheet and then cutting it into units. They also set wooden frames into which the clay was pressed. After the frame was removed, the bricks were left to dry until they were firm enough to stack in pairs. They were made in many sizes, but a brick size of around 12 in (30 cms) square by 1½ in (4 cms) thick is typical.

From the late 12th century, with the resurgence of brick making in Europe, two methods of moulding were introduced which continue to the present day.

Pallet Moulding: The mould used may be wood or metal and is in two pieces. The base or 'stock board' is nailed to the brickmakers bench. From the late 18th century the stock board had a raised 'kick' fixed to it which formed a 'frog' or recess in one face of the finished brick. The rectangular frame which shapes the body of the brick is called the 'mould'. Both mould and stock board are dusted with sand and placed together. Sand is sprinkled on the bench and a lump of high quality, very plastic clay called a 'clot' or 'warp' is rolled in it and 'thrown' into the mould, before being pressed down to fill each corner. The excess clay is struck off the mould, and the brick turned out on to a pallet board to be taken to a drying platform or 'hack'.

The bricks produced by this process are called sand-faced bricks and, although they are more expensive than machine made bricks, their attractive appearance means that there is still a demand for their use in modern buildings.

Slop Moulding: For this process, the mould is wetted instead of sanded, and placed directly on to the bench – without a stock. Very soft clay is pressed into the mould. The water acts as a lubricant to prevent the clay sticking to the mould when it is removed, but the bricks are so wet that they have to be left to dry on a sand-covered floor for a few days before being taken to the hack.

This method of moulding bricks was widely used until the 20th century, but it is not widely practised in many countries today.

Machine Pressed

Soft Mud: The soft mud process was developed in the 19th century as a form of mechanized pallet moulding, to produce sand-faced bricks which are a cheaper alternative to the hand-made variety.

A clay of high plasticity is forced by a powerful press into sanded moulds. The machine then releases the bricks and washes and resands the moulds. Bricks produced by this method do not have the handmade character of a true pallet moulded brick, but are nevertheless an attractive—and less expensive—alternative and many varieties are made.

Semi–dry and Stiff Plastic: The two processes are similar in that they suit shales and harder clays which are ground to a coarse powder and screened (sieved) to ensure consistency. In the semi–dry process, the natural moisture content of the clay is usually sufficient. The damp powder is pressed in a mould by powerful presses, producing a smooth, consolidated, almost dry brick which can pass straight to the kiln.

In the stiff plastic process the low plasticity of the clays and shales being used is assisted, after grinding and screening, with the addition of a little water to dampen the mix before it is pressed. Bricks produced by this method can usually pass straight to the kiln.

The smooth-faced bricks produced by this method are not now so popular as they once were. Surface textures can be made by sand-blasting or mechanical texturing or, alternatively, a sand-faced finish can be applied. In the latter case, the surface colour will also vary with the body of the brick and, if damaged, will cause an unsightly contrast.

Wire-cutting

The alternative to using moulds is to compress and extrude (ie, shape by forcing through a perforated block) long lengths of clay and then machine-cut them to the size required by a set of wires attached to a frame. This method, called wire-cutting, is the process by which the majority of bricks are now produced in industrialized countries, but it can be reasonably economic, even on the modest scale of production operated in developing countries.

The method was invented around the middle of the 19th century and most clays, except those with a high plasticity, can be used. It is the most efficient method of production in terms of output, with some wire-cutting machines capable of producing as many as 40,000 bricks per hour. Wire-cut bricks are made by extruding a continuous ribbon of moist clay through a dye and then cutting the emerging column by means of taut wires set at the required spacing. Most modern extruded wire-cut bricks are perforated to help reduce energy cost and to improve the uniformity of burning. Wire cutting often produces drag marks across the bed faces of the brick, and some bricks for facing or engineering quality are machine pressed following cutting to give a smooth face with sharper arrises. In addition, a range of surface finishes can be offered by mechanical texturing or sandblasting. On the whole, wire-cut bricks are cheaper and less dense than pressed bricks, and, unlike other bricks, they have no frog.

DRYING

—

Before firing, all bricks must be thoroughly dry. Bricks produced by the semi-dry or stiff plastic processes are firm to handle and their low moisture content is removed during firing without causing cracking.

The earliest method for drying bricks, and one still in use in developing countries, is to stack the bricks in 'hacks'. These are, in effect, open-sided sheds which allow free air circulation around the bricks. As the bricks harden they are 'skintled' – set diagonally and further apart – to speed drying, which, depending on the weather, can take 3 to 6 weeks.

In the early 19th century, hot floor driers were introduced, with the bricks set on a floor heated from underneath by hot air pipes. Later, chamber driers were introduced, in which the bricks were stacked on pallets and cool, humid air was circulated, followed by hot dry air. Temperature and circulation were adjusted to control humidity.

Today, high production brick manufacture uses the tunnel drier. This was perfected around 1900 and consists of a tunnel 83–116 ft (25–35 m) long, 4 ft (1.25 m) wide and 5 ft (1.5 m) high. Bricks are stacked on trucks which run slowly through the tunnel on rails. The trucks take about 3 days to pass completely through the tunnel. Hot air is admitted at the exit, and cooler, more humid air is extracted at the entrance, to expedite the drying process.

FIRING

—

To change dried mud into durable brick with a degree of vitrification, the bricks must be fired for several hours at a temperature greater than 900°C (1652°F). The precise temperature required depends on the type of clay used and the type of brick being produced. As the temperature rises, the character of the clay and its colour changes. For example, an engineering brick is fired at a prolonged and controlled high temperature to an advanced stage of vitrification, in order to produce a dense, hard and durable brick.

CLAMP FIRING

This is probably the oldest method of firing bricks, and one that is still in use today in many countries. It is a temporary structure requiring only the bricks themselves, some turf or mud from the site, and the addition of fuel, ideally wood. It used to be common practice for the clay to have half-burned ashes mixed in with it to assist the firing process.

Constructing a clamp entails stacking bricks so that tunnels are left for the wood fuel. The tunnels are covered with an insulating layer of mud or additional bricks. Ideally, a clamp should not hold fewer than 40,000 bricks, to limit the extent of uneven firing. Coal or clinker are sometimes used instead of wood, but with both these fuels the burning time is longer. Occasionally, waste oil is used.

The main problem with all unmechanized firing processes is the lack of control, which can result in bricks of variable quality – under burning at the edge, over burning near the fire, and variations of colour and texture.

In spite of these drawbacks, the convenience of producing bricks at the building site where they are required – the only equipment needed being a spade and a wooden mould – accounted for the widespread use of this process until well into the 19th century.

INTERMITTENT KILNS

Intermittent kilns, so-called because they were allowed to cool between firings to enable bricks to be loaded and unloaded, were the only method of firing bricks in a permanent kiln until 1858, when the Hoffman continuous kiln was introduced.

The Scotch kiln emerged at about the same time as the clamp. The method of firing is similar to a clamp, but the bricks and the fire holes at the base are contained within a permanent, roofless structure. This type of kiln is called an updraught kiln, and it was capable of firing between 20,000 and 50,000 bricks over a period of 3 to 4 days. Although inefficient, a few are still in operation because of the variety of beautifully coloured bricks which they can produce.

Downdraught kilns are more efficient than updraught kilns because they have an enclosed chamber which allows the amount of oxygen to be controlled enough to obtain particular colours in the bricks. Capacities vary from 13,000 to 100,000 bricks. They are still found in brickworks producing handmade bricks.

CONTINUOUS KILN

Friedrich Hoffman patented a continuous kiln in Germany in 1858. This design and its derivatives formed the basis of large scale brick production for almost a hundred years.

The continuous kiln has a number of independent chambers – typically 12 – which are interlinked with flues and dampers and linked to a central chimney. A continuous sequence of loading, firing, cooling and

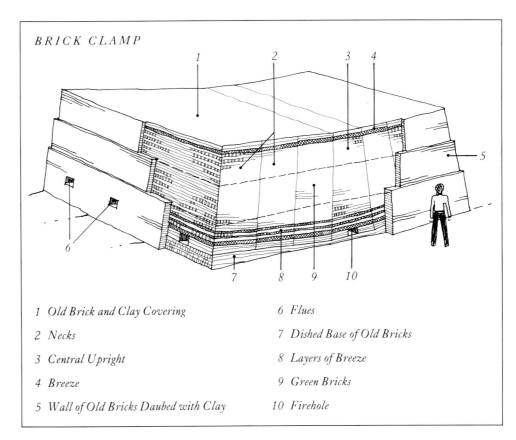

BRICK CLAMP

1 *Old Brick and Clay Covering*

2 *Necks*

3 *Central Upright*

4 *Breeze*

5 *Wall of Old Bricks Daubed with Clay*

6 *Flues*

7 *Dished Base of Old Bricks*

8 *Layers of Breeze*

9 *Green Bricks*

10 *Firehole*

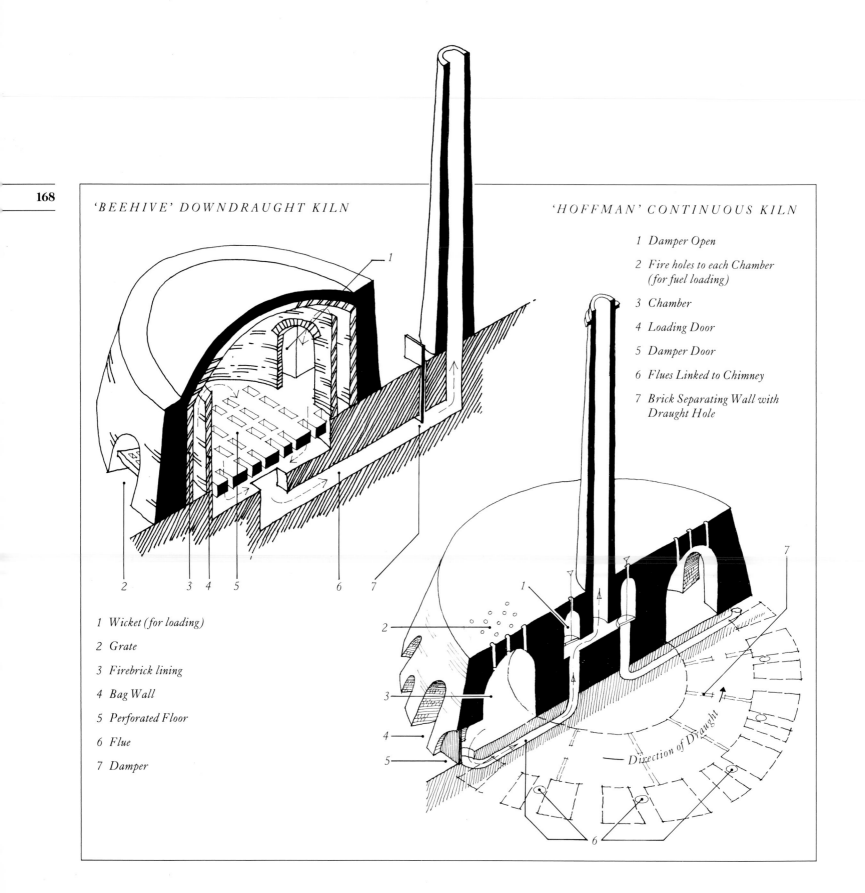

'BEEHIVE' DOWNDRAUGHT KILN

'HOFFMAN' CONTINUOUS KILN

1 Damper Open

2 Fire holes to each Chamber
  (for fuel loading)

3 Chamber

4 Loading Door

5 Damper Door

6 Flues Linked to Chimney

7 Brick Separating Wall with
  Draught Hole

1 Wicket (for loading)

2 Grate

3 Firebrick lining

4 Bag Wall

5 Perforated Floor

6 Flue

7 Damper

Direction of Draught

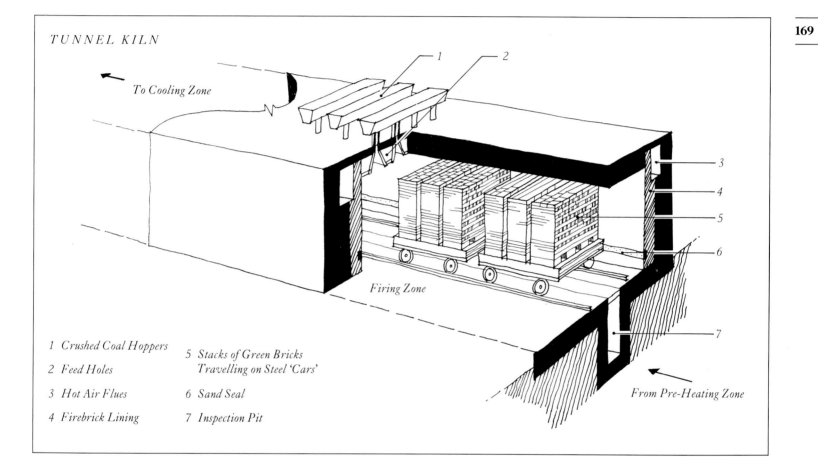

TUNNEL KILN

To Cooling Zone

Firing Zone

From Pre-Heating Zone

1 *Crushed Coal Hoppers*

2 *Feed Holes*

3 *Hot Air Flues*

4 *Firebrick Lining*

5 *Stacks of Green Bricks Travelling on Steel 'Cars'*

6 *Sand Seal*

7 *Inspection Pit*

unloading each chamber in sequence, effected by the operation of the dampers, enabled the fire to be taken from one chamber to the next, resulting in economy of fuel with considerable control of the firing process.

TUNNEL KILN

Modern, mass-produced bricks are usually fired in a tunnel kiln. Between 300 and 400 ft (90–120 m) long, the tunnel has three zones – pre-heating, firing and cooling. Fireproof trolleys loaded with around 1000 bricks, and sometimes many more, pass slowly through; the whole process taking about 3 days.

CHOICE OF BRICK

Hundreds of brick types are available and the majority will be suitable for most building projects. In some cases the choice of brick will be limited by technical criteria such as strength or durability, but aesthetic considerations, such as the appropriate colour and texture for a particular design, are likely to determine the final choice.

Clay bricks account for the majority of bricks used worldwide. The calcium silicate and concrete bricks, described earlier, have a small but consistent following. Their technical performance is comparable to a good quality clay brick and their use will again be determined by how appropriate their rather hard and mechanistic appearance is to the design of the building. They tend to be less expensive than clay bricks, which may be a further reason for their use.

In general terms, a good brick should be regular in shape, size and colour, have rectangular faces, a uniform texture (only one long face and one end need be textured), be well burned, reasonably free from lime, cracks and stones, and give a solid ring when struck with a trowel. The easiest and the most effective

170

way to assess these qualities is by experience.

There are, however, a number of other quantifiable factors that are used to assess a brick and its likely technical performance, and these properties are discussed next.

GENERAL CLASSIFICATION

Bricks suitable for one purpose may not be suitable for another. They are, therefore, classified according to either their intended use, physical appearance or quality.

Common bricks: These are sufficiently strong to enable them to support a normal load. In addition, they have a good shape and are moderately priced. Their dull texture and generally inconsistent colour are the reasons that their use is usually limited to internal and unexposed walls.

Facings: These make up the largest category type. They are of a consistent colour and texture, intended for the construction of fair-faced brickwork of attractive appearance. Most modern facings are specially made for the purpose, whereas formerly they were selected from batches of common bricks.

Engineering bricks: These are dense and exceptionally strong. These characteristics are produced by moulding under high pressure and firing with carefully controlled burning, to ensure that the bricks conform with defined water absorption and strength limits. They are typically red or blue in colour and are often used as facings, although, strictly speaking, they are not designed for this, as the manufacturer will not have selected them to be of consistent colour, texture and appearance.

Damp Proof Course Bricks: These are dense bricks with a low water absorption. They are similar to engineering bricks and are to be recommended for use at the base of free-standing or retaining walls to prevent rising

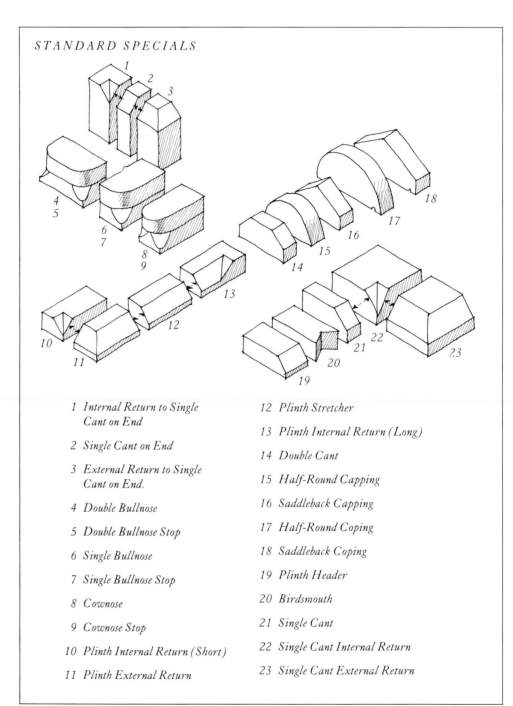

STANDARD SPECIALS

1 *Internal Return to Single Cant on End*	12 *Plinth Stretcher*
2 *Single Cant on End*	13 *Plinth Internal Return (Long)*
3 *External Return to Single Cant on End.*	14 *Double Cant*
4 *Double Bullnose*	15 *Half-Round Capping*
5 *Double Bullnose Stop*	16 *Saddleback Capping*
6 *Single Bullnose*	17 *Half-Round Coping*
7 *Single Bullnose Stop*	18 *Saddleback Coping*
8 *Cownose*	19 *Plinth Header*
9 *Cownose Stop*	20 *Birdsmouth*
10 *Plinth Internal Return (Short)*	21 *Single Cant*
11 *Plinth External Return*	22 *Single Cant Internal Return*
	23 *Single Cant External Return*

SPECIAL SPECIALS

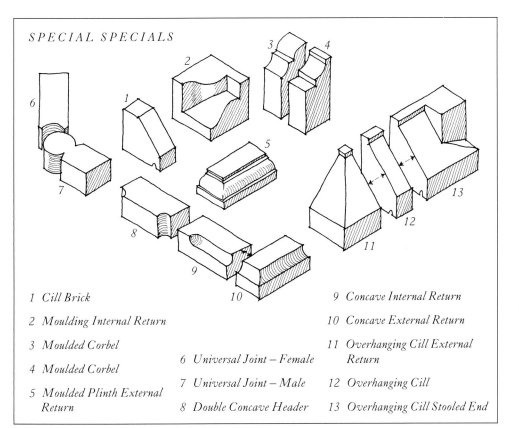

1 Cill Brick

2 Moulding Internal Return

3 Moulded Corbel

4 Moulded Corbel

5 Moulded Plinth External Return

6 Universal Joint – Female

7 Universal Joint – Male

8 Double Concave Header

9 Concave Internal Return

10 Concave External Return

11 Overhanging Cill External Return

12 Overhanging Cill

13 Overhanging Cill Stooled End

MATHEMATICAL TILES

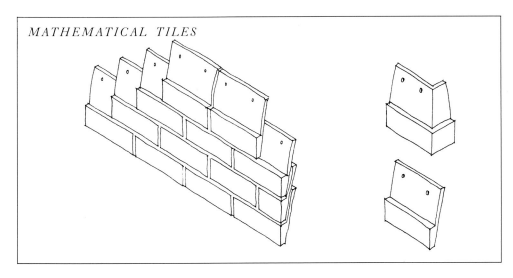

damp in cases where a horizontal sheet damp proof course would make the wall susceptible to being overturned.

Specials: Bricks of special shape or size for forming features or construction details that cannot be built from standard bricks without cutting them. 'Standard specials' are produced by most brickyards as standard items available from stock. Typical examples are: snap headers, King and Queen closers, half round and saddle back copings, a full range of bullnose and plinth bricks, culvert and radial bricks. 'Special specials' have to be produced to order.

Special Purpose Bricks: Paving bricks, fire-bricks, lightweight bricks, glazed bricks, enamelled bricks, mathematical tiles.

PHYSICAL APPEARANCE

Appearance is only important if the brick is to be clearly visible. If this is the case a 'facing' brick is the natural choice. Almost any type of brick is suitable, however, if the wall is to be rendered.

COLOUR

A brick's colour may be integral or superficial. Integral colour is determined by the chemical composition of the raw material and the effect of firing. There is a vast range of colours available today but they can be classified into five basic groups: red; red multi-colour; buff/yellow; grey/brown; blue.

In almost all cases, colour is attributed to the amount of iron compounds either naturally present in the clay or added during manufacture. Red bricks contain 4–5%, blue ones 7–10%, and large quantities of iron mixed with a small quantity of magnesium will result in black bricks.

The degree of firing also affects colour, with increasing temperature and duration of firing generally producing a darker colour. Control of the amount of oxygen during firing is also critical. Firing in an atmosphere of excess oxygen will produce various shades of red (iron compounds are converted to ferric oxide at the commencement of vitrification – about 900°C). A reducing atmosphere (reduced or no oxygen) will cause the iron compounds to form oxides such as magnetite or ferrous oxide, to produce bricks of a black or a blue-black colour.

Multi-coloured bricks which are produced by chance during clamp firing can also be produced by design, often in down-draught kilns. By a repeated process of reducing conditions and temperature and atmosphere control, bricks of an attractive appearance with red/blue/brown effects can be produced.

Superficial colour is obtained by treating the surface of the brick before the firing stage, usually with sand and oxide pigments, something which occurs naturally during the 'soft mud' process where sand is used as a mould release agent. Sand can also be applied to extruded products (wire-cut bricks) for a similar effect. The main drawback with this process is that the surface colour will vary from that of the body of the brick, and, if it is damaged, an unsightly contrast will result. It is also possible that the face of the brick may become detached from the body, again causing an unsightly finish. This last condition, if it occurs, may be aggravated or caused by poor constructional detailing or inadequate pointing.

TEXTURE

A brick's colour is both complemented and modified by its texture. The reflectiveness of a brick surface varies from a semi-vitreous brick with an almost shiny appearance, to a rustic (heavily textured) brick which absorbs the light to give it a matt quality. Different textures will also weather differently, with the heavy textures accumulating atmospheric particles and quickly acquiring the patina of age to give the building a mature look. A smooth-faced and perfectly regular brick will maintain its clean look indefinitely, provided there is low atmospheric pollution.

The textures of handmade bricks, even when smooth faced, tend to have a soft appearance. A slop moulded brick has a smooth face with a textured quality from the wet clay of which it was formed. Pallet-moulded bricks come as 'sand faced' (from the sand used as a release agent) either smooth, sand-creased (lines formed on the surface during moulding) or, if they are stock bricks, the surfaces may show areas of the burnt clinker which was added to the clay to assist the firing process.

With the exception of the remains of the burnt clinker, all the textures associated with a handmade brick can be approximated on machine pressed or extruded and wire-cut bricks, although they never quite achieve their subtlety or individuality.

There are many textures to choose from but a representative range would include:

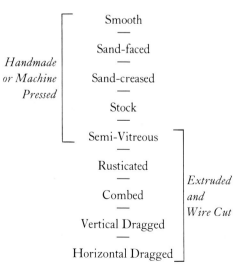

Handmade or Machine Pressed
- Smooth
- Sand-faced
- Sand-creased
- Stock
- Semi-Vitreous

Extruded and Wire Cut
- Rusticated
- Combed
- Vertical Dragged
- Horizontal Dragged

PHYSICAL PROPERTIES

Bricks are classified according to their physical properties and also given a designation to indicate a specific or minimum performance in various categories. The exact requirement and designation will vary from country to country, but the general categories are strength, water absorption, frost resistance and soluble salt content.

SIZE

The brick is one of the first examples of standardization and has changed little in size since the middle ages.

The governing dimension for the width is the maximum size that a human hand can hold; around 4.5 in (11.5 cms). The length will then be regulated by the geometry of bonding and the constructional necessity of breaking joints, giving a dimension of just over twice the width. The maximum weight that can be lifted easily by one hand is 10–12 lbs (4.5–5.4 kg), although a weight half that amount is preferable. The remaining dimension, the depth, has fewer restrictions. It is partly limited by weight and partly by the fact that with some clays, a great thickness will cause difficulties in the drying process. However, the main variation to the size of a brick over the years has been in the depth, varying from 1.5 to 3 in (4–7.5 cms).

Standard Brick sizes vary from country to country, and each country sets dimensional tolerances with which the finished article must comply. In general terms, this means that bricks should be reasonably rectangular with the beds and faces flat and at right angles to one another, well proportioned and with sharp arrises and uniform dimensions.

WEIGHT

In general terms, the weight of an individual

brick varies from around 4.25 lb (1.92 kg) for a common to 9 lbs (4.16 kg) for an engineering brick.

STRENGTH

Bricks, even from the same source, vary widely in strength. Compressive strength is measured by taking the average of the crushing strength of 10 samples. Although the minimum strength is 5.00 N/mm^2 for any brick, the compressive strength of an engineering brick may exceed 140 N/mm^2. Unless the bricks are specifically required for load-bearing purposes, such as for calculated brickwork or advanced structural techniques, the strength of 5.00 N/mm^2 is adequate for most buildings.

WATER ABSORPTION

The water absorption of a brick is measured as a percentage of the mass of the bricks as an average from a sample of 10. A typical requirement for an engineering brick and a damp proof course brick would be water absorption of less than 4.5% of its dry weight. Absorption below 7% usually indicates good frost resistance. There is no direct relationship between water absorption and durability.

DURABILITY

Frost Resistance

The destructive effect of frost is due to the 9% increase in volume that occurs when water at 0°C is converted into ice at the same temperature. The recurrent freeze/thaw action on saturated bricks causes failure, rather than the degree of frost that is experienced.

Correct detailing of brickwork to eliminate or minimise its saturation by water is the best solution to this problem. Where this is impossible, bricks of frost resistant quality should be used. For less severe conditions, bricks of moderate resistance may be used.

Soluble Salts Content

Clay bricks contain soluble salts which, in persistent wet conditions, can lead to detrimental chemical reaction with the mortar. This is called sulphate action and, if left unchecked, it may cause serious damage.

Bricks are graded with a low and normal designation for soluble salts content for use in damp conditions. In addition, a sulphate-resisting cement should be used for the mortar where normal bricks are used.

As with frost resistance, correct brickwork detailing, to minimize water saturation, is essential.

DEFECTS AND REMEDIES

EFFLORESCENCE

When soluble salts (particularly magnesium and sodium, and to a lesser extent calcium and potassium) migrate to the surface of a brick, they deposit a white crystal stain. The problem is most likely to occur in brickwork exposed to saturation and is prevented by keeping bricks dry during laying. The main determining factors, however, are the soluble salt content of the brick and the degree and frequency of saturation. Although unsightly, the effect of efflorescence is usually harmless—unless it lifts paint or plaster—and in time can be brushed off dry or with clean water.

CRYPTO-EFFLORESCENCE

Bricks which have a smooth and dense surface may be susceptible to crypto-efflorescence. Soluble salts become trapped below the surface of the brick and expand, causing the brick face to crumble. Serious disintegration may result if the brick is subsequently subjected to wetting and freezing. The only effective remedy is to cut out and replace the damaged bricks. However, this disorder is extremely rare.

LIME-BLEEDING

Soluble lime, from the setting reaction of cement in water, can be leached from brickwork if it becomes saturated when the mortar is newly laid. The resultant lime–bleed quickly reacts with the carbon dioxide in the air to produce an insoluble white stain.

Careful cleaning with a proprietary acid-based brickwork cleaner is the most effective means of removal.

SULPHATE ATTACK

The effects of sulphate attack on mortar may take several years before they become obvious to the naked eye. Most cases are caused by a reaction between the sulphates either in, or absorbed by, the brick, and the tricalcium aluminate present in ordinary portland cement. The reaction produces calcium sulphoaluminate (commonly known as *ettringite*), which crystallizes, then expands and leads to the gradual break up and eventual crumbling of the mortar. The areas of brickwork most at risk are foundations, retaining walls, parapets and chimneys, and for these it is advisable to use bricks with a low sulphate content or a sulphate-resisting cement in the mortar.

CONSTRUCTION TECHNIQUES

MORTAR

Bricks are rarely regular in either shape or size, and laid without mortar a wall of them would have uneven courses and look a mess. Mortar provides a plastic matrix in which the differences are lost to the eye and a jointing medium through which loads can be uniformly distributed.

From the bricklayer's point of view, a mortar should have good workability and remain plastic long enough for the bricks to be laid. In the longer term, it must be durable, bond with, and be of similar porosity to the bricks used with it, and be able to withstand the adverse weathering effects of rain and frost.

Mortar is normally a mixture of either sand and lime, or of cement and sand which may or may not include lime. Lime makes the mortar more workable. However, the proportion of cement in the mixture also determines the mortar's resistance to frost damage: the higher the proportion, the greater the resistance. All raw materials used in the preparation of mortar should be clean and free of contaminations and the cement should always be fresh.

Mortar types

There are three common types of mortar: cement, gauged and lime. The strongest of the three, cement mortar, is composed of cement and sand. It is only suitable for use with strong bricks and in structures subjected to exposure to frost damage. To ensure a good consistency, the cement and sand must be well mixed when they are dry. Setting begins soon after water is added to the mixture, so immediate use after mixing is vital. Cement mortar reduces in strength if it is disturbed after setting has commenced and for this reason it should not be 'revived' by being added back into freshly mixed mortar.

Gauged mortar is a mixture of lime and sand, 'gauged' with cement. The presence of lime helps the mortar retain a high level of workability and benefits bonding. The lime does, however, give a reduced strength and gauged mortar should be accurately batched, and specified with care in relation to exposure.

Lime mortar, made from a mixture of lime and sand, is the oldest—and the weakest—of the three types. Unlike the other types, lime mortar does not set, but gradually stiffens until

it gains a limited strength, normally after 24 hours.

Alternatives to cement have been used in binding matrixes developed in Europe over the past few years. Common substitutes are pulverized fuel ash (PFA) and blast-furnace slag. However, they should be used with caution, as their long-term performance is unknown.

Mortar Colours

The mortar in a stretching bond brick wall amounts to 17% of the total surface area. The percentage is even higher for the more decorative bonds, such as English and Flemish bond. By occupying such a high percentage of the total surface area, the colour of the mortar plays an important part in the overall perceived colour of a wall.

The colour of natural mortar (without added pigments) is determined by the colour of the sand. Using golden yellow coloured sands will result in a rich yellow-ochre coloured mortar, while whiter coloured sands produce a paler mortar. A black mortar can be formed by adding pigments or carbon black into the cement and sand.

The simplest way of colouring mortar is with pigment admixtures. Mixing the pigment with the mortar requires special care and attention, particularly if it is done on site, because any inconsistency will be detrimental to the general appearance of the finished wall: too much or too little will give a patchy effect. Ready-mixed mortar or ready-to-use retarded mortars may be more reliable because they are prepared in controlled factory conditions. However, their actual colour and strength may still vary from one bag to another and they can never be totally predictable.

Pigmented mortars newly applied to a wall need protection to ensure that the colour is not washed out during rainfall.

Plasticisers

These air-entraining agents increase the workability of mortar and are principally used in cement mortars in place of lime. They work by breaking down the surface tension of the water and lubricating the hard, sharp sand particles so that the mixture is easier to spread. The process is activated by the addition of water, which causes the plasticiser to foam, releasing minute bubbles which surround the particles. However, although plasticised cement gives good workability and improved resistance to frost at an earlier stage than gauged mortar, its bond strength is less. Particular care must be taken to ensure that the manufacturers' instructions regarding dosage and mixing are closely observed.

Frost inhibitors

The purpose of frost inhibitors is to accelerate the setting times and lower the freezing point of the water absorbed by the mortar. However, despite some manufacturers' claims to the contrary, no mortar admixture has been found that will satisfactorily act as a frost inhibitor – or 'anti-freeze' agent as they have become known – and not adversely affect the mortar. Admixtures based on calcium chloride can lead to wall dampness and corrosion of embedded metals such as reinforcement and wall ties. Similarly, the use of ethylene glycol to lower the freezing point of mortar is known to have a detrimental effect on the hydration of cement.

Non-hydrated cement in the finished brick joints may harden when subjected to rainwater, expand and fracture the mortar joints. Therefore, until a satisfactory agent is found, the use of frost inhibitors is not recommended.

Retarders

These are used to delay the onset of the setting process without significantly affecting the mortar's workability or strength. Sugars, starches, zinc oxide or boric oxide are commonly used basic ingredients. The withdrawal of water from the mortar by the absorption of the bricks triggers the setting process when these retarding waters are used.

Latex

This term is applied to all cellulose and polymer bonding admixtures. The purpose of latex mortar is to retard early setting and strengthening and to increase the material's flexibility and compressive strength. It is not advisable to use them in areas of brickwork exposed to persistently damp or harsh weather conditions.

Cellulose ethers are particularly useful in rapid drying conditions because they ensure that plasticity is maintained for longer than is usual with other kinds of mortar. They help the mortar to retain a higher water level and thereby resist suction from the bricks.

Polymer bonding admixtures are essentially polyvinyl acetate (PVA) and natural or styrene-butadiene rubber (SBR). Only SBR is suitable for external use. Polymer bonding admixtures improve a mortar's bond strength and waterproofing properties and are particularly appropriate for exposed areas such as copings and cills. It is claimed, too, that they reduce shrinkage in strong mortars. Polymer bonding admixtures require careful usage—failure to follow the manufacturer's instructions may undermine the performance of the mortar to such an extent that the result is worse than no admixture at all.

LAYING BRICKS

The object of bedding is to ensure that all horizontal joints (beds) and vertical joints (perpends) are thoroughly flush and filled with mortar. This can be achieved by trowelling, larrying, grouting or dip laying.

Placing mortar with a bricklayer's trowel is the method adopted for most walls. The trowel is used to spread mortar on the upper course of bricks and on to one header face of the new brick, which is then pressed into position. Excess mortar which oozes out as a result of this pressure is 'struck' away by the trowel.

Larrying: A technique sometimes used for thick walls. The face bricks are first laid one course at a time on a trowelled mortar bed in the normal fashion, to ensure that a good quality finish to the face brickwork is obtained. A semi-fluid mortar is then poured into the spaces between the bricks. The central or filling bricks are then pushed into the fluid mortar with less care so that the excess mortar displaces to fill the side joints and interstices. This process is much more haphazard but makes the building of thick walls cheaper and quicker. If the level of mortar does not rise to the top of the joints, the empty areas are filled when the next course is larried.

Grouting: A general term which describes pouring mortar or concrete into a cavity. When used in the context of bricklaying it refers to filling the vertical joints (perpends) after the bricks have been laid.

Dip Laying: This technique is used for gauged brickwork with rubbers. The brick is 'floated' on its bedding faces on the surface of the putty lime in the dipping box, taking care to keep the face clean. It is slid into position on the wall, or arch, a small bead of putty is pressed out and this is usually left and rubbed down on completion. No other jointing technique is necessary.

JOINTING AND POINTING

Exposed sections of fresh mortar (beds and perpends) can be finished, or shaped, in a variety of ways to produce a range of effects. The finish and profile of these mortar joints influence both the visual appearance of a structure and its resistance to water penetration. The correct choice of mortar joint is, therefore, very important.

Jointing

Jointing is the process carried out when the mortar is still fresh (wet). In the case of the simple joint shape such as the flat or flush joint, the jointing can be done at the time of laying the brick.

Flat or Flush joints: These are formed by the bricklayer as work proceeds, by scraping the exposed end of the wet mortar with the trowel until the surface is flush with the surface of the brickwork. This type of joint provides the maximum bearing area and is especially appropriate for fair-face internal work because it does not collect dust. It is often favoured for use with coarse or textured bricks, although following the line of irregular faced bricks may give the joint an irregular appearance. However, because it is flush with the face of the bricks, it does not throw a shadow and can give the wall a dull appearance.

Jointed Flat joints: These are similar to flush joints except for the addition of a semi-circular groove along their centre. The groove is formed after the mortar has begun to set by running a jointing tool along the mortar, using a straight edge (such as a metal ruler). Jointed flat joints are also known as scored or ruled joints.

Struck or Weathered joints: These have a recessed top and flush lower edge. The tooling action compresses the mortar into intimate contact with the brick to produce a smooth, water-resistant surface. The joint also protects the upper edge of the lower brick and ensures that water does not collect but runs off. It gives an attractive appearance and throws a sharp shadow.

The lower edge of this type of joint is often struck back to produce an effect known as an overhung struck joint. This creates a sharp line on the joint's upper edge and eliminates shadow. Although it may enhance the brickwork's appearance, this joint leaves a ledge on which water may collect, ultimately causing discolouration and leaving the brick vulnerable to frost damage. It is, therefore, not recommended.

Keyed joints or Bucket-handle joints: These give a concave appearance and are formed by drawing a tool with a curved edge along the mortar. Like struck and weathered joints, the tooling action compresses the mortar and seals the surface, increasing its resistance to water. The concave shape also throws a soft shadow within the joint which is very attractive. If the wall is to be rendered, this term is also used to describe a joint left recessed or raked out in order to give a key to the finish.

Recessed joints: These are formed by raking out some of the face mortar. This produces a pleasing and deep shadow which adds considerably to the character of the brickwork with a negligible loss of strength. However, recessed joints suffer increased rain penetration, particularly if the mortar is textured as a result of the raking. If this joint is used at all, the mortar should always be tooled or rubbed to a smooth finish. There is also an increased risk of rainwater saturating the brick arrises, leaving them vulnerable to frost damage.

Masons' joints: These are traditional, but rarely used today. They are essentially decorative and are unusual in as much they are the only jointing technique which projects from the face of the bricks.

Pointing

Pointing is the process whereby freshly laid joints are allowed to stiffen before being partly raked-out and replaced with fresh mortar. Re-pointing is similar to pointing except that it occurs after the mortar joint has set, and is,

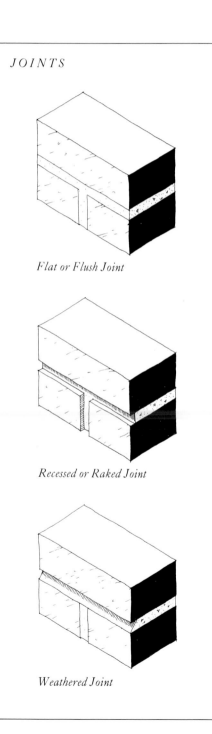

JOINTS

Flat or Flush Joint

Recessed or Raked Joint

Weathered Joint

therefore, a remedial treatment for the repair and restoration of existing brickwork.

Pointing is a particularly useful means of correcting any frost damage caused to a mortar joint. Unless the damage is severe or the mortar was laid during frosty weather (in which case the whole joint should be cut out and replaced), the damage is usually restricted to the exposed outer edge of the joint. In these circumstances, it may be sufficient to rake out the damaged area and point it up with fresh mortar.

The joints are usually raked-out about ¾in (20 mm), dusted and wetted to ensure maximum adherence to the new mortar. It is essential that pointing mortar be of the same strength or weaker than the original mortar. Stronger mortars impose an increased load on the brick face, which can lead to cracking.

Most pointing and re-pointing is finished with a flush joint, although any of the joints explained here can be used. In situations where the brick arrises are ragged, either through the deterioration of the bricks or from careless raking out, the bricklayer may prefer to use the time-consuming and therefore more expensive alternative, tuck pointing or its variant, bastard tuck pointing. Both of these joints include a thin projection which casts a fine shadow line on the mortar and gives the appearance of a sharply defined joint.

Tuck pointing: This is formed in the same way as any pointing technique, in that the affected mortar is raked out to a suitable depth and then filled with a 'stopping' of hard-setting lime or cement mortar, which is coloured to match the surrounding brickwork. A fine line is cut into the horizontal and vertical joints and pointed with lime putty, set to project beyond the mortar face with regular square arrises. The contrasting whiteish colour of the lime putty and the fine shadow cast by the projection combine to give the effect of fine joints in high quality brickwork. It is not a method of pointing in common use, except for refurbishment work. Effective when first done, it will soon weather and the pigment will be lost.

Bastard tuck pointing: This is the term used when the pointing ridge is formed on and of the stopping itself. Seen from a distance, the fine dark shadow cast by the projection gives the appearance of a thin joint. However, a projection of any kind exposes the joint to the danger of water collecting on it, and ultimately damaging both the mortar and the brickwork.

BONDS AND BONDING

The term bonding is applied to the regular arrangement of bricks in a wall. A wall built by simply stacking bricks one on top of another with a series of continuous vertical joints would be unstable. Unity and rigidity are obtained by overlapping one brick on another, so that each brick binds on, and is supported by at least two bricks below it. This means that no vertical joint in one course is directly in line with a vertical joint in the course immediately above or below it. The minimum overlap between two bricks should be one-quarter of a brick length.

Additional strength is provided in walls which are one brick or more thick by laying headers across the wall, at right angles to the face. This bond increases the stability of the wall, and also assists in spreading stresses from point loads above. In practice, however, the merits of the various bonds are usually assessed more on their appearance and ease of workmanship than for their effect on the strength of the wall.

The exceptions to this general observation are the quetta bond, used where vertical steel reinforcement is incorporated into the wall for earthquake resistant structures, civil defence structures or for post-tensioned brickwork. The other is the rat-trap bond, which creates discontinuous cavities within the wall thickness and has properties of thermal insulation and resistance to rain penetration.

BONDING TYPES

There are many different types of bond, the most common of which are detailed below. Other widely used types are described in the glossary to this book.

Stretching bond is probably the simplest and most common type of bond. Courses of stretchers are laid so that one half their length overlaps the brick immediately below, to produce single or half-brick thick walls.

Heading bond produces a one-brick thick wall. The bricks are laid across the thickness of the wall so that their headers show on the wall face.

English bond is a combination of stretchers and headers, laid in alternate courses on the face. This bond is particularly suitable for one-brick thick walls or thicker arrangements where variation in each course is necessary to

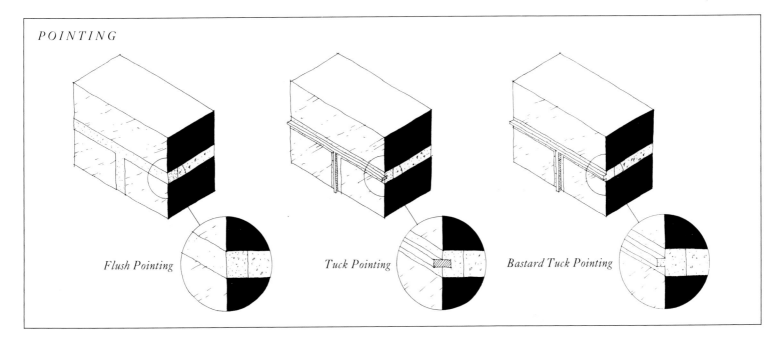

POINTING

Flush Pointing   *Tuck Pointing*   *Bastard Tuck Pointing*

WALL BONDS

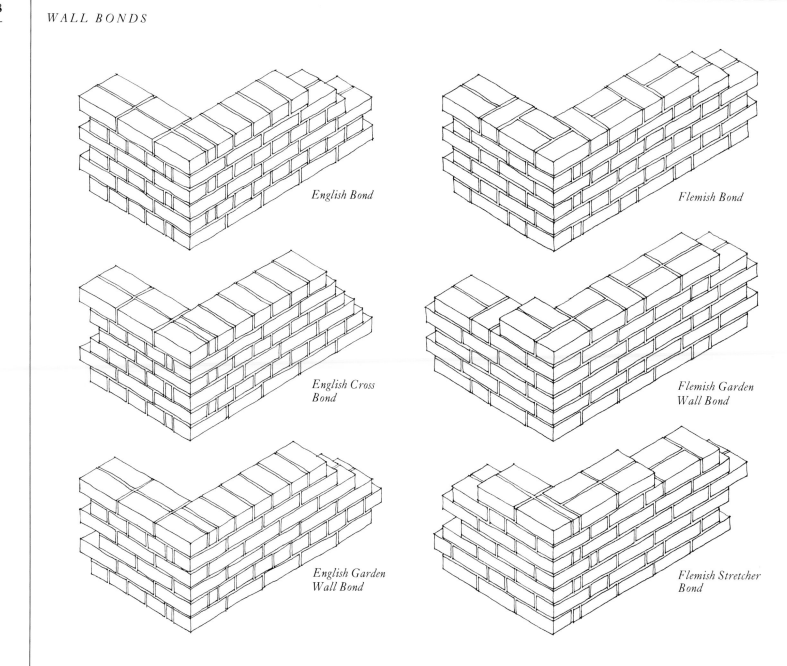

English Bond

Flemish Bond

English Cross Bond

Flemish Garden Wall Bond

English Garden Wall Bond

Flemish Stretcher Bond

Monk Bond

Rat Trap Bond

Header Bond

Dearne's Bond

Stretcher Bond

Loudon's Hollow Wall

maintain a good bond. English bond is considered to be the strongest of all the bonds because it secures the wall both horizontally and vertically across its length and depth and has no straight joints.

Flemish bond has headers and stretchers laid alternatively on every course, with each header placed centrally over the stretcher below. In double Flemish bond, both the internal and external wall faces show the arrangement. The visual appearance of Flemish bond is its main advantage over English bond. Although it is a strong bond, the arrangement contains a number of straight joints which make it weaker than its English counterpart.

Garden-wall bonds are imperfect variations on the English and Flemish types. They are, generally, cheaper and easier to build than regular English or Flemish bond, particularly when both faces of the wall are exposed. They are most suitable for one-brick thick walls, such as garden and boundary walls, hence their name. English garden-wall bond has the same general arrangement as English bond except that heading bricks are used in every fourth or sixth course and the courses in between are built up in double stretching bond. In Flemish garden bond, three stretchers are laid to one header in every course.

Rat-trap bond involves laying bricks on edge in a Flemish bond arrangement. It is most suitable for one-brick thick walls which are to be clad with tiles or rendered. This bond has a saving of about 25% in materials over one-brick thick Flemish bonds.

DESIGNING FOR MOVEMENT

All buildings and building materials have to be designed to accommodate the effects of thermal expansion and contraction, and moisture movement. Unless they can do this, abnormal stresses will occur which will eventually lead to cracking and disfiguring.

Movement can be accommodated by the incorporation of expansion (movement control) joints at specific locations in the structure. Stress concentrates at various points in a structure, such as where there is a change in height or thickness of the wall, and where there are large chases or grooves in the wall. The frequency with which these joints are included depends very much on the individual situation, but will range from every 20 ft (6 m) on freestanding and parapet walls to 40 ft (12 m) on the enclosing walls of a large building.

There are two types of expansion joint. The first is designed to cope with compressive and tensile stresses and is mainly used in vertical surfaces. It is usually formed as a butt joint between two bricks or between bricks and other materials. The joint is sealed with a flexible sealant which also covers the flexible joint filler. The second type of joint is designed to cope with shear stress and is mainly used in horizontal situations. This joint can be as simple as a strip of flexible material, such as bitumen felt, with a sealant cover.

The degree to which brickwork may be affected by thermal movement largely depends on the level and means of restraining the wall, the internal friction and the temperature difference across the thickness of the wall, and all of these factors should be taken into account at the design stage to ensure that the problem of cracking is avoided. Precautions should be taken: never fully restrain a wall between a structural frame, position restraints at regular intervals along the length of the wall, provide sufficient expansion joints and always assume the maximum possible temperature range and consequent horizontal movement.

All fired bricks expand over time with the absorption of water, although the degree to which this occurs depends on the quality of the brick. Their most susceptible period is soon after emerging from the kiln, when the dry brick absorbs atmospheric moisture. As a result of this, manufacturers recommend that bricks should not be used within 48 hours of firing—the reality of manufacturing and distribution makes this unlikely in any case. The effect of any moisture expansion should be easily accommodated by the expansion joints.

All building materials react in their own ways to changes in temperature and moisture content. Differential movement is caused by disparate materials coming into contact with each other, a problem which can be avoided by inserting a suitable expansion joint between the materials.

Heavy vertical loads in a structure can cause a wall to deflect or bow, producing a movement called 'creep'. This problem rarely arises if the brickwork is supported on a frame or foundation. Brickwork which is supported on a lintel or 'toe' may require the addition of a horizontal expansion joint between the bearing and the brickwork.

Setting mortar can shrink by as little as 0.04% or by as much as 0.10%, depending on the mix. Generally speaking, the higher the percentage of cement in the mix, the greater the mortar shrinks. Strong mortars (those containing a high proportion of cement to sand) are more likely to shrink than weaker mixes, and should not be chosen unless they are really necessary.

PAVING

Brick is a suitable paving surface for most locations, both interior and exterior. Where bricks are to be used in a sheltered position with light traffic, there is a wide selection of colours and textures available from a range of 'special quality' pavers produced to a thinner than standard depth. Well-burnt hard bricks may also be used.

For more extreme conditions where the paving will be subjected to heavy wear, wet conditions or exposure to frost, or where chemical resistance is required, a dense brick with low water absorption should be used. In practice this means a brick which has been fired to a high degree of vitrification such as a Dutch 'klinker' brick or an engineering brick.

Brick pavers are also made in interlocking shapes, which are particularly suitable for large areas of hard standing for cars, and a variety of kerbs, radii and rain-water channel units, to provide a brick edge to roads and paths.

Where pavers are 2 in (50 mm) thick or less, a continuous cement mortar bed should be laid using a weak mix with little cement. Thicker pavers can also be laid in the same way, particularly if heavy traffic is expected; however, it may be preferable to lay them on a flat bed of sand which is quite stable, provided that the sub-base has been levelled and covered with a layer of hard-core if used externally or a level concrete slab (with damp-proof coursing) if laid internally. The sand-bed method gives a degree of flexibility to the surface, allowing for a degree of settlement without unsightly surface cracks appearing. In all cases, jointing between the pavers may be in mortar or with dry sand.

Drainage should always be provided in external conditions, with the bricks laid on a small slope to allow water to drain. Even when laid on a sand-bed with sand filled joints, the brick surface will act as an impervious sheet in conditions of moderate or heavy rainfall.

STRUCTURAL TECHNIQUES

∞

BUILDING WALLS

It is essential that a new wall is built off foundations adequate for its intended load, and that each course is kept perfectly level during

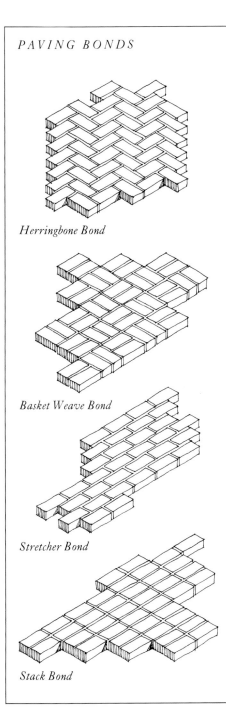

PAVING BONDS

Herringbone Bond

Basket Weave Bond

Stretcher Bond

Stack Bond

construction, with the corners and both faces carefully plumbed as the wall gains in height. It is also desirable that both the length of the wall, and the position of any features should relate to the joint pattern of the brick bond chosen, to ensure an even, attractive appearance unmarred by unsightly cut bricks.

To ensure a plumb and level structure the corners of the walls should be built up to a height of around 3 ft (1 m), extending the base courses and racking back as the work proceeds. The corners should be checked for plumb and the base course levelled with a spirit level. To construct the intermediate portion, a line pin is inserted into the mortar joint at each corner, one course above the bed joint of the course to be laid. A line is stretched between the pins and the new course is built with the outside upper edge of the brick abutting the line. The whole wall should be built up together in stages which do not exceed three feet, to allow the mortar to set.

SOLID WALLS

Before load-bearing brick walls were calculated on a scientific basis, if a wall was to be built high, the thickness at the base was increased accordingly, the calculation being made by rule of thumb and experience.

A one-brick thick solid wall is not now regarded as rain-resistant without cement render, timber weather boarding or another material applied as cladding, and it is therefore no longer used much for external walling, except when building on to an existing structure.

The techniques described in the following sections were first developed in conjunction with solid walls – the construction used for most, if not all, of the buildings constructed before 1918. This is not to say that some of the techniques are not applicable to cavity walls and brick cladding described later.

FOOTINGS

The term footings describes an expanded wall base in brickwork, the purpose of which is to increase the area at ground level in order to distribute the wall pressure over a greater area of foundation. They are now obsolete for this purpose as it is more effective, cheaper and easier to form a foundation in concrete.

Footings are built up in header courses. Stretcher courses have a tendency to tilt and become detached from the footing, especially under high loads. If their use is unavoidable, they should be placed as near to the centre of the wall as possible. Well-designed footings have the lowest course of bricks set at twice the thickness of the wall and step up in quarter-brick wide offsets at successive courses. Footings to two, or more, brick thick walls were traditionally constructed with a double bottom course for additional strength.

PLINTHS

A plinth is a projection at the base of a wall which extends downwards to the foundations and horizontally for the full length of the wall or around a building. The additional thickness gives the wall greater strength as well as providing it with protection from damage. Today, advances in calculating the strength and thickness of brickwork make the plinth redundant for all but decorative purposes.

The simplest way to form a plinth is by using a 'plinth' brick produced as a standard special, with a 2⅜ in (55 mm), 45° chamfer to the top edge on either the stretcher or header.

These bricks will form the top course of the plinth, projecting one quarter of a brick length from the wall face. To construct a bigger projection, each course underneath must be faced with a plinth brick projecting by a

further quarter brick length, until the required projection is achieved.

Whatever the profile of the plinth, the horizontal projections formed as it steps away from the wall face must have a sloping or chamfered edge so that water will drain away from the building.

An alternative to using a plinth brick would be to use a bullnose brick – also a standard special – which has a rounded edge of a similar dimension to the chamfer.

PIERS

Brick piers are rectangular pillars which take one of two forms: isolated, or attached. Isolated piers are freestanding and constructed to support beams or arches, and to transfer the load vertically to the foundation.

The height of an isolated pier should not exceed its smallest dimension multiplied by

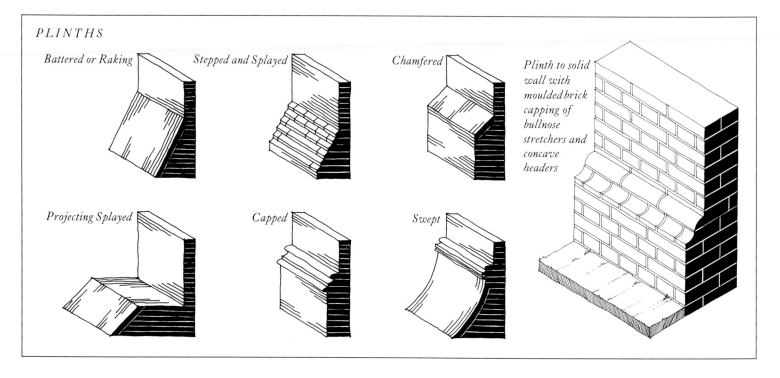

PLINTHS

Battered or Raking

Stepped and Splayed

Chamfered

Plinth to solid wall with moulded brick capping of bullnose stretchers and concave headers

Projecting Splayed

Capped

Swept

PIERS

Isolated Pier   *Attached Pier*

an arch or vault, or the steep pitch of a roof. Buttresses are also used to provide stability to walls of considerable height and length.

The profile of buttresses varies from a flattish projection for the complete height of the wall, to the offset buttress which steps outwards in stages from top to bottom (the bold profile is an essential feature of Gothic architecture). Its forms culminate in the flying buttress, which is an arch resting on a detached pier – although this particular form is generally constructed in stone. Buttresses may also be constructed with a batter or sloping outer face.

The top of the buttress is sometimes built up above the wall parapet to form a row of pinnacles, or it may finish just below the eaves or parapet line. In every case, the top face of the buttress must be protected with a coping or capping which usually has a severe slope to throw off any water. Materials used are brick, terracotta, stone, slate, clay tiles or concrete. Any dense, smooth-faced brick, given an adequate fall, will prove satisfactory if the brick is

eighteen. The advisable minimum width is one and a half brick lengths, so that any variety in the length of the bricks can be accommodated within the joint thickness to produce straight sides. Isolated piers must also be properly bonded by reversing alternate courses or turning them through 90° otherwise the structure will be weakened.

An attached pier is an integral part of a wall, used to provide increased stability at a point where a particularly large load is imposed. It is also used to give additional lateral restraint. Junctions between an attached pier and the wall should be arranged so that headers in the pier bond with the stretching course of the wall. This may require the use of special-shaped bricks such as bats and king and queen closers in order to avoid straight joints.

BUTTRESSES

A buttress is a projection built on to the face of the wall for the purpose of resisting a lateral pressure. This may be the sideways thrust of

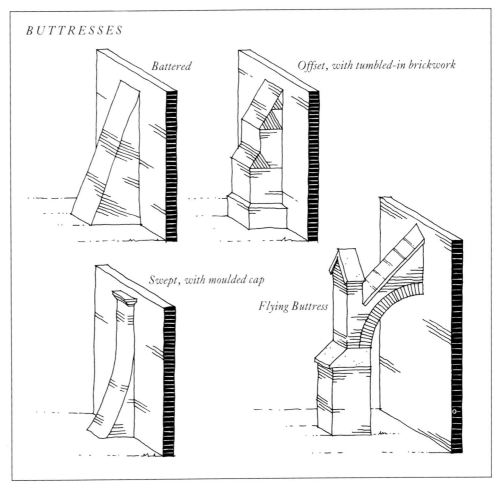

BUTTRESSES

Battered   *Offset, with tumbled-in brickwork*

Swept, with moulded cap

Flying Buttress

set 'on edge' (ie, bedded on the stretcher with a stretcher forming the outside face), or set at right angles to the slope, a process which is known as 'tumbling-in'.

The junction between the buttress and the wall should avoid straight (unbonded) joints between the bricks. The principles involved here will be discussed in the next section.

JUNCTIONS AND EXTENSIONS

A junction may be defined as the place where two walls meet and either one, or both, of them continue. If only one wall continues, such as where an internal wall of a house meets an external wall, the joint formed at the point where they meet is called a T-junction, if both walls continue after that point, such as when two internal walls cross at the corner of four rooms, the term cross-junction is applied.

The simplest junctions to form are in thin walls (not more than 1 brick thick) which are built of simple bonds.

The maintenance of adequate bonding is the test of a good junction. This can be especially difficult to achieve if the intersecting walls are either thick, of varying thicknesses, unusually angled, or constructed in a complex bond. In all these circumstances, it may be necessary to cut bricks or to use special shaped bricks, such as king or queen closers in order to achieve a proper bond between the walls. This is necessary with T-junctions where the intersecting wall must stop at the face of the through wall without disturbing the through wall's bond arrangement. The bond is obtained by placing a queen closer in every alternate course in the through wall, thus leaving a recess for a similar projection from the intersecting wall.

The easiest way to achieve a cross-junction is probably by alternating the through courses. This appears on plan as though the bonding of one wall is continuous on every odd-numbered course, while the bonding of the second wall is continuous on every even-numbered course.

The extension of an already completed wall regularly occurs when a building is enlarged. Before work begins, consideration must be given to matching the colours and textures of the old brickwork. Adequate bonding between the old and new brickwork is essential, but the techniques for achieving this differ from those described above, where the bond between the two walls is made as the work proceeds. Matching the bond of the new wall to that of the existing one can be achieved either by 'toothing' the brickwork or by using a connection plate system.

Toothing entails cutting a number of rectangular recesses to one half brick in depth and bonding the new wall into the pocket formed with cement mortar. If the wall is extended at the corner, the recesses are formed by alternately removing the headers of one wall and insetting or tailing in the ends of the new bricks. Walls which connect at right angles to an existing face wall are traditionally toothed by alternately removing three brick courses of the existing wall to the width of the new wall. The remaining courses are retained between the pockets to receive the new brick courses, which are again bedded in cement mortar to create the bonding between the new and old brickwork. The distance of three courses between pockets must be maintained to minimise the risk of bricks cracking during cutting.

The majority of the proprietary tying-in systems are in the form of stainless-steel plates which are screwed or shot-fired to the old wall. Adjustable, serrated anchor ties are set at right angles to the plate and bedded into the mortar joints of the new brickwork to provide lateral support, while permitting a small degree of vertical settlement. These systems provide a simpler cleaner and cheaper alternative to toothing. The ability to adjust the position of the anchor ties makes the system more flexible than the traditional toothing system, making it especially useful in walls with uneven courses, and where the new and old courses are unlikely to match because the new bricks are larger or smaller than the old.

CORBELLING AND CORNICES

Corbelling is the term applied to the projection of one or more brick courses from the face of a wall in increments of either one half or one quarter bricks, usually in header course, to form an overhang for either decorative or weathering devices such as cornices, string courses or cills, or to make a bearing for an applied load such as a timber beam or any other weight.

The disadvantage of corbelling is that it makes the wall less stable by taking the centre of gravity away from the centre of the wall. Where loads are light and spread evenly along the whole length of the wall, as with floor or roof joists, the stress is negligible. Where larger loads have to be concentrated on one point, such as a main girder, brick corbelling may not necessarily be the best solution. A general rule for the maximum projection of a corbelled wall is that it should be one third of the thickness of the wall immediately below. Where corbels are used principally for decorative effect and only have to transmit their own weight to the wall underneath, this rule is frequently disregarded, and there are many examples of cornices constructed in corbelled brickwork with a cantilever equal to the wall thickness.

Cornices serve the dual purpose of throwing rainwater clear of the wall face and providing a strong and decorative horizontal line where the roof springs from the wall or at the base of the roof parapet. When constructed in brick, additional support to the corbel may be given by brackets of either stone or steel encased in decorated stucco. The brickwork may also

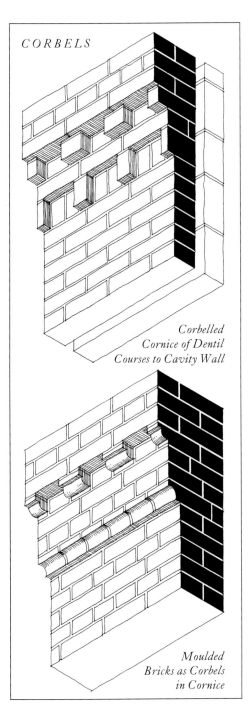

CORBELS

*Corbelled
Cornice of Dentil
Courses to Cavity Wall*

*Moulded
Bricks as Corbels
in Cornice*

have metal cramps built into the mortar joints and be tied back to the main wall. The brackets beneath the cornice are called modillions, sometimes made from moulded or carved brick.

The brickwork for decorative corbels and cornices is often in carved or moulded rubbers which have adequate strength and durability

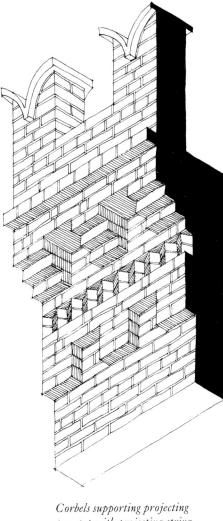

*Corbels supporting projecting
parapet with projecting string
course and dog-tooth brickwork*

for the task. Plinth bricks, or bullnose bricks laid with the moulding on the bottom face, also give an attractive finish. As the main stress is in the wall face, any facing brick being used is quite satisfactory for forming a cornice. The top face of the cornice should have a slight fall to throw off water, but the large surface area will need some protection to prevent water seeping into the brickwork. This is often a stucco finish, and other materials used are tiles, terracotta, slate, lead, copper and zinc.

COPINGS

A wall which is not covered by a roof, or one that is taken beyond the roof line in the form of a parapet, must be capped to prevent rain saturating its exposed top surface and causing efflorescence or frost damage. This protects the joints in the top course of brickwork and prevents rainwater from penetrating the mass of walling. Strictly speaking, the term coping refers to a cap which overhangs the wall to give it protection from rainwater. Where the edges are flush with the wall, the correct term is capping, though generally the term coping is used to cover both types.

Copings can be made of almost any material, provided that it is capable of resisting rainwater absorption. Typical materials include ordinary and special-shaped bricks, a combination of bricks and tiles, concrete, metals, stone or terracotta. Copings are named according to their external shape – for example, half-round or saddleback. The bricks for copings should be dense, with a low water absorption, and have a good shape, undamaged faces and, preferably, a slight glazed surface for improved weathering.

Brick copings are formed by laying bricks on their stretcher face in cement mortar. The cheapest coping is made with standard shaped bricks laid in this fashion, but bullnose, or other shaped bricks are a great improvement.

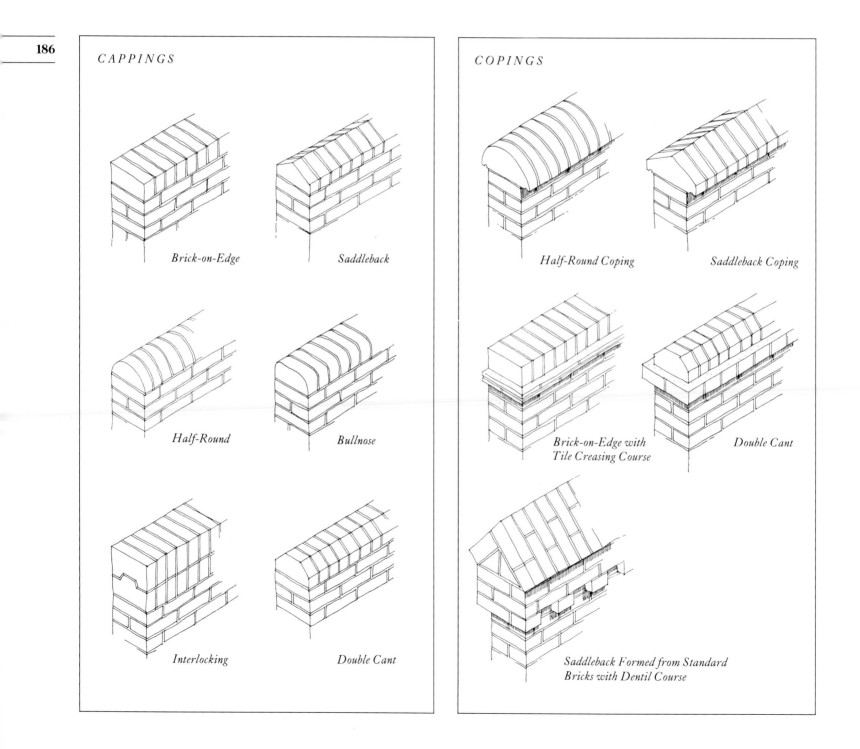

CAPPINGS

Brick-on-Edge

Saddleback

Half-Round

Bullnose

Interlocking

Double Cant

COPINGS

Half-Round Coping

Saddleback Coping

Brick-on-Edge with
Tile Creasing Course

Double Cant

Saddleback Formed from Standard
Bricks with Dentil Course

If a standard shaped brick is used, the coping should be slightly canted in one direction so that the rainwater can drain. Bricks laid with a flat top retain water in their surface imperfections and this eventually permeates the brickwork to cause deterioration of the joints. This type of coping can be improved by laying one or two courses of roofing tiles called 'creasing tiles' under the coping brick, with an angled cement fillet known as a 'weathering' above the tile to prevent rainwater collecting and possibly freezing on the flat tile surface. The edges of the tiles project beyond the face of the wall to enable the rainwater to drip clear of the wall face.

Special brick shapes which can be used with the above technique are double bullnose, half-round and saddleback cappings. Other special shapes are produced which oversail the wall faces and incorporate a groove (known as a drip) on the underside of the outer edge to prevent water running back into the mortar joint. Two readily available shapes are half-round and saddleback copings which are both designed to be used straight on top of the wall.

Saddleback copings can also be formed using common bricks set in cement mortar. The wall should terminate with a course of three-quarter bat headers set projecting from the wall face. Standard shape bricks are bedded on this course, on edge, at an angle of 45°. The inclining bricks are bonded together by alternating the full-length brick and the bat and setting them over a triangular brick core with a right angled apex. In a well constructed saddleback coping the exposed edges will project beyond the coping bed so that rainwater running off it will drip clear of the wall face.

Due to the importance of copings in ensuring and maintaining the longevity of a brick wall or parapet, brick manufacturers have developed many coping systems in answer to the need. Amongst these are interlocking systems which comprise two shaped bricks which interconnect, placed top and bottom. The lower is bedded on to the wall in cement mortar. The upper is bedded on top, also in cement mortar. The interlocking shape is intended to secure the lateral stability of the upper 'coping' brick to prevent it from being dislodged.

CAVITY WALLS

A wall constructed from two skins of brickwork either side of an air space, or cavity, is known as a cavity wall. Since the late 19th century, cavity walls have taken over from solid walls to become the most common form of external walling for domestic buildings. The main function of the cavity is to prevent rainwater from reaching the inner wall. In a solid wall, rain can penetrate right through to the inner face, either through the pores of the bricks or by capillary action through cracks in the joints between the mortar and the brick. Penetration through the pores of the bricks or mortar requires long or frequent periods of heavy rain so that the wall becomes saturated. Penetration through the cracks can occur as readily with dense, non-porous bricks and a strong mortar, as the rain running down the surface is not absorbed and is easily drawn into the cracks of joints, passing straight through to the inner face. A cavity wall eliminates this problem. In its simplest form, a cavity wall consists of two half-brick walls separated by a 2 in (50 mm) cavity. To obtain stability between the two leaves, horizontal metal or polypropylene ties known as wall ties are set across the cavity and bedded in the mortar joints of each wall. The accepted maximum distance between each wall tie is 3 ft (900 mm) horizontally and 18 in (450 mm) vertically. This improves the stability of the cavity wall to almost that of a solid wall of the same thickness. These are designed so that water cannot creep across them, and during construction they must be protected from mortar droppings which otherwise might form a bridge for water to pass from the outer to the inner leaf. For the same reasons, a physical waterproof break must be made between the two leaves where they are brought together for constructional reasons. Such details are at lintels above door or window openings, at jambs, cills and thresholds, and where the wall meets the ground. In all these locations a continuous and impervious damp-proof course must be built into the joint for its full width, and in horizontal locations it should be sloped outwards to throw water away from the inner leaf. There are many proprietary damp-proof courses on the market, the most common being those with a bitumen or lead component.

A traditional 11 in (280 mm) thick cavity wall will also give slightly better sound and thermal insulation than a one brick thick 8½ in (215 mm) solid wall, but only just. Thermal insulation, which is a legal requirement in most developed countries today, is not met by two skins of brickwork and a cavity. The two principal methods used to improve the thermal performance of the cavity wall are the substitution of a lightweight concrete block for the inner skin of brickwork, and the insulation of the cavity.

Blocks made out of aerated concrete are manufactured as 'thermal blocks'. They come in various thicknesses, but to achieve the necessary standard a thickness of at least 5⅞ in (150 mm) is required. If the design solution is to insulate the cavity, this can be achieved by the addition of an insulation material such as glass fibre, mineral fibre or polystyrene, set within the cavity thickness. To be wholly effective, that insulation must extend over the whole width and height of the cavity, including the jambs, heads and cills of openings. The insulation material should be firmly held against the inner wall, usually by the wall ties, and should maintain an air space of 2 in (50 mm) between the insulation and outer wall.

For buildings of two to three storeys a cavity wall of two half brick leaves or one half brick leaf and an inner leaf of 5⅞ in (150 mm) lightweight block will be sufficiently strong.

For buildings of a greater height, the brick leaves could be increased in thickness to one brick or they could be used in conjunction with a reinforced concrete frame, designed to support the outer, half-brick skin at each floor level.

As the outer wall is one half brick thick and this is not bonded to the inner skin, the obvious, and only way, if bricks are not to be cut, is to lay them in stretcher bond which has a relatively lifeless and uninteresting face-pattern. It is possible to vary this by constructing the wall in both whole bricks and half bats laid to any particular bond pattern. This is not often done due to the extra time and cost involved, but it does mean that buildings constructed with a cavity wall rely on the individual characteristics of the brick alone rather than interesting bond patterns. For a building of three storeys high with light domestic loads, strength is not a consideration. Nor, as has been demonstrated, is porosity. Above all, the choice is probably determined by cost and availability.

DIAPHRAGM WALLS

A diaphragm wall is a recently developed and highly cost-effective structural technique for strong and robust brickwork.

It looks like a wide cavity wall with each brick skin connected at regular intervals, not by metal ties but by brickwork ribs bonded to each skin and forming a series of box sections. The sections can be treated as an integral unit for the purpose of structural calculation: the

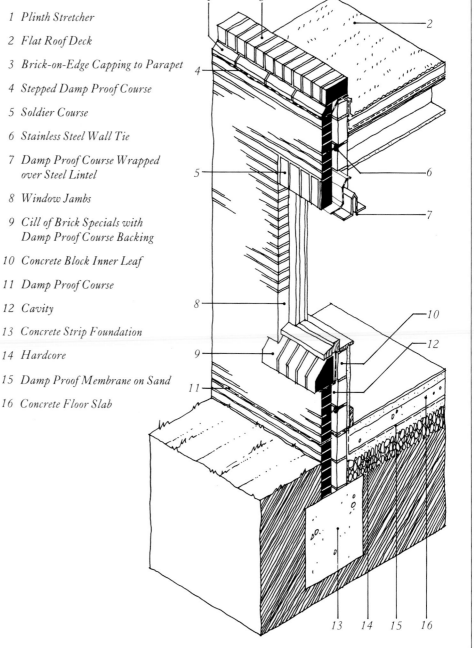

CAVITY WALL

1 *Plinth Stretcher*

2 *Flat Roof Deck*

3 *Brick-on-Edge Capping to Parapet*

4 *Stepped Damp Proof Course*

5 *Soldier Course*

6 *Stainless Steel Wall Tie*

7 *Damp Proof Course Wrapped over Steel Lintel*

8 *Window Jambs*

9 *Cill of Brick Specials with Damp Proof Course Backing*

10 *Concrete Block Inner Leaf*

11 *Damp Proof Course*

12 *Cavity*

13 *Concrete Strip Foundation*

14 *Hardcore*

15 *Damp Proof Membrane on Sand*

16 *Concrete Floor Slab*

parallel walls function as a flange and resist bending stress, while the web-like cross-ribs withstand shear stress.

Diaphragm walls can be used for heights up to 40 ft (12 m) and their construction becomes more economical as the height increases. They are particularly suitable for high single-storey structures and typical applications are for factories, auditoriums and sports halls. Diaphragm walls are becoming increasingly popular as quicker and cheaper alternatives to traditional steel or concrete frames. They provide an all-in-one structure, cladding, lining and fire-protection and represent a significant saving over other traditional frame structures, plus an attendant saving in construction time by eliminating another building trade and reducing the requirement for sheet finishes.

The overall thickness of a diaphragm wall is normally between two and three bricks. The precise width is determined by the wall's overall height and its expected loading. The number of diaphragms is also influenced by loading, and normally occur at intervals of every fourth or seventh brick. As the distance between the cross ribs increases, so the strength of the wall and its ability to withstand loads decreases. Additional stability is provided by applying the weight of the roof directly on to the wall as a uniformly distributed load.

Consideration must be given to the effects of strong winds on the outer skin of brickwork. If this bends, perhaps as a result of the cross-ribs being set too far apart, stress will occur at the junction of the cross-rib with the main wall and, in time, will cause a shear fracture. The tendency to bend can be greatly reduced by bonding the diaphragms into alternate wall courses, or by securing the two by means of non-ferrous or stainless-steel wall ties. The junction between the top of the walls and the roof should normally include a reinforced in-situ concrete capping beam.

Precast beams can be used when concrete spillage may be a problem. Capping beams have three functions: to give a positive connection between the wall and the roof, safely to transfer roof loads on to the walls and to resist horizontal loads. Most beams are hidden behind overhanging eaves or a parapet wall.

Wall openings are easily accommodated in diaphragm walls by incorporating an appropriate lintel across the thickness of the wall. In situations where an opening has to be wider than the distance between two diaphragms, the lintel must be suitably reinforced to transfer the increased load on to the wall jambs. This is usually done by thickening the jambs with a secondary cross-rib.

A horizontal damp-proof course is only necessary at cross-rib and internal wall junctions; experience has shown that moisture penetration from the external face is minimal and unlikely to reach the inner skin, provided that the cells are ventilated with air bricks. The damp-proof course should be of a type that can resist horizontal movement and squeezing under a vertical load. Vertical damp-proof courses are only necessary at openings.

The cellular configuration of the diaphragm wall allows water, gas, drainage pipes and electrical cables to be accommodated within the voids. The provision of removable panels (such as a small door giving access into one of

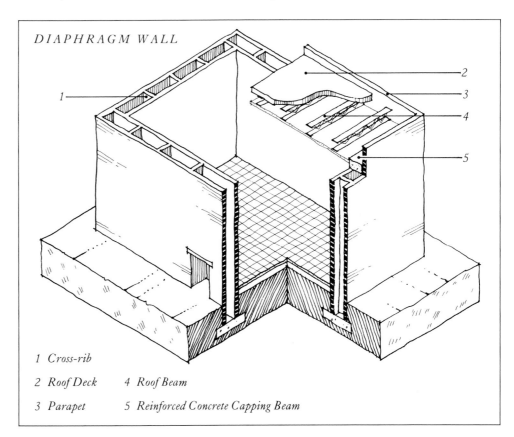

DIAPHRAGM WALL

1 *Cross-rib*

2 *Roof Deck*   4 *Roof Beam*

3 *Parapet*   5 *Reinforced Concrete Capping Beam*

the cells) is therefore essential for maintenance. Insulation materials can also be fixed within the cells and tied to the inner skin. Even without this additional insulation, the resistance of heat through a wall (U-value) in most cases can be about 10% better than that achieved in a normal cavity wall construction. The difference is largely due to the larger volume of trapped air in the voids and the mass of solid material of the cross-ribs across the voids.

For long expanses of walling, the effects of thermal movement can be controlled by incorporating an adequate number of expansion joints. In practice, this usually means providing joints at around 40 ft (12 m) intervals and to accommodate them by building a double rib, with one rib on either side of the joint.

As with normal cavity walling, the diaphragm wall uniformly distributes the loading on to its foundations. The bearing pressure on the foundations is low and nominal concrete strip foundations are normally adequate in all but weak or soft ground situations. This type of foundation represents a considerable saving on the expensive concrete pad foundations and reinforced ground beams required for framed structures.

FIN WALLS

A development of the diaphragm wall system, fin walls are essentially standard cavity walls incorporating a series of equally spaced piers or 'fins' for additional strength. They share the diaphragm system's suitability for tall single-storey structures which require a large and uninterrupted floor plan, and also eliminate the need for an additional frame structure of steel or concrete, an applied external cladding system and internal lining to the walls. The 'fins' perform a similar function to that of attached piers or buttresses.

The principal visual difference between diaphragm walls and fin walls is that the structural fins are visible on the outside of the building. They add a regular and aesthetically pleasing arrangement of vertical features to what would otherwise be a plain brick wall. The fins may be shaped in a number of ways or they may be designed with a brick arch linking them at roof level.

Fin walls gain their strength from their plan arrangement of T-shaped brick columns. The role of the fins and the adjacent external brickwork is to support the weight of the roof. Horizontal stress is borne equally by the fins, the outer wall and the inner skin, and distributed across the cavity by wall ties. The ties themselves provide little protection against

shear failure. This could occur at the junction of the fin and outer wall as a result of strong horizontal wind forces, causing the wall to bend, but the calculations made to justify the structure would include a wind load for the area in question and the necessary reinforcement at the junction.

Fin walls should be provided with a reinforced in-situ or precast concrete capping beam, especially when the structure has a lightweight roof with a low profile. Such roofs are susceptible to pressure from strong winds which may cause the roof deck to lift. The purpose of the beam is to provide a means of anchoring the roof to the fins, both to secure the roof from up-lift and to increase lateral

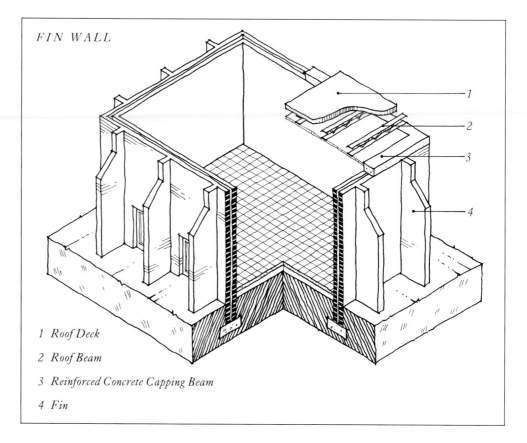

FIN WALL

1 Roof Deck

2 Roof Beam

3 Reinforced Concrete Capping Beam

4 Fin

stability in the walls. The capping beam or the roof may also be extended to cover the tops of the fins. Where this is not done, the exposed brickwork must be protected by a coping.

Unlike diaphragm walls, fin walls provide little cavity space in which water, gas, drainage and electrical services can be concealed. It is possible to form an occasional hollow fin to act like a service duct, but it would have to be made wider than the others so that it still performed its structural duty. However, the physical difficulty of gaining access to the inside of the hollow fin for inserting or maintaining the necessary pipework and cables would be difficult, and the suggestion is not recommended.

Normal strip foundations are adequate for most fin walls, unless the ground is weak or soft. Fin walls occupy less plan area than diaphragm walls and thus require a smaller foundation area, even allowing for the projections under the fins. The savings, however, ultimately depend on the overall thickness of the wall.

The requirement for long lengths of walling to be able to accommodate thermal movement – and thus incorporate expansion joints at intervals – is as relevant to fin walls as it is to the diaphragm system, the traditional cavity wall and the solid wall. The joints can be accommodated within a double-thickness rib, although this may not be visually acceptable.

POST TENSIONING

Post-tensioning (pre-stressing) is a method of increasing a brick wall's resistance to eccentric loading, lateral wind forces and bending stresses by giving the brickwork the ability to resist shear and tensile stresses in addition to the compressive stresses which it is capable of resisting on its own. There are some examples of post-tensioned brickwork in use, but not so many as to indicate its general acceptance. This

is possible due the belief that it is a costly technique which necessitates not only sophisticated design, materials and equipment, but also a specialist workforce. In fact, it is a relatively straightforward and economic way of increasing the structural capabilities of a wall.

The first step is to anchor steel pre-stressing cables into the foundation and then build a hollow wall or pier around the cables: either a diaphragm wall, cavity wall or fin wall, with regular hollow piers.

The steel cables are taken up inside each hollow cavity of the wall and extended until they pass through a reinforced concrete capping beam. The cables should be protected within a plastic sleeve to enable grout to be placed within the cavity without it impeding the free movement of the cables during the post-tensioning. The cables are then fitted with a capping plate and nut, and torqued (tensioned) with a hand-held torque wrench. The amount of tensioning is decided by the likely wind loads and estimated distortion caused by bending. In most circumstances it is preferable for the capping beam to be located and hidden within a parapet so that any torque adjustments and repairs can be performed without affecting the building's watertightness.

In many cases, post-tensioned brick walls are quicker and cheaper to construct than walls made with reinforced or pre-stressed concrete, because there is no need to erect costly and time-consuming shuttering (ie, formwork, usually in sawn timber or plywood, which encases the concrete as it is poured). Although they must be carefully designed, post-tensioned brick walls are simpler to construct than traditional reinforced brickwork and present a practical alternative to it. Avoiding the traditional frame system eliminates many of the internal piers and columns which not only take up floor space, but also restrict the potential use of that

part of the building. The combination of this with the simple logic of the post-tensioned system (particularly when coupled with the diaphragm wall) has appealed to many architects and developers, which is why it is becoming popular throughout the world.

BRIDGING OPENINGS
—
BUILDING ARCHES

An arch is a structure designed to span an opening, composed of individual bricks (or stone blocks) which are joined together so they are self-supporting and able to carry a superimposed load. This is achieved by placing the bricks mainly in compression and exerting a sideways diagonal force at the springing point, thus transferring the load on to the jambs (ie, the walls at either side of the opening). The strength of this lateral force is dependent on the span and rise of the arch and the load carried. For the arch to function properly, it must be resisted by an abutment or buttress of equal or greater weight and width, or by the placement of a similar arch next to it to form an arcade.

Arches can be classified in two ways: firstly, by their method of construction or function (e.g. Rough, Gauged, Relieving, Squinch) and secondly, by their shape or architectural style (e.g. segmental, flat, Gothic, Moorish).

CONSTRUCTING AN ARCH

An arch is composed of individual elements which only act as a homogeneous structure when they are all assembled, so some other means of support must be used during construction. The most common method is for a curved template of wood, called a 'centring', to be placed in position. The brick voussoirs, which form the arch ring, are then bedded over it, using the centring for temporary support.

These may be ordinary uncut bricks, in which case the arch is referred to as a rough arch, or they may be formed to a tapered shape to make a thin even joint between each voussoir. This arch is referred to as a gauged arch, and the voussoirs may be shaped by rubbing, axing or by using special shaped bricks.

Rough arch

The tapered joint between each uncut brick voussoir is provided by the mortar joint and to avoid an unpleasantly wide joint towards the extrados, stretchers are rarely used, the arch being constructed in heading bond in one ring or with the perpends overlapping in two or more rings.

Stretchers are occasionally used as skewbacks to distribute the thrust from the rings on to the abutments, or as lacing courses if the arch is several rings thick. However, the necessary cutting of the headers in this instance reduces the ease of construction which is the purpose of the rough arch.

Rough arches are relatively inexpensive to build, but the untidy appearance their name suggests has tended to limit their use to facing work at locations where it is not of prime importance, or where they will be concealed completely. They are often used as relieving arches, above a flat timber lintel, to window and door openings with a rendered finish or behind a half brick thick gauged arch.

Gauged arch

The true gauged arch is formed from soft sandy-textured bricks, sawn to shape and rubbed to give a flat bed joint and produce a number of regular-shaped tapered bricks. To obtain such precision, the arch is first drawn full size to determine the number of voussoirs required, the correct curve and the joint width, which is usually formed in lime putty.

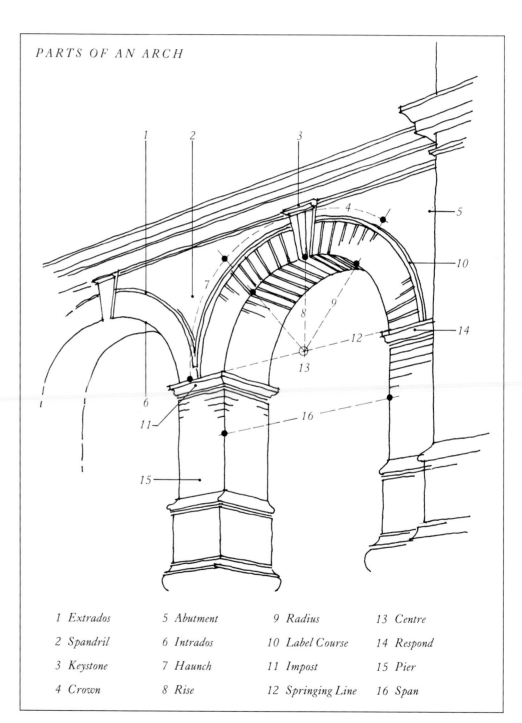

PARTS OF AN ARCH

1 Extrados	5 Abutment	9 Radius	13 Centre
2 Spandril	6 Intrados	10 Label Course	14 Respond
3 Keystone	7 Haunch	11 Impost	15 Pier
4 Crown	8 Rise	12 Springing Line	16 Span

The thickness of joint can vary from an almost 'dry' joint of less than $\frac{1}{32}$ in (1 mm) to between $\frac{1}{10}$–$\frac{1}{7}$ in (2.5–3.5 mm) depending on the appearance required. If thicker joints are required, the finish between voussoirs does not have to be so precise and, another, less expensive method of shaping the brick may be used.

Axed arch

This is an alternative method of forming a gauged arch using ordinary bricks. The voussoirs are prepared by marking the brick from a template and a mechanical mark is then made on the face to give a precise line of finish. For accuracy this would be a cut of around $\frac{1}{8}$ in (3 mm) depth made either by saw or powered carborundum disk, and the unwanted part of the brick would then be removed by striking it with a bricklayer's axe or scutch.

A less accurate, though acceptable, cut is made by tapping the face of the brick with a hammer and bolster on the line of the proposed cut to form a slight indentation. The unwanted part of the brick is then given a sharp blow and generally splits cleanly along the prepared line. Any waste can be trimmed by axing.

The cut arrises and bed joints of the brick voussoirs are not so precise as those of a rubbed brick. Nevertheless, an even joint of no greater than $\frac{3}{8}$ in (10 mm) can be achieved to give a neat appearance.

Special shapes: Arch bricks

Most brick manufacturers include a selection of shaped brick voussoirs in their range of standard specials. Typically these would be double taper headers or double taper stretchers to form arches or vaults for a given number of standard radii. The limitations are that the arch must be designed to this standard radius and that the arch ring can only be one brick thick.

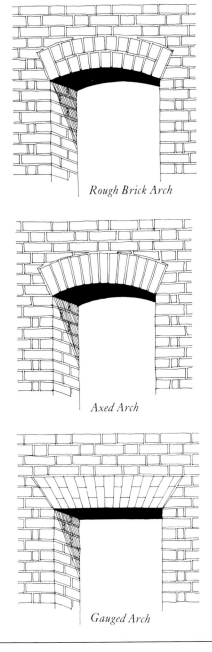

ARCH TYPES

Rough Brick Arch

Axed Arch

Gauged Arch

Alternatively, if the number of voussoirs required justifies the cost of production and there is sufficient time for the manufacture and delivery, the brickworks will produce special shaped voussoirs, on request, to suit a particular project.

Flat arch

This is constructed in gauged brickwork and also known as the 'Camber' or 'Georgian' arch. Although flat, its stability relies on the structural principles for arch construction described earlier, that is, on placing each voussoir in compression. The arch requires individually shaped voussoirs with skewbacks at either end to ensure that the bed joints are at right angles to the line of thrust.

Although this arch has been used extensively above window openings, particularly in the Georgian period, it is a weak form of construction and is prone to settlement, with cracks becoming apparent in some of the joints, especially at the key or centre bond. To help to overcome this, the arch is often constructed in one half brick in thickness with a lintel or relieving arch behind it to carry the inner thickness of the wall. The width of opening spanned was generally limited to $3\frac{1}{4}$ ft (1.3 m) or less.

If the camber arch is constructed with the soffit (intrados) perfectly level, it appears to sag. To overcome this illusion the centre point needs to be raised by $\frac{1}{8}$ in (3 mm) for every 1 ft (300 mm) of span. The extrados was generally cut level with a masonry saw to align with the adjoining horizontal brick courses.

LINTELS

A lintel is a horizontal beam which spans an opening in a wall and which performs the same structural function as an arch.

The brick is a unit which, in this context, is of relatively small size and has little strength in

Failing this, the steel may be coated with a rust protecting and inhibiting primer followed by a thick coat of bituminous paint. Providing this coating is undamaged, the steel will not corrode. However, it is sometimes difficult to avoid damage through careless handling.

Support for the facing skin of brickwork can be achieved in several ways. The simplest is by providing a 'toe', on which the bricks sit. Where a metal angle or preformed metal lintel is used, this is the only method of support. It can also be used in the case of a reinforced concrete lintel, either by bolting a metal angle to the face of the beam or, more usually, forming a concrete toe on the lintel, the thickness of one brick course, called a 'boot lintel'.

Another method of supporting brickwork from a concrete beam involves setting a soldier course of facing bricks in a horse, with galvanized or non-ferrous metal wall ties set every third joint and projecting from the rear face. The concrete beam is then cast behind the row of bricks and, when set, it acts with the bricks as a lintel.

Recent years have seen the development of mechanical fixing and support systems for brickwork. This has evolved in response to the desire to clad concrete framed buildings with a single brick skin, together with the ability to form decorative features. The systems use a combination of stainless-steel channels and brackets which are either bolted or cast into a concrete beam or panel. Additional stainless steel 'fish tail' ties and sliding anchors are set with one end in the channels and the other in the mortar joints of facing brickwork. These systems offer increased versatility and flexibility in setting out external brickwork, and the manufacturers will give any technical assistance required as well as providing drawings showing fixing positions, to ensure that the installation is both correct and safe.

JAMBS, CILLS AND THRESHOLDS

Jambs

The vertical surfaces at the sides of an opening in a wall are known as jambs. These are usually defined by the function of the opening: eg, door-jamb, window-jamb, fireplace-jamb. The term jamb is also used to describe the wooden uprights of a door frame but in the context of this section it will be used to describe the sides of an opening for a window or door in an external wall constructed in facing brickwork.

Jambs are formed by returning (ie, changing the direction of) the brickwork at an angle to the face of the wall and, in the case of a cavity wall, closing the cavity at the opening. There are three types of jambs, which are named according to their shape: plain, rebated, or splayed.

Plain, or square, jambs are returned on one plane and at right angles to the face wall. Timber frames may be set at any distance from the face within the overall wall thickness. In practice, windows in particular were often set close to the face to present a flush appearance.

In rebated jambs, the facing brickwork forms a projecting 'nib' on either side of the opening. The timber frame would be positioned one brick thickness back from the face and set into the recess formed by the two nibs. This construction gave the frame protection from wind and rain, and was particularly suited to housing the sash weight boxes of vertically sliding windows.

Splayed jambs are similar to plain jambs except that they are set at angles (normally 45° or 60°) to the face wall. They are mainly used in thick walls to help reflect daylight into the interior of a room, as well as providing modelling and a visual 'feel' for the wall thickness.

The main consideration in forming a jamb is to retain a full bond with the adjacent brickwork, so that an unbroken bond can be maintained. This is best achieved by designing the brick openings to coincide with a brick 'dimension' for the bond being used. If this is not possible, bricks will have to be cut as necessary to make up the dimension, or a special shaped brick used. Where walls are thick or the jambs are shaped, special shapes must be used if the jamb is to have an exposed brick finish. If the jamb is to be rendered with sand and cement, then the bricks can be cut approximately to size by 'axing'.

In a cavity wall, the outer course of bricks is turned towards the inner course at all jambs, to preserve the wall's weathering ability and thermal integrity. This technique is known as 'closing' the cavity, and a butt joint is used to connect the two brick walls. A vertical damp proof course should be fixed within the thickness of this joint to prevent bridging by rainwater.

Cills and Thresholds

A cill is the term applied to the external covering of a wall at the bottom of a window opening; the same detail at the bottom of a door is called a threshold. Both cills and thresholds share the same function, which is to prevent rainwater from collecting beneath the opening. This is achieved by setting the top surface of the cill or threshold at an angle so that the water will drain.

A number of different materials can be used to form both cills and thresholds, including stone, concrete, timber and, of course, brick and terracotta. If terracotta is used, provision should be made for a recessed drip or throating on the underside of the cill. This will direct discharged rainwater away from the face of the wall below and also prevent it being blown back by the wind or drawn back by capillary attraction. Unless they are specially manufactured for the purpose, brick cills and thresholds do not include a throating because the physical action of cutting a throat on a fired brick is likely to split the brick itself.

Brick cills and thresholds should be constructed using a dense brick with low water absorption to assist weathering, and should be set to overhang the wall surface by at least 2 in (50 mm). Bricks typically used for cills and thresholds are king closers or bull-nose bricks set on edge as a row of headers. The joint between the cill or threshold and the frame is normally sealed with a water-proof mastic. In some cases it is also advisable to set a galvanised or stainless steel strip, called a water bar, between the cill or threshold and the window or door frame. The water bar is set on edge in a waterproof compound such as mastic or white lead, and prevents draughts and rainwater from passing beneath the cill during stormy or windy conditions. It is normally set-in so that one half of it sits in a groove on the underside of the frame and the other half sits in a similar groove on the brick or terracotta unit.

ENCLOSING SPACE

Having constructed the walls of a building, there remains the question of how to cover it. Nowadays there are many different materials and methods for spanning large distances. Before the development of steel, reinforced concrete and detailed structural calculations, there were really only two: bulk timber beams or vaults and domes using bricks, tiles or stone blocks in conjunction with cement.

VAULTS

The construction of a vault is identical to that previously described for arches. A barrel vault, the simplest vault form, is a semi-circular arch extended at right angles to the span.

A vault is formed on a centring from either shaped voussoirs or standard bricks laid to present a bond on the intrados, or exposed face of the vault. As only one face of the brick is visible, standard bricks are the simplest way to form a vault as the splayed mortar joints – visible on a rough arch – will not be seen.

Brick is not an ideal material to form cross vaults such as those developed during the Gothic period, which used a skeleton of stone ribs to collect the pressures of the vault and concentrate them on the piers. A cross vault (also known as a groin vault), where two barrel vaults intersect at right angles, is formed in brick by cutting each brick to shape where they meet on the diagonal line across the intersection.

As with an arch, a vault carries its load by exerting a sideways diagonal force at the springing point. This force must be restrained

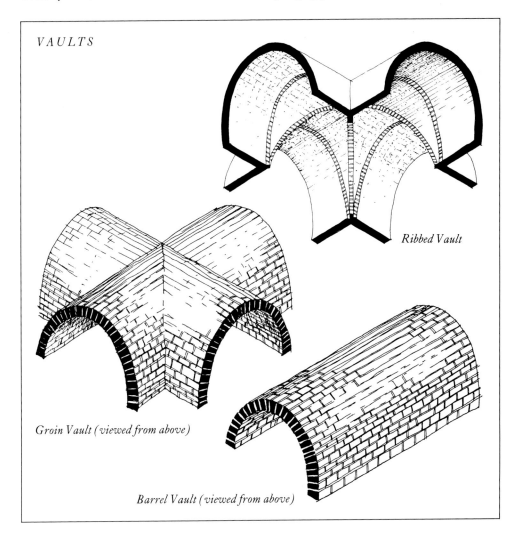

VAULTS

Ribbed Vault

Groin Vault (viewed from above)

Barrel Vault (viewed from above)

if the vault is to stand and this may be achieved by placing another vault alongside, by a buttress or by an abutment.

Today a brick vault is not the simplest way to enclose a space. It is interesting to note, however, that in some parts of the middle east, brick vaults are constructed without centring, using a traditional method. The tradition

Construction of Barrel Vault without using centring

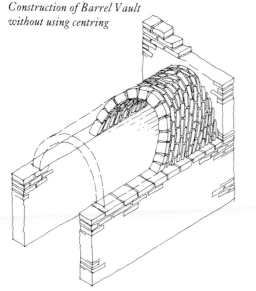

developed in Mesopotamia and Iran where there is little timber and forms of building had to be adopted using brick in compression. An arch of bricks is constructed by laying it at an angle against a vertical end wall. Subsequent arches are laid parallel, and cemented to the brick faces of the preceding arch until a long barrel vault is created. A course of brick is then laid flat along the top, followed by two more courses of bricks on edge to create a sufficient thickness in the vault to take a load. By the same method a groined vault could be built and also, on a square plan, four sloping barrel vaults.

DOMES

The Byzantines constructed brick domes from large flat bricks, which were usually around 1½ in (38 mm) in depth, like the Roman ones. They were laid on a thick bed of mortar composed of lime, sand and crushed pottery, tiles or bricks. M. Choisy in *L' Art de Batir Chez les Byzantins* (1883) has illustrated the method by which they constructed domes without centring, by means of a central post to which rods were attached, free to move in any direction. The thrust of a dome can be reduced by making it flatter. It can also be restrained by grouping a number of smaller domes around it. One of the beauties of Byzantine Churches is that the dome and vaults had no additional outer covering; the actual brick structure is visible inside and out. The problem of setting a dome on a square base is solved by the Byzantine device of the pendentive. Another method is to place a series of squinch arches one on top of another.

In western building, small domes were sometimes constructed in half-brick gauged brickwork, cut and rubbed to a wedge shape and bonded to an outer shell of ordinary brickwork. They were constructed around a dome-shaped timber centring.

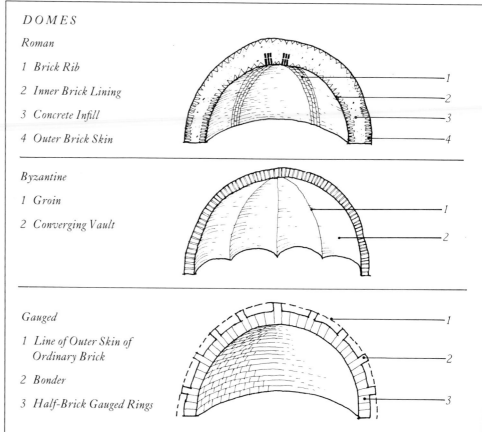

DOMES

Roman

1 *Brick Rib*

2 *Inner Brick Lining*

3 *Concrete Infill*

4 *Outer Brick Skin*

Byzantine

1 *Groin*

2 *Converging Vault*

Gauged

1 *Line of Outer Skin of Ordinary Brick*

2 *Bonder*

3 *Half-Brick Gauged Rings*

The 'Beehive' down-draught kiln provides a further interesting example of a brick dome. These were constructed from firebricks and fire clay mortar. The builders were reputed to build them without centring, judging the curve only by eye and relying on the adherance of the mortar to bond the bricks.

However, the use of brick for domes has never been very common in the west, and today they would certainly be constructed in concrete.

CONSERVATION OF OLD BRICKWORK

Regard for historic buildings is sometimes overcome if the site they occupy is wanted for redevelopment, but in the main, buildings which are considered important either in their own right or as a part of a nation's cultural heritage have been looked after and kept in a good state of repair. Brick is a durable building material, but, as with any other material, some maintenance is necessary.

Brickwork often deteriorates because another material has failed or a detail needs attention. Water penetration is one of the main causes of trouble and where this occurs, the source should be found and corrected without delay. Locations which may require attention are the tops of chimney stacks, copings to parapet walls and flashings. Checks should also be made to ensure free running and undamaged rain-water gutters, hoppers and pipes. Brickwork that is kept dry, or, that is allowed to dry out quickly when damp will last for many years without requiring maintenance.

Another source of trouble is structural movement, which may lead to cracking and thus to another point for water ingress. The cause of the movement must be established and

remedial action taken. It is rare for the wall or building to become so unstable that it must be demolished. Most buildings constructed up to 1900 have been built with what is now termed 'soft construction'. This means lime mortar, brick, and timber which is built in as lintels, wall plates (a horizontal piece of timber built into a wall on which the timber floor joists rest) or bonding timbers (built in to give stability to the structure). This flexibility of construction has enabled many old buildings to accommodate movement without failure, and now 20th-century technology and methods are available to give them a further lease of life. The repair of any building should be judged on its own merits, and, in the case of intricate and highly specialized gauged, moulded or carved brickwork, terracotta, or faience, expert advice should be sought on the methods proposed.

The essence of conservation today is to understand the materials used, and how they are assembled, and to maintain or repair, if necessary, using the same principles. This may be done using similar materials if they can be obtained—if not, substitutes must be considered. Much damage has been done to old buildings over the years by crude repairs to the fabric, although the methods used were considered at the time to be the most advanced. It is quite acceptable to take advantage of modern methods and materials, provided that stringent tests have shown that they will not affect the original fabric.

RE-POINTING

Re-pointing is the most frequent of remedial repairs to brickwork and will eventually become necessary however well a building is maintained. Current opinion is that if the mortar joint is intact and has no recesses which may harbour water, then even if the mortar is 'soft' it is better to leave it a few years until it actually breaks down before raking out and

repointing, as it is still performing its task.

Where the joint has broken down, or to remake any repair made with 'hard' mortar that has subsequently pulled away from the soft bedding mortar, re-pointing should be carried out. First, the joint should be raked out with a hooked metal implement. Where the wall has been deeply repointed in a hard mortar this method is not possible. Cutting out mortar with a bolster and hammer may damage the bricks, as may the modern powered carborundum disk cutter. It is better to leave it and wait until the mortar joint eventually breaks down.

Mortar for repointing should be of a weak mix. For standard conditions a 1:1:6 cement: lime: sand mix; for softer bricks a 1:2:9 mix of the same ingredients, or for old, historic buildings a lime mortar of one part lime putty to one part fine sand.

Where the building is of architectural interest, the original mortar can be replicated – even to the extent of finding the same colour of sand from the same local source. Using this method, patch pointing (ie, repairs to localized areas of damaged pointing) can be done. The problems which arise with old buildings vary, but a typical example would be a 16th-century brick building which was repointed in the 17th and 18th centuries by different methods. If examples of both survive in reasonably good condition, the decision must be taken as to which method would be historically correct for use in any repair work. Clearly, there is no one correct answer, but this example does illustrate that a building may well be altered and added to over the years.

With gauged brickwork, the question of whether to repoint or not is even more difficult. However it is sometimes necessary and should be carried out with the lime putty mixed with a little silver sand to a stiff consistency, flattened to a fine edge, and pointed in.

REPLACING BRICKS

Where the faces of a number of bricks have begun to disintegrate, it may be preferable to replace them individually rather than to rebuild the whole wall.

One method of repair is to cut the spalled face back to a solid base and to repair the brick with a coloured mortar, using either a patent colouring powder or some brick dust from the facings themselves. Each brick is repaired individually, and the mortar is compacted, left to set and the joints pointed. This method of repair tends to be disparaged by conservation specialists. It is, however, an inexpensive way of extending the life of the wall and does no harm to the surrounding bricks. For small areas which would otherwise remain untreated or for polychrome brickwork where it is not feasible to obtain an accurate colour match from a replacement brick, it has much to commend it.

Failing this, the brick must be cut out and replaced. Brick facings in old work are generally a half-brick thick cladding, and the cutting-out to this depth should be done carefully with a sharp brick-chisel to avoid damaging the sound brickwork and also to try to preserve the damaged brick, as it may be possible to reverse it and put it back in the wall.

Replacement bricks must match the existing bricks in every respect. With old buildings, this invariably means that new bricks must be specially made to the same size as the originals. The artificial weathering of new bricks is a frequent cause for debate amongst conservationists. If a small quantity of wood shavings are mixed in with the clay, they will burn on firing, leaving the face of the bricks pitted and subtly weathered. Another frequently used method for toning bricks is by applying a wash of soot and water—it is always best to treat a small sample first to assess the effect.

Many brickworks will make special bricks to match the existing ones, but pre-planning is essential, as manufacture and delivery will take a long time.

Where the expense of having specials made cannot be justified, other sources of bricks to use for repair are second-hand bricks, either from the locality, or from the building itself, or from collapsed boundary walls or outbuildings.

The difficulty of repairing gauged brickwork has been previously touched upon when dealing with re-pointing. Again, the advice must be to leave well alone unless repairs are absolutely essential. If they do become essential, any of the methods described above may be used.

CRACKS AND BULGES

Before any remedial work is started, structural movement in a building must be accurately assessed and corrected. It is beyond the scope of this section to discuss all the reasons for movement, but the majority of structural cracks and bulges in old buildings are caused by a small range of problems associated with 'soft construction' which it is useful to mention.

Timber lintels, wall plates and bond timbers built into external walls which in many cases have contributed to the building's flexibility, are also prone to rot. This causes local subsidence of the brickwork, the fracture of lintels and other cracks.

The typical brick facing was a 4 in (100 mm) skin in Flemish bond with a softer, irregular-shaped brick backing-wall of 4 in (100 mm) to 18 in (450 mm) thick. Although constructed in Flemish bond, most of the headers were snapped, so that the two skins were held together only by the occasional header. Both skins were bedded in lime mortar of varying strengths. There was often a difficulty in obtaining a satisfactory bond between the rough brick inner skin and the room partitions and party walls, and bulging frequently occurs at these locations.

Before undertaking any action it is as well to consider just how long the building has stood without failure. Its method of construction is both its strength and its weakness, but it is unlikely to be in such a severe state of disrepair that demolition is the only option.

Where the cause of movement has been corrected, or the movement has ceased, simple cracks may be left alone, provided that they are not a source of water penetration. If they are, or if they are unsightly, then a local repair should be made by carefully cutting out and re-pointing around the cracks, employing the methods previously discussed.

Bulging facing bricks can be tied back to the inner wall with stainless-steel bars set into pre-drilled holes through both the facing bricks and the inner wall, and bonded in position with resin. Stainless-steel expanding bolts may also be used, but it is often difficult to make a precise hole in the rough brick inner skin and the bolts might induce stresses and split the softer brickwork. Often a resin bond is a surer method of fixing.

In conditions where the whole facing wall (inner and outer skins) has become disconnected from a party wall, sections of concrete may be cast behind the facing, linking the inner skin to the party wall. Rotten bonding timbers may be cut out in sections and replaced with brickwork, timber wall plates can also be cut and replaced in a similar fashion and the timber joists which they supported re-hung on metal joist hangers.

All the treatment is linked with the provision of stainless-steel ties (described above) and fractures and cracks may be cut out and new brickwork 'stitched' in, bonding to the existing facing bricks.

Rebuilding in serious cases, where the wall bulges or leans to an unacceptable degree (a good rule of thumb is that the wall should not be out of plumb by more than 1 in (25 mm) per storey height), a structural repair may be necessary. It must be carefully taken down, salvaging all re-useable material, and rebuilt with the original coursing, bonding and joint profile. Thorough preparation is required before taking down, and the joints and bond pattern may be marked on a polythene sheet pinned to the wall. Gauged brickwork should be recorded, and drawings prepared of gauged arches together with arch centres constructed to the original profile. Cut and moulded bricks should be carefully numbered on the back as they are taken down, and all materials should be protected from damage and placed in dry conditions while awaiting re-assembly.

CLEANING

Even if it is in a weathered condition, a brick building can be brought back to its original appearance by cleaning, which will allow colour contrasts in the materials and shadow lines to be seen as they were originally intended. At the same time, great damage can be done to a brick façade through carelessness and inexperience, and poor understanding of the cleaning methods.

The methods for cleaning large areas of brickwork are: washing, chemical cleaning and abrasive cleaning. In addition, small areas of paint, oil or grease or other complex stains which may have been absorbed into the body of the brick, can be removed with a proprietary chemical poultice.

Washing

Before starting, all points where water might penetrate the building must be sealed. Washing is best carried out using a very fine spray of water which produces a fine mist against the brick surface. This will be sufficient to clean moderate soiling, but heavy soiling may require a greater flow of water – possibly leading to saturation of the brickwork. This should be avoided as it will mobilize soluble salts in the brick which will become visible as efflorescence as it dries. High pressure water jets which will damage the brick surface must never be used.

Washing may be assisted by mechanical brushing, but it must be remembered that even a bristle brush will scratch the surface of soft facing bricks. A nail brush of natural bristle is ideal for these. For harder bricks, a brush of bristle or phosphor bronze wire may be used.

Chemical cleaning

As with washing, all water ingress points must be sealed, and all glass, paint and polished surfaces must be covered.

The cleaning fluid used contains hydrofluoric acid and it should be used in a weak concentration of around 1%. Test patches should be carried out in unobtrusive areas before work commences. The fluid is generally applied with a water lance and before application the brickwork is wetted to encourage the chemical reaction to remain on the surface. Application time is from 2 to 5 minutes, following which the chemical must be washed off thoroughly. If the chemical is left on the brick for too long, there is a danger that a white bloom will form, but if this method is carried out correctly, the results can be excellent.

Abrasive cleaning

The methods used for this type of cleaning are compressed air and abrasives such as sand, or a carborundum disk which is spun against the surface of the brick.

In both cases, the weathered surface of the brick is etched or scoured away, so even with careful, experienced operators this is a method best avoided. The eroded brick face provides an easy catchment for future soiling and the removal of the weathered 'skin' will cause an accelerated rate of decay.

Abrasive papers such as sand or emery can be used to clean small areas of gauged brickwork quite successfully, but, as always, the skill of the craftsman will determine the level of success.

GOOD SITE PRACTICE

Although it demands little more than common sense, good site practice is a rarity in the modern construction industry. Adherence to the following guidelines, which are all too frequently ignored, should ensure both a reduction in the time spent on a job and in the waste of expensive materials.

ORDERING BRICKS

The first step is to ensure that the bricks are ordered well before building is due to commence. Very few facing bricks will be available 'ex stock' and most manufacturers have a minimum order period, especially for non-standard and special bricks. In times of high demand, even small quantities of bricks can only be supplied over a long time-scale. It is equally important to order the right quantity of bricks. Over-ordering is expensive, wasteful and, if excessive, it can affect the profitability of a project. Under-ordering will disrupt the work schedule and inevitably add to the contract time and cost. The normal practice is to calculate the number required (based on the area) and allow an additional 5% for wastage. There is a danger, too, that new batches of bricks will differ visibly from the initial batch, and create an unwanted variation in the colour of the building's elevations.

Some builders find it useful to agree a delivery programme with a supplier whereby, although only one consignment is ordered, the bricks are delivered to the site in manageable batches. This has the advantage of reducing the problem of on-site storage, as the materials are delivered when they are needed.

DELIVERIES AND STORAGE

The off-loading of bricks at the site should be done carefully. The best way is to lift the pallets of bricks mechanically from the lorry on to a firm, dry, level piece of ground. This should be as close to the working area as possible, so that handling is kept to a minimum. Loose bricks are particularly susceptible to damage as they are often transported around the site in a dumper truck and thrown into the dumper's bucket or tipped out wholesale on to the ground close to the work area. Significant waste can occur as a result of such treatment, especially in the case of special bricks, which are easily damaged by rough handling.

Fortunately, most bricks arrive on site safely bound together in polythene wrapped packs, stacked on wooden pallets. This reduces the risk of bricks becoming dirty and wet before use as the pallets raise the bricks above any pools of water. Once the pack has been opened, the bricks should be covered with a tarpaulin to avoid any problems with staining should they become saturated.

It is a wise precaution to keep separate storage areas for commons and facing bricks, so that the more expensive bricks do not get mixed up with the commons and possibly used in areas where a common brick would suffice.

MIXING BRICKS

Many bricks have attractive natural variations in colour. However, a finished building should have a subtle gradation of shades and not a sharp line across a wall surface. To achieve this, the bricks should be mixed on site. On large projects, it may be preferable to receive as many bricks as possible at an early stage to ensure colour consistency throughout the project.

MORTAR PREPARATIONS

Mortars are invariably mixed on-site with the proportions of cement, sand and lime worked out by the number of shovelfuls, and the water content estimated by eye. Where possible, correct proportioning of the ingredients by gauging – a standard volume achieved either by batching boxes or buckets – is preferable. This will ensure a consistent mortar which will give adequate strength, avoid colour variation, and produce a good brick-to-mortar bond.

Where great consistency is required, the sand for mortar may be ordered from one source at the commencement of the project.

SETTING OUT AND BRICKLAYING

Accurate brick coursing is essential, and walls should be built using gauge rods or profiles at corners. Unless the doors or windows are built in as work proceeds, a profile should also be used for openings.

Freshly laid brickwork should always be protected against wind and rain as it has little tensile strength and is susceptible to wind damage. This is particularly true of free-standing elements such as gables and single leaf walls, which should always be strutted until they are tied to the roof structure. Rain will cause efflorescence in newly laid brick-work, and may also cause lime to leach from the mortar and stain the brick face.

Hot dry weather presents problems of abnormal water absorption and evaporation for any type of wet construction work. In brick-work, the main problem lies with the mortar, which will lose its strength and eventually fracture if it is allowed to dry too rapidly. The principle cause of water loss is absorption by dry bricks; the relatively small amounts lost through evaporation can be replaced by pre-paring a wetter than normal mix. It is advis-able, therefore, to dampen bricks before bedding and to remove all dust from those surfaces that will come into contact with the mortar.

In winter, bricklaying should be suspended if the temperature falls below 3°C (37.4°F) and frost is imminent. If damaged by frost, fresh mortar will disintegrate, endangering the stability of newly laid bricks. If building work has to continue during a cold spell, a cement mortar with an anti-freeze additive may be used, but this should be discouraged unless it is absolutely necessary.

The drying and suction rate of brick is lower in winter, so all mixes of mortar should be as stiff, or dry, as possible. Freshly laid bricks need protection overnight or if work is to be suspended for longer periods. Hessian, together with an additional over-covering of plastic or other waterproof material, should be used for this purpose. By itself, hessian is useless and can cause serious staining and efflorescence if it becomes wet. All coverings should be propped away from the brickwork, to prevent the mortar sweating and then smearing over the faces of the bricks. When the weather improves, the covers should be removed to allow the brickwork to dry out.

Care should be taken in the immediate aftermath of an icy spell. In particular, brick-work on which new work is to be laid must first be checked to ensure that its temperature is above freezing point. If the temperature of the brickwork is below freezing point, any fresh mortar laid on it may be damaged.

GLOSSARY

ABUTMENT: A solid brick or masonry pier, from which an arch or vault springs, and which counteracts lateral thrust from the arch or vault.

AIR BRICK: A perforated brick which is used to provide ventilation.

ANNULET COURSE: A course of moulded bricks, usually semi-circular in section and circumscribing a column.

APRON: A projecting brick panel below a window cill. The panel is often ornamented by using shaped or carved bricks.

ARCADE: A line of arches which are supported on piers or columns. They can be either blind (attached to a wall) or free-standing.

ARCH: An arrangement of small blocks to bridge an opening. The blocks are normally wedge-shaped and support each other when loaded.

ABACUS: The moulded crown of a capital on which an arch or lintel is supported.

ARCH BRICKS: Special bricks which are tapered (tapered headers, tapered stretchers) to the required shape of an arch and which serve as voussoirs.

BED JOINTS: The joints between the voussoirs.

CROWN: The highest segment of the extrados, including the keystone.

EXTRADOS: The outside curve of an arch or vault.

IMPOST: The upper part of a pier or abutment on which the arch rests and from which it springs. Imposts are usually moulded and project beyond the face of the wall.

INTRADOS: the inner curve or underside of an arch or vault, also called a soffit.

KEYSTONE: The central and uppermost voussoir of an arch or rib vault. They are normally larger than other voussoirs and the last to be set in position so that they 'key' or 'lock' the other voussoirs in position.

LABEL COURSE: A course of projecting bricks around the extrados which throw off rainwater running down the face of the wall. They are often returned at the springing line to form a drip.

LACING COURSE: A radial course of stretchers in a large arch, built of half-brick rings.

PIER: The intermediate supports of an arcade.

RADIUS: The line of curvature of the intrados (applies to circular arches only).

RESPOND: A corbel or half-pier projecting from a flank wall and supporting the end arches of an arcade.

RING COURSE: The outer course (nearest the extrados) of an arch which is of several courses in depth.

RISE: The vertical distance between the springing line and the highest point of the intrados.

SKEWBACKS: The sloping face of an abutment on which the springers rest.

SOFFIT: See *Intrados*.

SOMMERING: The radiating joints of a flat brick arch.

SPAN: The horizontal distance between the supports for an arch or the two springing points of the intrados.

SPANDREL or **SPANDRIL:** The triangular filling to the right and left of an arch, and measured from the springing of the extrados to the level of the crown.

SPRINGER: The first and last voussoirs of an arch. They are bedded on the springing line and their upper surface is called a skewback.

SPRINGING LINE: The line connecting the springing points of the intrados.

SPRINGING POINT: The points from which an arch begins.

VOUSSOIR: Wedge-shaped bricks or stone forming the units of an arch.

ARCHES: There are many types of arch. They are classified in two ways: 1. By method of construction or function. 2. By shape or architectural style.

BASKET ARCH: An arch with a rise of less than half the span, and formed by a segment of a large circle continued left and right by two segments of much smaller circles.

CAMBER ARCH: An arch which has a level extrados and a slight rise on the intrados to counteract the visual appearance of sagging. Also known as a Flat arch, Georgian arch, Skewback arch or Straight arch.

CONCEALED ARCH: A circular arc passing through the crown of a Camber arch. It is struck from the centre of the arch and from it the voussoirs radiate.

DEPRESSED ARCH: See *Four-centred arch*.

DROP ARCH: A pointed arch with a radius less than its span.

EQUILATERAL ARCH: A pointed arch with a radius equal to the span.

FALSE ARCH: An arch which is formed by cantilevering bricks from both springing points, and from normal brick coursing so that the horizontal joints remain. The arch can follow many formats, i.e. elliptical, pointed etc., with the cantilevered edge cut or shaped to the line of curvature.

FLAT ARCH: See *Camber arch*.

FLORENTINE ARCH: An arch with a semi-circular soffit and a pointed or Gothic shaped extrados to increase its strength at the crown.

FOUR-CENTRED ARCH: An arch formed from four arcs, with the lower arcs centred on the springing line, and the higher two from centres below the springing line. The arch is similar to a Tudor arch. Also known as a Depressed arch.

FRENCH or **DUTCH ARCH:** A flat brick arch with only the central voussoirs wedge-shaped.

GEORGIAN ARCH: See *Camber arch*.

GOTHIC ARCH or POINTED ARCH: An arch formed by two arcs springing from the springing line and which meet at a central point. There are three types: equilateral, drop and lancet.

MOORISH ARCH: A characteristic feature of Saracenic architecture. The soffit consists of two segments struck from centres set above the springing line. When one centre only is used, the soffit is a little more than a semi-circle and is called a Horseshoe arch.

OGEE or OGIVAL ARCH: A pointed arch with each side formed from two arcs.

RAMPANT ARCH: An arch whose springings or abutments are on different levels.

RELIEVING ARCH: An arch built above a lintel to carry a load. It is normally formed using rectangular bricks and tapered joints.

ROMAN ARCH: An arch formed in a semi-circular shape, also known as a Semi-circular arch.

ROUGH ARCH: A relieving arch formed of half-brick rings of uncut bricks and generally covered by other work.

SEGMENTAL ARCH: An arch formed of a circular arc less than a semi-circle.

SEGMENTAL GOTHIC ARCH: A flatter Gothic arch.

SKEWBACK ARCH: See *Camber arch*.

SOLDIER ARCH: A flat arch constructed of uncut bricks on end. There are many techniques for supporting the arch, including its construction above a lintel or with wire hangers fixed between the cement joggles and hooked round the reinforcement in an in-situ concrete lintel. They are a common feature of modern architecture.

SQUINCH ARCH: A pendentive arch set at the corners of a structure and used, for example, to transfer the load of a square tower on to an octagonal one.

STRAIGHT ARCH: See *Camber arch*.

THREE-CENTRED ARCH: See *Basket arch*.

VENETIAN ARCH: 1. A lancet arch where the intrados and extrados of one side respectively spring from the intrados and extrados of the other side. The result is that the voussoirs are thicker at the crown than at the springing. 2. A combination of a central, semi-circular arch and two flat arches, in a single window; sometimes supported by brick mullions or piers, but structurally not sound.

ARRIS: The corner where two surfaces meet and form a sharp edge.

ASHLARED: Blocks of masonry which are carefully hewn to a regular shape and size. The term is more generally applied to stone walling but can be used to describe walls set with finely dressed courses of brick, particularly with regard to Gauged brickwork. In the USA, ashlar is also applied to walls constructed of burnt clay blocks. They are larger than standard bricks and could include terracotta.

ATTACHED PIER or COLUMN: One that is bonded to a wall. It usually projects by a maximum of three-quarters of its diameter.

BASKET WEAVE: Ornamental brick panels containing alternate squares of three bricks on end and three on flat.

BAT: A manufactured, broken or cut portion of a brick, which is larger than a closer and known according to its fraction of a whole brick, i.e. half bat or three-quarter bat. A bat which is cut so that its severed face is at an angle to the header is known as a bevelled bat. Also see *King* and *Queen closers*.

BATTER: The inclined face of a retaining wall.

BAY: A vertical and often regular division in a building, normally marked by fenestration, buttresses, piers or units of vaulting.

BED JOINT: The horizontal joint between brick courses. In batter walls, the bed joint is at right angles to the batter.

BISCUITING: Secondary burning of glazed bricks after an initial firing to 'biscuit' condition.

BLIND/BLANK DOOR or WINDOW: A recess in a wall which gives the appearance of a bricked-up door or window. The recess includes the arch, cill, head and jambs, but omits the frame and glazing. It is mainly employed to maintain symmetry to an otherwise asymmetrical facade.

BOLSTER: A brickmaker's cutting chisel.

BOND: The arrangement of bricks in a regular pattern so that each brick binds and bears upon two or more other bricks below it to give strength and stability, or for decoration.

AMERICAN BOND: A term used in the USA for English garden-wall bond.

BROKEN BOND: The irregular arrangement of bricks in a wall to form a bond, but with no regular pattern, and often found as a filling between piers.

BURGLAR BOND: See *Projecting headers*.

DEARNE'S BOND: A wall formed using alternate courses of headers and bricks set on edge in a one-brick thick wall. The bricks on edge provide shallow cavities and rely on the header courses for lateral restraint. The wall is more economical than a solid wall of the same width but has an irregular appearance. Often used in low-cost houses, it was also known as Dearne's hollow-wall bond.

DIAGONAL BOND: An arrangement where the internal headers of every fifth course are placed diagonally across a wall to give lateral bonding to thick walls. An example of a raking bond.

DOG-TOOTH BOND: A section of brickwork where courses of headers extend diagonally beyond the face of a wall, giving a jagged appearance. Also known as Saw-tooth bond.

DOUBLE FLEMISH BOND: A wall showing Flemish bond on both sides.

DUTCH BOND: A confusing term which actually describes St. Andrew's bond or Flemish bond. It is formed by staggering alternate courses by half a brick and known in the USA as Staggered Flemish bond.

ENGLISH BOND: An arrangement consisting of alternate courses of headers and stretchers. This wall is the strongest of the brick bonds because of the absence of straight joints running vertically through the wall. However, it is difficult to lay and expensive. The bond is created by using a closer next to the quoin header.

ENGLISH CROSS BOND: See *St. Andrew's bond*.

ENGLISH GARDEN-WALL BOND: Similar to English bond but with more than one course of stretchers between two courses of headers. It has many of the advantages of English bond but is generally cheaper to form. In the USA, it is also referred to as American bond or Common bond.

FACING BOND: A loose term used to describe any bond which uses mainly headers.

FLEMISH BOND: An arrangement consisting of alternate headers and stretchers in each course. It is generally regarded as more decorative than English bond, but is weaker. Although it takes its name from Flanders, the bond is rarely seen there. See *Single Flemish, Double Flemish* and *Flemish garden-wall bond*.

FLEMISH CROSS BOND: Similar to Flemish bond, but where occasional stretchers are replaced by additional headers to increase the wall strength. The group of headers form a cross shape, from which the bond takes its name.

FLEMISH GARDEN-WALL BOND: The formation of a Flemish bond, but with three (or four) stretchers between two headers in each course. It is also known as Sussex bond.

FLEMISH STRETCHER BOND: A bond formed by inserting three (or more) courses of Stretcher bond between two courses of Flemish bond brickwork. The actual number of stretcher courses varies, but is usually limited to a maximum of six and a minimum of three. It is sometimes referred to in the USA as American with Flemish bond.

HEADER or HEADING BOND: Brick bond formed by all headers set centrally over the joint of the brick below. The bond has great strength and is traditionally used for footings, engineering works, curved walls and for brick sculpture walls.

HERRINGBONE BOND: A raking bond. It is used to give longitudinal bond to thick walls and for ornamental panels.

HOOP-IRON BOND: A term used for any of the major brick bonds, but with a tarred and sanded, galvanized steel or stainless-steel hoop-iron set in the horizontal beds to increase its longitudinal strength.

MIXED GARDEN BOND: Modified Flemish stretcher bond with the headers set in an irregular pattern.

MONK BOND: A variation of Flemish bond where two stretchers are set between two headers, and repeated in every course. Also known as Yorkshire bond and Flying bond.

QUARTER BOND (Raking stretcher bond): A variation on Stretcher bond where the introduction of a Queen closer (or three-quarter bat) at each quoin forms a quarter brick overlap on the brick below.

QUETTA BOND: A wall, usually Flemish bond, where continuous gaps are left in the middle of the wall. It is similar to Rat-trap bond except that the bricks are not laid on edge. The voids usually house vertical reinforcement rods and are filled with mortar or a cement grout.

RAKING BOND: See *Diagonal* and *Herringbone bond*.

RAT-TRAP BOND: A one-brick thick wall formed in a similar fashion to Flemish bond with alternate headers and stretchers, but with the bricks laid on edge. The wall contains a series of staggered voids between opposite stretchers and is weak as a result. The wall is, however, light in weight and cheap to construct because it uses less bricks. It is also known as Chinese bond, Rowlock bond and Silverlock's bond.

ST. ANDREW'S BOND: A delicate variation on English bond where a header is placed next to the quoin stretcher in the stretching course in order to break the straight joint.

SINGLE FLEMISH BOND: The arrangement of a Flemish bond wall greater than one-brick thick, in which Flemish bond shows on one face only.

STACK BOND: A wall built of bricks set on end and with continuous vertical joints. The wall has no load-bearing strength and is used as a lining to a concrete panel.

STRETCHER BOND: The arrangement of courses of stretchers only. Each stretcher sits centrally over the vertical joint between the two bricks below. Stretcher bond walls are usually restricted to half-brick thickness because of the absence of cross bonding and are the usual bond for cavity walls.

BONDING BRICKS: Bricks which are used for tying together the two leaves of a cavity wall, instead of wall ties and tie rods. The bricks are cranked so that the end which is built into the outer leaf is in a lower course, in order to prevent water bridging the cavity to the inner leaf.

BRACKET: A brick which projects beyond the vertical surface of a wall to provide a horizontal support. See *Corbel* and *Cantilever*.

BREAKING JOINT: The avoiding of a vertical joint in consecutive brick courses.

BREEZE: Finely broken coke or cinder. 1. Partially burnt, it was added to clay to assist combustion. 2. Fully burnt, and usually from a furnace, it is mixed with cement to form a building block. They are used for internal walls. This technique is now seldom used.

BRICK-EARTH or BRICK CLAY: See *Clay*.

BRICKS: Rectangular blocks of burnt clay, calcium silicate or concrete. Bricks differ widely in quality, colour and texture, according to the composition of the clay and means of manufacture, and can be handmade, machine made, pressed, extruded or wire-cut. Most countries specify standard dimensions and shapes for their bricks, although special bricks can be manufactured to any size or shape.

BRICK-ON-EDGE: A brick bedded on its stretcher face.

BRICK-ON-END: A brick bedded on its header face.

BRICK SET: An American term for a Bolster or brickmaker's cutting chisel.

BRICK SLIPS (FACING SLIPS): Thin facing bricks to match headers and stretchers to give the appearance of a continuous brick wall.

BRINDLES: Bricks of a non-uniform or stippled colour, caused by contact with other bricks in the kiln. The term is sometimes applied to second quality blue bricks with irregular reddish markings, and not as vitrified as the best quality.

BRIQUE-ET-FER: A French term for reinforced brickwork. From the French *brique*, meaning brick and *fer*, meaning iron.

BUILDING BLOCKS: Types of slabs and blocks which are used for partitions and walls. They are made from concrete, clay or Moler earth and may be solid, hollow or reinforced. The clay blocks are known as 'bricks' in most Alpine and Mediterranean countries.

BULLNOSE BRICKS: A brick with one rounded arris. Bricks with two rounded arrises are sometimes referred to as double bullnose. They are used in situations where a sharp arris is not required or is susceptible to damage, and as capping bricks.

BULLSEYE: A circular aperture in a brick wall, formed by voussoirs, normally tapered to give regular joints.

BURRS: Partially melted bricks which have run and fused together from excessive heat, through being near the 'live' holes in the kiln.

BUTTRESS: A mass of masonry or brickwork projecting from, or built against, a wall to give additional support. The purpose of a buttress is to resist lateral thrust from an arch, roof or vault.
ANGLE BUTTRESS: Two buttresses which meet at right angles and at the corner of a building.
CLASPING BUTTRESS: A buttress which wraps around the corner of a building.

DIAGONAL BUTTRESS: A buttress which equi-angularly meets at a right angle corner of a building.
FLYING BUTTRESS: An arch or half-arch which connects a point of lateral thrust and transmits it to an outer support or buttress.
LATERAL BUTTRESS: A buttress which stands at the corner of a building but on the axis of one wall.
PIER BUTTRESS: An exterior pier counteracting the thrust of a vault or arch.
SETBACK BUTTRESS: A buttress set slightly back from the angle.

CALCIUM SILICATE BRICKS: Bricks made from sand or crushed flint, and mixed with hydrated lime. The bricks are compressed and allowed to harden in a sealed autoclave. They continue curing when exposed to the atmosphere and thereby increase their strength. Because they are made from carefully selected and accurately proportioned materials, they are more regular and more consistent in quality than clay bricks.

CALLOW: 1. The overlying soil stratum above superficial clay deposits. 2. The inferior layer of clay over deep bed clay deposits.

CANT BRICK: A brick which includes a splayed corner, but not a right angle. Bricks with two cants are called double cant bricks.

CANTILEVER: A beam or unit which is supported at one end only – the other end is free.

CAPITAL: The head of a column or pilaster set immediately below the entablature of a Classical building. Each architectural 'order', such as Greek Doric, Ionic, Corinthian, Tuscan, Roman Doric and Composite (a mixture of Ionic and Corinthian), has its own distinctive style of capital. The word is from the Latin *capitalis* meaning head.

CAPPING BRICK: A shaped brick serving as a cap (coping) to a wall, but without oversailing the wall face. See *Coping*.

CARVED BRICKWORK: Brickwork which is laid with very fine joints, like gauged brickwork, and carved with a hammer and bolster, and brought to a fine finish with rubbing.

CASINGS: Bricks which are used as the outer cladding to a clamp.

CAVITY BRICKS: Bricks, usually large, which when laid over one another leave a hollow cavity in the middle of the wall. Most are extruded bricks where the cavity recess replaces the usual frog. Many countries have attempted to perfect a cavity brick for every day construction applications. However, whilst cavity walls are faster and cheaper to construct using this method, the examples have not been popularly received by the professions and public.

CAVITY WALL: A wall constructed of two separate leaves with an air gap between, and bound together at regular intervals with tie-bricks or wall ties. They are principally used to prevent moisture penetration to the inner leaf, and to give a slight improvement to the thermal insulation of the wall.

CHAMFERED: A corner which is bevelled so that the arris is removed equally from each face of the brick. If the cuts are unequal in length, it is called a bevel.

CHEQUERED BRICKWORK: A regular design formed by building small square panels of different coloured bricks into a wall. The term is also applied to the introduction of other materials in a square pattern, such as flint or chalk, and provides a similar appearance to that of a chessboard.

CHEVRON: A carved zigzag moulding.

CHIMNEY STACK: The section of brickwork which stands above the roof level and which contains the flues.

CHUFFS or SHUFFS: Those bricks which are very soft or full of cracks as a result of exposure during burning. They normally disintegrate when removed from the kiln and are unsuitable for construction work.

CILLS: The lowest horizontal member of a door or window. They may be in either timber, brick or stone. In the USA, the word is spelled sill.

CLADDING: A non-loadbearing structure or skin applied to the walls and roof to keep the weather out. In the USA it is known as siding.

CLAMP: A stack of unfired bricks and fuel which is fired to produce stock bricks.

CLAY: A mixture of extremely fine rock particles, formed from the decomposition of other rocks. The principal minerals are a mixture of hydrous silica and alumina (sand and aluminium) which are capable of absorbing and losing moisture. When moist they become plastic and are capable of being moulded into shapes. Varying amounts of other minerals may also be present, typically chalk, iron-oxide, and manganese dioxide.

ALLUVIAL CLAY: A clay containing alluvium (deposit of earth and sand) and used in the production of Portland cement.

BALL CLAY: A very plastic clay which vitrifies without changing shape, used for pottery.

BOULDER CLAY: From glacial deposits. The clay used in the production of bricks and tiles. Boulder clays are impure mixtures of clay and sand (loamy clay), or clay and chalk (marly clay) etc.

BRICK-EARTH or BRICK CLAY: The term is officially used to describe the thin deposits of silty clays from the Pleistocene period (Ice Age). However, it is more commonly applied to any clay from which bricks are made.

CALCEREOUS CLAY: A clay which contains a high proportion of calcium carbonate.

CARBONIFEROUS CLAY: A term for clays which evolved during the Paleozoic era containing particles of coal.

FIRECLAY: A refractory clay which is rich in quartz and alumina, and used for making firebricks and setting grates in boilers etc.

GAULT: A stiff strata of clay found between the layers of greensand in chalk formations, and used in the manufacture of gault bricks.

KAOLINITE CLAY: A primary or pure china clay which has poor plasticity. Derived from the decomposition of feldspar in granite, it is used for the manufacture of porcelain.

LEAN CLAY: A clay containing a high percentage of silica.

LOAM: A clay containing sand or gravel (also with an organic contact – humus). They are known as mild clays and produce bricks which are less susceptible to warping and shrinkage than those produced from strong clays.

LIAS CLAY: Blue argillaceous limestone, rich in fossils – the high carbon content saves fuel in firing.

MALM: 1. An artificial marl which is obtained by adding chalk to clay. 2. A rich chalky clay, or marl.

MARL: A calcareous clay or loam, often rich in iron. Consolidated marl is called marlstone.

MILD CLAY: A loamy or sandy clay containing free silica.

PLASTIC CLAY: Clay which is soft and easily moulded into shape.

PRIMARY CLAYS: Those found at considerable depth at the place of formation by the decomposition of rocks. They are usually lean clays.

RED CLAY: A clay obtained from felspathic rocks which contain iron oxides.

REFRACTORY CLAY: A clay which is difficult to fuse and which can resist very high temperatures.

SHALE or CLAY SHALE: Shale is formed from fine-grained sedimentary rocks which have been compressed and laminated together. Clay shales have a high proportion of carbonaceous matter and therefore require little added fuel for burning. They may disintegrate in water but do not become plastic.

SILICEOUS CLAY: A clay with a high proportion of silica.

STRONG CLAY: Pure clay which is free from other substances, such as sand etc.

CLINKER: Fused ash, known as slag, from furnaces. It is used in the manufacture of clinker bricks and blocks.

CLINKER BRICKS: A special type of hard-burned and vitrified brick which is principally used for paving. Also known as Dutch clinkers.

CLOSER: A cut or moulded part of a brick, used to make up a dimension in the face of a wall to complete a band pattern. See *King Closer, Queen Closer*.

COMBED: Surface scratching to provide a key for a plaster or rendered finish.

COMMON BRICKS: A cheap local brick which is generally not used for facing and loadbearing situations. In the USA they are known as building bricks.

CONCRETE BRICKS: Bricks moulded from a cement and sand slurry and annealed in ovens. They can be tinted to almost any colour.

CONTINUOUS KILN: See *Kilns*.

COPING BRICK: A brick, stone or terracotta unit used on the top of a wall for protection and ornamentation, and made so that the ends overhang the wall faces to throw rainwater clear.

CORBEL: A projecting support on the face of a wall.

CORBEL COURSES: The courses of bricks or stones forming a corbel.

CORBEL TABLE: A projecting course, or courses, usually of stone supported on corbels and forming a parapet.

CORNICE: 1. A moulding at the top of an internal wall covering the joint between the wall and ceiling. 2. An overhang at the top of an external wall to throw water away from the face of a wall.

COURSE: A horizontal row of bricks between two bed joints. It is measured as one brick and one joint high.

COWNOSE BRICKS: A brick with a semi-circular end.

CRAZING: The term applied to fine cracks in cement, terracotta and glazed surfaces.

CREASED: The folds of clay on the surface of a handmade brick, usually formed as a result of stiff clay being thrown into the mould with insufficient force.

CREASING: A double row of tiles projecting beyond the face of a wall and usually set under a brick-on-edge coping. It is designed to throw off rainwater and is often combined with a triangular shaped cement fillet to prevent the water from lodging.

CRINKLE-CRANKLE WALL: A wall, usually only a half-brick width, with a serpentine (snake-like) plan, from which it derives its stability. It is known in the USA as a Serpentine wall.

CROSS JOINT: The inner joint between two stretchers in a one brick (or more) thick wall, running at right angles to the face of the wall. Joints which run parallel to the wall face are called *Wall joints*.

CROSS VAULT: See *Groin vault*

CROW STEP (CORBIE STEP): Forming a gable coping by a series of horizontal steps.

CRYPTO-EFFLORESCENCE: A rare defect caused by soluble salts which are trapped behind the face of a brick. The salts expand when hydrated and create an unsightly crumbling of the brick's face.

CUT BRICKS: A brick which is axed (cut) to shape using an axe or bolster. The cut face is usually of a rough texture making it unsuitable for face work.

CUTTERS: See *Rubbers*.

DAMP-PROOF COURSE: A layer of impervious material usually set just above ground level and below any inside timbers to prevent moisture from rising up the wall. It is commonly referred to as a d.p.c.

DENTILS: 1. Rectangular projections on the face of a moulding. 2. In brick construction, dentils are formed by projecting alternate headers beyond the face of the wall.

DENTILATION: The presence of dentils.

DIAPER: A regular and repeated decorative motif of different coloured bricks set in a lozenge or square pattern on a plain wall.

DIAPHRAGM WALL: A structural wall system which is similar in form to a cavity wall except that each brick leaf is set either side of a wide cavity and connected at regular intervals by brick cross-ribs called diaphragms. The wall resembles a continuous series of box or 'I' sections and is suitable for tall single-storey structures. See *Fin wall*.

DOG-LEG BRICKS: An angled brick where the angle between two stretcher faces is not a right angle.

DOG-TOOTH BRICKWORK: A course of bricks laid diagonally so that one corner protrudes from the face of the wall, forming a series of triangular projections. It is placed under an Oversailing course and is known in the USA as Hound's tooth brickwork.

DRESSINGS: Projecting or moulded masonry to form quoins at the corners of buildings, or cills and reveals around openings, and normally formed of brick or stone, to present a superior material and finish to that of the main wall. Brick walls often have stone or gauged brick dressings.

DRIP: A groove or projection under an over-hanging edge, such as a window cill, cornice or coping, designed to throw off rainwater at the outer edge of the building and prevent it from running back to the wall face.

EAVES: The lowest part of a sloping roof, and which projects beyond the face of the wall.

EAVES COURSE: A projecting brick course immediately below the eaves.

EFFLORESCENCE: An unsightly, but usually harmless, white staining on the surface of a brick wall, caused by the drying out of soluble salts on, or just behind, a brick's surface. It normally comprises one or more of the carbonate and sulphate compounds of calcium, magnesium, potassium or sodium and occurs where bricks have become saturated.

EGG AND DART MOULDING: A style of moulding consisting of alternate oval and arrowhead motifs.

ENGINEERING BRICKS: Dense, well-vitrified bricks, of uniform size. They have high crushing strengths and low porosity.

EXPANSION JOINTS: Special flexible joints in brick and block walls which allow for expansion and contraction through temperature changes or where structural settlement is anticipated. An expansion joint breaks the continuous bond of a wall.

FACE or FACE SIDE: The exposed vertical surface of a brick.

FACING BRICKS: Those bricks which have good weather-resisting properties and a pleasing appearance, and selected for use on the external face of a wall. There is a large assortment of types and they vary widely in colour, texture and quality. They are often referred to simply as facings.

FAIENCE: A term applied to a glazed terracotta slab. It is produced by the twice-fired process: once without and once with the glaze. It is often loosely used to describe any glazed terracotta finish.

FIN WALL: A development of the diaphragm wall system and having similar properties. Fin walls are essentially cavity walls which obtain additional strength through being connected to a series of equally spaced piers called fins. The system is suitable for tall single-storey structures requiring a large and uninterrupted floor plan such as warehouses or sports halls. See *Diaphragm wall*.

FINIALS: Formal decorative ornaments, usually pointed, crowning a canopy, gable, spire or pinnacle.

FIREBRICKS: Bricks which are capable of resisting high temperatures and used for lining fireplaces, kilns and chimneys. They are made from fireclay and burnt at a high temperature.

FIREHOLES: Small chambers in the walls of a kiln which are packed with coal or wood and ignited to start the firing.

FISHTAIL TIES: A metal bar, the ends of which are split and twisted, resembling a fish's tail. When built into a mortar bed (or concrete) the twisted end resists movement caused by tensile loads.

FLARED BRICKS: Bricks which have dark patches at one end, caused by being placed near to the fire during burning. They are laid as headers to form patterns in the brickwork such as diaper or chequerboard.

FLAUNCHING: A strip of mortar applied to the top of a chimney or brick ledge and acting as a weathering to prevent rainwater settling.

FLETTONS: Common bricks made from deep bed clay. The clay has a natural moisture content and a high carbon content which provides nearly enough fuel to burn the bricks, hence they are cheap and have a controlling effect on other brick prices. A large proportion of bricks produced in the UK are Flettons made of Lower Oxford clay.

FLUX: Any substance which causes metals or minerals to flow or fuse together, or which dissolves impurities during calcination. Typical fluxes applied to brick clay are lime, potash, soda and common salt.

FOIL: A leaf-shaped curve produced by the cusping of an arch or circle. The number of foils involved is indicated by the prefix, eg, trefoil (3), quatrefoil or quadrifoil (4), cinquefoil (5), hexafoil (6) and multi-foil or plurifoil (many).

FOOTINGS: Bricks which are stepped out at the base of a wall in order to spread the wall load over a greater foundation area.

FRET MIXTURE: A decorative pattern made by the continuous repetition of two or more materials in a straight line. The finished effect is similar to a chequer or interlacing pattern.

FROG: An indentation on the bedding surface of a brick. It is done to reduce the brick's weight and provide a key for the mortar. Wire-cut bricks do not have a frog; handmade bricks have one frog; semi-dry machine pressed bricks usually have two.

GABLE: The portion of the end wall which follows the profile of the roof, from the eaves to the ridge. The design can be as simple as a triangle or as complex as Gothic scrollwork. A Dutch gable has curved sides crowned by a pediment. See *Crow step*.

GALLETING: A decorative technique of inserting small pieces of coloured stone or flint into soft bedded mortar.

GAUGED BRICKWORK: Brickwork in which the bricks have been cut and rubbed to a required shape and size, and set with fine joints. Also referred to as gauged or gaged brickwork.

GAULT BRICKS: Bricks made from gault clay (chalk and sand) and usually pale yellow or white in colour.

GLAZE: A transparent glass-like coating (slip) applied to bricks, tiles and terracotta etc. The glaze can be made from various materials, but is chiefly a composition of china clay and a colour additive, and is fired at high temperatures.

GLAZED BRICKS: Bricks which have a salt-glazed stretcher and/or header face.

GREEN BRICKS: Semi-plastic moulded bricks before they are burned.

GROG: An aggregate or binding material formed from finely ground burnt bricks or clay waste. The grog is added to fresh clay for the manufacture of some types of bricks. The grog required for making terracotta is formed from finely ground fired terracotta or pottery.

GROIN: The sharp edge formed at the intersection of two vaults crossing one another.

GROUT: Cement mortar in a fluid state. It is used for filling crevices or forming a key when jointing together new and old cement work.

GROUTING: Filling the crevices of brickwork and stonework with grout.

HACKS: Stacks of bricks arranged for drying after moulding. The hacks are allowed to stand for a few weeks before burning. They are protected from the weather by lightweight moveable roofs or permanent sheds with open sides known as hack houses.

HANDMADE BRICKS: Bricks which are made by hand as opposed to those which are machine-made. They are made by a brickmaker throwing high quality, semi-plastic clay into a mould or templet and are regarded as more aesthetically pleasing, because of their non-uniform appearance, for use as facings. Handmade bricks generally have one frog.

HARD-BURNT: A description which is applied to bricks, tiles etc., that have been fired at a high temperature. They are durable, and have good compressive strength and low water absorption.

HEADER: 1. The short end of a brick. 2. The end of a brick showing on the face of the wall.

HEADING COURSE: A course of headers. It is mainly used in English and Header bond brickwork, and in the construction of brick footings.

HERRINGBONE BRICKWORK: Bricks which are laid diagonally with each brick pillar sloping in different directions. It is most often used to fill the space between a timber frame. See *Nogging*.

HOLLOW BRICKS: Those bricks containing large holes or cavities which represent more than one-quarter of the brick's total volume. They are light in weight and have good insulation properties. They are also suitable for introducing reinforcement rods and cement grout within the voids to resist lateral loads.

HONEYCOMB WALLS: A wall where alternate headers are omitted to allow the free passage of air. They are commonly used below timber floors to allow ventilation and reduce the risk of wet and dry rot, when they are known as sleeper walls.

HYDRATED LIME: Lime which has been slaked, dried, and ground to a powder. It is used in the same way as cement and mixed dry with sand before adding the water to make it plastic. It should, however, be prepared a few days before use.

INSULATING BRICKS: Bricks which are used for retaining heat within a kiln in order to reduce fuel consumption. The clay is mixed with combustible material that burns away to leave a porous brick.

JAMB: The side of a door or window opening between the frame and the face of the wall. It is normally set at right angles to the face of the wall. Jambs which are not at right angles to the face of the wall are known as splayed jambs.

JOINT: The mortar between two bricks.
BED JOINT: 1. The horizontal mortar joints. 2. The radiating joints of an arch.
CROSS JOINT: The vertical mortar joints set perpendicularly to the face of the wall. In the USA they are known as Head joints.
WALL JOINT: A mortar joint set parallel to the face of the wall.

JOINTING TOOL: A bent steel tool used for forming brickwork joints when pointing.

JOINTING: The process of finishing mortar joints while the mortar is still fresh.
FLUSH JOINT (FLAT JOINT; BAG-RUBBED JOINT): A mortar joint pressed flush with the brick surface by a trowel.
GRAPEVINE JOINT: A popular joint in the USA and bearing many similarities to the scored mortar joints which are prominent in 18th-century Britain.
KEYED JOINT (BUCKET-HANDLE JOINT): A concave-shaped joint, formed by drawing a curved-edged tool along the mortar joint.
MASONS' 'V' JOINT: Pointing so that a small triangular wedge of mortar projects beyond the face of the wall.
RAKED JOINT: A joint where the mortar has been raked out a reasonable depth from the face of the wall. This is often done for decorative reasons or as a precursor to repointing or rendering.
RUBBED JOINT (RAG JOINT): A flush joint where the excess mortar is rubbed off with a piece of rag, rubber or other soft material.
RULED JOINT: A flush joint in which a groove is placed along the centre of each joint with a bricklayer's jointer. In 18th-century Britain, the scoring was traditionally made with the edge of a penny and obtained the nickname of 'penny round joint'. The effect of light and shade was similar to the more expensive 'two-coloured tuck pointing'.
STRUCK JOINT: An inverted Weathered joint. It is created by pressing the trowel along the lower edge of the joint to form a recessed bottom. The mortar is flush with the arris of the upper brick.
WEATHERED JOINT: It is created by pressing the trowel along the upper edge of the joint to form a recessed top. The mortar is flush with the arris of the lower brick.

KEY: A tool for jointing brickwork, and used for keyed joints.

KEYED BRICK: A brick with one stretcher face indented to provide a key for a plastered or rendered finish.

KEYSTONE: 1. The central voussoir at the crown of an arch. 2. The top stones of a vault. 3. The boss of a dome. See *Arch*.

KILNS: A furnace in which bricks are burnt. Kilns work on an intermittent or continuous process and rely on a downdraught or updraught system.
BEEHIVE KILN: A cylindrical-shaped brick kiln with a cupola cap and a chimney, and so named because of its resemblance to a beehive. It is an intermittent kiln which operates on the downdraught principle: hot gases reach the cupola and are drawn down again through the bricks being fired by the drawing action of the chimney.
CONTINUOUS KILN: A kiln containing a number of chambers, and in which the sequence of operations – loading, sealing-up, firing, cooling and unloading – is uninterrupted. The fire is allowed to move to a neighbouring chamber when the brickmaker is ready and this reduces the high cost of reigniting the kiln before each firing. See *Hoffman kiln*.
DOWNDRAUGHT KILN: An intermittent kiln which comprises a square or circular chamber with a vaulted or domed top, and a chimney. The hot gases from the burning fuel are drawn upwards and, with the draw from the chimney, deflected down again from the vault or dome.
HOFFMAN KILN: A continuous kiln for brickmaking. It is normally circular on plan and contains between 12 and 16 chambers. By careful setting of the dampers, each

chamber is at a different temperature, rising from a chamber being loaded to another where the bricks are burnt, and then descending to the one being unloaded. The continuous system means that a new batch of bricks can be produced each day and is therefore the most efficient.

INTERMITTENT KILN: A small kiln which has to be loaded, heated to firing temperature, cooled and unloaded again at every firing. They tend to be popular in situations where the demand for bricks is low, and in less-developed countries.

TUNNEL KILN: A continuous tube-shaped kiln in which green bricks are placed on carts at one end of the tunnel and travel slowly through the kiln on a moving conveyor. The bricks undergo a preheating, firing and cooling process within the kiln and emerge at the far end as burnt bricks. Temperatures and track speeds can be varied.

UPDRAUGHT KILN: An intermittent kiln in which the hot gases rise up through the kiln chamber to the open air. Examples include Newcastle, Scotch and Suffolk kilns.

KING CLOSER: A three-quarter brick with a diagonal section cut off one corner.

KISS MARKS: A fault on the surface of a brick which is caused by bricks touching one another in the kiln, usually as a result of poor stacking. The contact causes unequal burning and the discolouration on a brick's surface.

KNAPPED FLINT: Flints which are broken through their middle to reveal a darker coloured centre and give a flat face to a wall.

LACING COURSE: 1. A course of bricks, stones or tiles used to level up and strengthen a wall built of another and irregular material, such as rubble, flints etc. 2. See *Arch*.

LARRYING: A method of setting bricks in thick walls. The face bricks of the inner and outer walls are laid on a mortar bed in the normal fashion. Semi-fluid mortar is then poured into the space between and the central bricks are pushed into position. Excess mortar is displaced and fills the side joints and interstices.

LEAF: A thickness of walling, generally half of a cavity wall.

LIME: The product of burning calcium carbonate or limestone. The process leaves an oxide of calcium known as quicklime, used for mortars and plasters. Its quality depends upon the constituents of the limestone. When soaked in water, quicklime becomes hydrated lime. Pure lime derives from burning chalk and is used for lime (plasterer's) putty and whitewashing. It has poor setting qualities. Grey stone lime is used for mortar for general building purposes. Hydraulic lime is used in damp situations as it is able to set under water – some of its qualities match that of cement. Slaking of lime generates great heat and causes the lime to expand. All limes, except hydraulic lime, should therefore be slaked some time before they are required for use.

LIME PUTTY: It can be produced from sieving slaked lime (in order to remove lumps and grit), or from wet hydraulic lime soaked for a minimum of 12 hours. It is used for jointing gauged brick arches.

LINE PINS: Steel pins with a long blade-like shank and large head. They are inserted into a bed joint at each end of a wall with a line of cord tied to both to provide the bricklayer with a horizontal bed level.

LINTEL: A horizontal beam or slab spanning an opening and supporting the wall above it.

JOGGLED LINTEL: A flat arch, usually of stone or terracotta, formed by a series of small blocks united with joggle joints.

LOUDON'S HOLLOW WALL: A means of building a one and a quarter brick thick wall in Flemish bond with a central cavity. Each leaf is formed in half-brick walling and is tied across the cavity by a header and a quarter closer behind. The technique is not suitable for domestic use because of the number of bricks bridging the cavity.

MAGNESIA: Oxide of magnesium. When present in brick-earth it gives the bricks a yellow tint.

MALM BRICKS: Bricks made from marl or malm. They vary in colour from red to buff and white – the best malm bricks are nearly white.

MASONRY: The pure definition of the term is the preparation and fixing of stone, although many countries choose to include heavy engineering work in brickwork and concrete blockwork.

MODILLIONS: A bracket, generally carved or moulded, projecting in rows beneath a cornice.

MOLER: A brick made from diatomaceous earth and used for the manufacture of insulation bricks.

MORTAR: The plastic jointing and bedding matrix between bricks. It helps to distribute the load, make the joints watertight and unite the bricks. Most mortars are composed of a ratio of cement and sand, to which water is added, although lime may also be introduced for extra plasticity.

BLACK MORTAR: A mortar containing crushed ash as a substitute for most of the sand content. It has a dark grey appearance and is normally used in thin joints.

CEMENT MORTAR: A strong mortar composed of cement and sand.

GAUGED MORTAR: A cement-lime mortar. Also known as Compo.

HYDRAULIC MORTAR: Mortar made with hydraulic lime and used in wet situations.

LATEX MORTAR: A new term used to describe cellulose and polymer bonding admixtures. Their purpose is to retard the setting of mortar.

LIME MORTAR: A weak mortar composed of lime and sand.

MORTAR MIX: The ratio of components creating the mortar.

PLASTICISER: A liquid air-entraining agent which increases the mortar's workability. It is mainly used with cement mortar as a lime substitute. Plasticisers are suitable for moderate strength mortars.

RETARDER: An admixture which is introduced to mortar in order to delay its setting time.

MOULD: A timber or steel templet in which clay is formed into bricks of a set shape and size. The templet is like an empty box with no top or bottom plate. It is placed over a separate stock board with a moulding for forming the frog, so that the moulded brick can be removed easily.

MOULDED BRICKWORK: Bricks which are moulded before firing and built into a wall to form an ornamental detail.

MULLION: The thin vertical dividing member between two frames. The term is more typically applied to timber windows but can equally be used to describe a thin shaft of brickwork between two windows.

MULTICOLOUR BRICKS: Bricks which have a non-uniform colour. They can be created from handmade, rough, smooth or sand-faced facing bricks and are achieved by careful mixing and burning to produce the varied effect. See *Rustic bricks*.

NOGGING: Brickwork infill, often ornamental, between the studs of a timber frame.

OVERHAND WORK: The erection of a brick wall from inside a building by men standing on the floor or a scaffold.

OVERSAILING COURSE: Applied to brick courses which project beyond the face of a wall.

PALLET BOARDS: Thin boards on which green bricks sit before being taken to the hacks.

PALLET MOULDING: A process for moulding bricks in which they are formed by the introduction of sand as a lubricant to the mould before throwing in the clay. The sand adheres to the wet clay and provides an attractively soft, yet rough, surface. They can be machine or handmade and are extensively used for facings. In addition to pallet moulding, sand-faced bricks may be made from common bricks (e.g. flettons) by sanding one face and one end before firing.

PAMMENTS: Thin and square paving bricks.

PARAPET: A low wall or balustrade which protects the edge of a platform or a roof.

PAVING BRICKS (PAVIORS): Special hard-burned bricks or stones (setts) used for forming pavements and roads.

PEDIMENT: A low-pitched gable above a portico in classical architecture, which may be either straight-sided or curved segmentally.

PENDENTIVE: A concave spandrel (triangular curved surface) set between a pair of supporting arches. It is one of the methods by which a dome can be constructed over a square or polygonal base and was used in Byzantine and occasionally Romanesque architecture, and often in Renaissance, Baroque and later architecture.

PERFORATED BRICKS: Bricks containing vertical perforations, introduced to save material and weight without materially affecting the brick's strength and to allow a solid mass of clay to burn evenly. Most perforated bricks are wire-cut.

PERPENDS: The vertical joints between two bricks, except in batter walls where the perpends are set parallel to the batter, and arches where they are normal to the curve of the arch.

PILASTER: A rectangular or circular pillar which projects about 1/6th of its breadth beyond the face of a wall. It acts like a pier and provides ornamentation.

PINNACLE: A slender turret, usually pointed or cylindrical, and ornamenting the crown of a buttress, gable, spire or tower.

PISÉ or PISÉ DE TERRE: Cob or dry earth mixed with gravel, which is rammed between shuttering whilst the mix is still plastic, and once used for the walls of country cottages and farm buildings.

PLACE BRICKS (PECKINGS): Defective (underburnt) stock bricks which are cheap and used for temporary work.

PLAT BAND: A projecting and unmoulded string course usually indicating the division.

PLINTH: 1. A projection at the base of a wall to give it added strength and rigidity. 2. The lowest member of the base of a column, generally chamfered or moulded at the top.

PLINTH BRICK: A brick with a chamfered edge, mainly used for corbelling or for reducing the thickness of a wall over a plinth. Bricks with a chamfered header are known as plinth headers, and those with a chamfered stretcher as plinth stretchers.

PLUGGING: The removal of mortar from a brick joint with a plugging chisel and the driving in of wood plugs for fixing joinery.

POINTING: The process of raking-out of mortar joints after they have been allowed to stiffen and replacing them with a fresh and richer mortar, usually coloured, before finishing.
FLUSH POINTING: Joints which are pointed but where the excess mortar is rubbed smooth with a piece of rag, rubber or other soft material.
BASTARD TUCK POINTING: Tuck pointing in which a projecting fillet or ridge of the same material is left.
TUCK POINTING: A decorative method of pointing in which the joints are filled with lime putty and a fine joint tuck is cut to give an impression of thin joints.

POLYCHROME BRICKWORK: Coloured bricks set in a regular pattern or arrangement.

POST TENSIONING: A method of compressing a wall in order to increase its resistance to wind forces and bending stresses. The technique requires the anchoring of steel tie rods to the foundation, running continuous rods through the cavity wall, grouting them in, and then torqueing up at the capping beam.

PRESSED BRICKS: Bricks which are moulded under considerable pressure in metal moulds before burning. The best quality pressed bricks are Engineering bricks with smooth faces, frogs and sharp regular arrises.

PROJECTING HEADERS: A decorative technique where the headers project beyond the face of a wall. When the arrangement follows a regular pattern it is reminiscent of diaper work. The regular arrangement of protruding headers has given the technique its nickname of Burglar bond.

PUG: A ball of clay in a plastic state for brickmaking.

PUG MILL: A machine which contains revolving knives to cut and convert stiff brick clays to a uniformly plastic state.

PURPOSE-MADE BRICKS: Bricks which are specially moulded for their particular purpose, as opposed to standard bricks being cut and rubbed to shape. They are chiefly produced for arches and general circular and angular work.

PUTLOG or PUTLOCK: Short horizontal bearers which support scaffold boards. One end is built into the brick wall as it rises and the other is tied to one of the ledgers (uprights) of the scaffold.

PUTLOG HOLES: The small holes in the brickwork or perpends left by the putlogs. They are usually filled after the scaffold is removed but can provide an attractive decorative feature if left blank.

QUEEN CLOSER: A brick which is cut to half the width of an ordinary brick.

QUOINS: 1. The external corners of a wall. 2. Projecting brick panels at the corner of a building imitating dressed stone quoins.

RACKING BACK: The stepping back of each brick course during the erection of a wall for completing or joining up to later.

RADIAL BRICKS: Brick specials which are tapered along their length and used for forming curved or circular work.

RAKING OUT: The removal of mortar from brick joints, usually as a precursor to re-pointing.

REFRACTORY: A term applied to materials, such as clay, which are difficult to fuse and able to resist high temperatures. Typical substances include oxides of silicon, aluminium or magnesium.

REINFORCED BRICKWORK: Brickwork which is strengthened with metal. For additional horizontal strength, expanded metal lath or mesh can be set along the bed joints. Additional horizontal and vertical strength requires the use of perforated bricks where steel reinforcement bars are set within the cavities and surrounded in cement mortar.

RENDERED BRICKWORK: An area of brickwork which is covered with a form of plaster or stucco. It can have numerous finishes, including smooth, rough-cast, scraped or pebble-dash (the application of small washed pebbles on to the wet cement).

RENDERING: The application of plaster or stucco on to a wall.

REPOINTING: The raking out of old and defective mortar and pointing up in fresh mortar.

RETAINING WALL: A wall which supports (retains) a volume of earth or water. It is normally battered.

RETARDERS: Substances which are introduced to hinder or prevent the setting of cement.

RISING COURSE: A row of bricks which taper over a given distance to take up the difference in level between two other courses. They are usually introduced where the course level of two separate brick faces are different.

RUBBED BRICKWORK: See *Gauged brickwork*.

RUBBERS: Soft bricks which are manufactured from sandy loams, and which are suitable for cutting and carving. They are fine grained, uniform and usually available in various colours.

RUSTIC BRICKS: Bricks which have a rough-face. The roughness is achieved by either sand-blasting the face of the brick, impressing a pattern on the green brick, or cutting the green brick with a wire to remove the clay surface. Careful mixing and burning also produces varied colour tones. See *Multi-colour bricks*.

RUSTICATION: A method of emphasizing the large-scale nature of stone blocks in order to give a rich and bold texture. There are six main types: banded (smooth facings with recessed horizontal joints); cyclopean (rough-hewn to resemble quarry cut rocks); diamond-pointed (the cutting of each stone to a point or mini-pyramid); frosted (blocks carved to resemble icicles); smooth (blocks which are neatly finished to present a flat face, and with chamfered edges emphasizing the joints); and vermiculated (blocks carved with shallow and curling channels to resemble work tracks). Banded and smooth rustication is occasionally simulated in brickwork by sinking every fourth or fifth mortar bed, and chamfering (where necessary) the edges of adjacent bricks.

SADDLEBACK COPING BRICK: A brick which includes a two directional slope on its top bed. See *Capping brick* and *Coping brick*.

SAND: Fine particles or siliceous and other stones. Sand which is used to make mortar (or concrete) should be graded, clean and sharp – dirty or greasy sand reduces the mortar's strength. It is used to increase a mortar's bulk for cheapness, counteract shrinkage, increase cohesion and allow air to penetrate the mortar to improve the setting power of lime. Sea sand is not suitable as the high concentrations of sea salts cause efflorescence.

SCROLLWORK: A decoration developed in the 16th century in which the masonry (usually brick or stone) is shaped to resemble a scroll.

SCUTCH, SCUTCHER or SCOTCH: A bricklayer's cutting tool. It resembles a hammer but with a cross peen at either end.

SHALE: See *Clay*.

SHIPPERS: Hard and sound stock bricks, often imperfect in shape, and so named because of their use as ship's ballast.

SILICA: Oxide of silicon. One of the commonest minerals, occurring naturally as quartz, flint etc., it also forms about 60% of brick-earth.

SLAG: The waste product from a blast furnace and used as an aggregate in the manufacture of slag bricks. The presence of sulphur, vitrified metal and glass, fluxes etc, means that it must be used carefully.

SLAG BRICKS: Bricks which are made from blast furnace slag and ground with hydrated lime. These bricks are regular in shape and durable. They are no longer manufactured.

SLOP MOULDING: Applying water as a lubricant to a brick mould to prevent the clay from sticking to the mould.

SOFT BURNT: Clay bricks which are fired at a low temperature. They have low strength and high absorption.

SOFT-MUD PROCESS: The mechanical equivalent of pallet moulding.

SOILING: The application of a sandy loam or cinder dust layer over the clay within settling tanks when brickmaking.

SOLDIER COURSE: A course of bricks on end, so named because they resemble a line of soldiers standing to attention.

SPECIALS: A brick of a non-standard size or shape, and which normally needs to be specially ordered. Special bricks which are normally kept in stock are known as standard specials; those which must be specially made are called special, or non-standard specials.

SPLITS: Bricks which are less than the standard thickness and used in a split course.

SQUINTS: Special moulded or cut bricks which have a corner removed for decorative or bonding purposes. They usually have three-quarters of one stretcher face and one-quarter on a header remaining.

STIFF PLASTIC PROCESS: A process in which a clot of ground, screened and wetted shale is pressed into a smooth-sided rectangular brick shape for firing.

STOCK BOARD: The base of a brick-making mould, which is fixed to the brick maker's bench.

STOCK BRICK: The most commonly available hand moulded bricks with ground fuel additive to aid firing in a clamp. The term is now used to describe the ordinary facing brick from any manufacturer.

STRAIGHT JOINT: 1. A butt joint. 2. A point where two consecutive vertical joints are in the same plane. They inevitably exist in short lengths within thick walls and in some bonds, but should be avoided on face brickwork.

STRAPWORK: A form of decoration which resembles interlocking straps, fretwork and leather, and originating in the 16th century. In brickwork, it is generally produced from carving or rubbing bricks.

STRETCHER: A brick laid with its long face parallel to the length of the wall.

STRETCHING COURSE: A course of stretchers.

STRING COURSE: A continuous plain or moulded projection from a wall to provide a decorative band or dividing line between two parts of a facade.

STUCCO: A plaster which is made from a mixture of lime, marble dust and an adhesive. It is easily moulded but can be applied as a smooth finish, and sets quickly.

TEMPERING: The mixing and preparation of the brick-earth into a homogenous mass before moulding.

TEMPLATE or TEMPLET: A wood or metal pattern or mould.

TERRACOTTA: Building blocks which are made from specially selected and extremely fine refractory brick-earth. They can be moulded to almost any shape before being burnt to vitrification. Terracotta, like bricks, varies in colour according to the chemical composition of the brick-earth. Sand, or ground glass or grog, is sometimes added to prevent excessive shrinkage; the blocks are made hollow with walls and webs (diaphragms) for the same reason, and usually filled with concrete before fixing. It is available as unglazed, glazed or faience, according to the means of firing.

THRESHOLD: The horizontal member, usually timber, at the bottom of a door. In the USA it is also known as Sill or Saddle.

TIE PLATES: A shaped, and often decorative, metal plate placed at the end of each tie rod.

TIE RODS: A steel or wrought iron rod which is threaded through a building and which, when tightened to a state of tension, holds two brick walls together and prevents them from 'bellying' out. Tie rods are often used in place of a tie beam.

TOOTHING: 1. Leaving the end or corner of a wall unfinished by leaving alternate courses to project. This allows a wall and its bond to be extended without further cutting. 2. Removing alternate courses, or several courses together, at intervals in a wall to provide bond for new work.

TRANSOM: A horizontal bar, usually in timber or stone, across the opening of a window or vault.

TUFA: A grey and porous building stone formed from volcanic dust and common in ancient Roman architecture.

TUMBLING or TUMBLING-IN: A term used to describe courses of brickwork which are inclined at right angles to the pitch of a gable or wall until it intersects with normal horizontal brick courses.

VAULT: An arched ceiling or roof, usually composed of brick or stone, and built over an enclosed area such as an underground chamber. Vaults are divided into three main divisions: barrel (tunnel), groined, and ribbed vaults, and elaborated into conoidal, fan, lierne and stellar. The outline may be cylindrical, elliptical, pointed (Gothic) or spherical.

BARREL VAULT: The simplest form of vaulting consisting of continuous semi-circular arches unbroken by cross vaults. Also known as a Tunnel vault or Wagon vault.

CROSS VAULT: See *Groin vault*.

DOMICAL VAULT: A dome which rises direct on a square or polygonal base. In the USA it is known as a Cloister vault.

FAN VAULT: A vault composed of a series of inverted concave-sided semi-cones which meet at the boss of the vault. The cones and flat ceiling area between are normally decorated to give an appearance of highly pronounced ribs. They were a particular feature of the Perpendicular Style of architecture found only in the United Kingdom.

GROIN VAULT: A vault created by the intersection of two identical barrel vaults meeting at a right angle.

PLOUGHSHARE or STILTED VAULT: A vault resulting from the springing of wall ribs at a higher level to the diagonal ribs.

QUADRIPARTITE VAULT: A vault where one bay is divided into four quarters (cells).

RAMPANT VAULT: A barrel vault with abutments and springing points at different levels.

RIBBED VAULT: A vault in which a series of ribs support the cells covering the structure between them.

SEXPARTITE VAULT: A quadripartite vault where one bay is transversely divided into two sections so that each bay has six sections.

STELLAR VAULT: A vault with a series of ribs, liernes and tiercerons in a star pattern.

TUNNEL VAULT: See *Barrel vault*.

'V' BRICK: A large perforated clay brick conceived by the British Building Research Station as a quick and cheap alternative to the traditional cavity wall. Unfortunately, the bricks demanded careful bedding to prevent the mortar from filling the perforations or from extending over the bridging pieces between the perforations. They are no longer produced.

VITRIFIED BRICKS: Bricks which have been glazed on one face through being placed in the hottest part of the kiln, or through the introduction of salt in the kiln during the firing process. The resulting bricks are impervious, and acid and damp-proof.

VOUSSOIRS: See *Arch*.

WALL JOINT: The inner joint between two stretchers in a wall of one or more bricks' thickness, running parallel to the face of the wall. The joint at right angles to the wall face is called a Cross joint.

WALL TIES: Shaped straps for tying together the two leaves of a cavity wall and usually of plastic, galvanized steel, or tarred and sanded iron.

WEEP HOLE: An open vertical joint between two bricks, left to allow water to drain.

WIRE-CUT BRICKS: Extruded clay cut into brick shapes by taut wires.

ASHURST, J. AND N., *Practical Building Conservation*, Volumes 2 and 3, Gower Technical Press, Aldershot 1988

BIDWELL, T. G. (edited by Robert G. D. Brown), *The Conservation of Brick Buildings: the Repair, Alteration and Restoration of Old Brickwork*, Brick Development Association, London 1977

BRASSINGTON, K., [et al], *Brickwork Arch Detailing*, Butterworth Architecture, London 1989

BRUNSKILL, R. W., *Brick Building in Britain*, Victor Gollancz, London 1990

BRUNSKILL, R. W., with ALEC CLIFTON-TAYLOR, *English Brickwork*, Van Nostrand Reinhold Co., London 1977

CASSELL, M., *Dig it, Burn it, Sell it!: The Story of Ibstock Johnsen 1825–1990*, Pencorp, London 1990

CHABAT, P., *La brique et la terre cuite: étude historique de l'emploi de ces matériaux, fabrication et usages, motifs de construction et de décoration choisis dans l'architecture des differents peuples*, Morel, 2 volumes, Paris 1881

CLIFTON-TAYLOR, A., *The Pattern of English Building*, Faber and Faber Ltd, London 1972

CONDIT, C. W., *American Building: Materials and Techniques from the First Colonial Settlements to the Present*, University of Chicago Press, Chicago 1968

COX, A., *Brickmaking: A History and Gazetteer*, Bedfordshire County Council and Royal Commission on Historic Monuments, Bedford 1979

DAVEY, N., *A History of Building Materials*, Phoenix House, London 1961

DAVIS, C. T., *Treatise on the Manufacture of Bricks, Tiles and Terracotta*, Philadelphia 1895

DETHIER, J., *Des Architectures de Terre*, Éditions du Centre Pompidou, Paris 1986

GAULDIE, E., *Cruel Habitations: A History of Working Class Housing 1780–1918*, George Allen and Unwin Ltd, London 1974

GURCKE, K., *Bricks and Brickmaking*, Moscow (Idaho, USA) 1987

HAMMOND, M., *Bricks and Brickmaking*, Shire Publications Ltd, Aylesbury 1990

HANDISYDE, C. C. with B. A. HASLETINE, *Bricks and Brickwork*, Brick Development Association, Windsor 1974

HAUPT, R., *Kurze Geschichte des Ziegelbaus und Geschichte der deutschen Ziegelbaukunst bis durch das zwölfte Jahrhundert*, Heider Anzeiger, Heide in Holstein 1929

HAYWARD, R., *Brick Book*, B. T. Batsford Ltd, London, 1978

HILLIER, R., *Clay That Burns: A History of the Fletton Brick Industry*, London Brick Company, London 1981

HOLLESTELLE, J., *De steenbakkerij in de Nederlanden tot omstreeks 1560*, Van Gorcum & Comp. N. V., Assen 1961

HUDSON, K., *Building Materials*, Longmans, London 1972

JENKINS, D., *Architectural Brickwork*, Studio Editions, London 1990

KEELING, P. S., *The Geology and Mineralogy of Brick Clays*, Brick Development Association, London 1963

KLINKOTT, M., *Die Backsteinbaukunst der Berliner Schule: von K. F. Schinkel bis zum Ausgang des Jahrhunderts*, Mann, Berlin 1988

KNIGHT, T. L., *Illustrated Introduction to Brickwork Design*, Brick Development Association, London 1975

LACROUX, J., *La Brique Ordinaire*, Durcher et Cie Editeurs, Paris 1878

LLOYD, N., *A History of English Brickwork: with examples and notes of the architectural use and manipulation of brick from Medieval Times to the end of the Georgian Period*, H. Grenville Montgomery, London 1925

LYNCH, G. C. J., *Gauged Brickwork: A Technical Manual*, Gower Technical Press, Aldershot 1990

McWHIRR, A. (ed.), *Roman Brick and Tiles: Studies in Manufacture, Distribution and Use in the Western Empire*, British Archeological Reports, No. 68, Oxford 1979

MANG, LE I., *Die Entstehung des Backsteinbaues im Mittelalter in Nordost-deutschlands*, J. H. Ed. Heitz, Strassburg 1931

MITCHELL, G., *Elementary Building Construction*, B. T. Batsford Ltd, London 1961

MITCHELL, G., *Advanced Building Construction*, B. T. Batsford Ltd, London 1963

220

MITCHELL, G. (ed.), Brick Temples of Bengal: From the Archives of David McCutchion, Princeton University Press, Princeton 1983

Per Kirkeby: baksteensculptuur, exhibition catalogue, Rotterdam 1987

PIERS, G., *Uit klei gebouwd*, 2 Volumes: I. *Baksteenarchitektuur van 1200 tot 1940*, and II. *Baksteenarchitektuur na 1945*, Lannoo, Tielt (Belgium) 1979–1982

POWELL, C. G., *An Economic History of the British Building Industry 1815–1979*, Architectural Press, London 1980

ROSS WILLIAMSON, R. P., 'The Progress of Brick Through English History', *Architectural Review*, May 1936

STREET, G. E., *Notes of a Tour in Northern Italy*, Waterstones & Co., London 1986

TREIBER, D. with E. FALK, *La brique et le projet architecture au XIXe siècle*, Ecole Nationale Superieure des Beaux-Arts, Paris 1984

VRIEND, J. J., *The Amsterdam School*, Amsterdam 1977

WACHTSMUTH, F., *Der Backsteinbau der Neuzeit: Die abendländische Backsteinbaukunst vom 15. Jahrhundert bis in die Gegenwart*, N. G. Elwertsche Universitäts und Verlagsbuchhandlung, Marburg 1942

WEISSMAN, A. W., *De gebakken steen*, Ipenbuur & Van Seldam, Amsterdam 1906

WIGHT, J. A., *Brick Building in England from the Middle Ages to 1550*, Baker, London 1972

WOODFORDE, J., *Bricks: To Build A House*, Routledge & Kegan Paul, London 1976

ZANTEN, D. VAN, *The Architectural Polychromy of the 1830s*, Garland Publishing Inc., New York 1977

The publishers wish to thank all individuals, photographers' institutions, and photographic agencies who have kindly supplied photographs for publication in this book.
© Ampliaciones Reproducciones MAS, pages 19, 145. © Ancient Art and Architecture Collection, pages 17, 97, 138, 155. Arcaid/© Mark Fiennes, pages 9, 20/21. Architectural Association/© Caroline Hanbury, page 63 (bottom); © Jo Kerr, pages 104/105; © Mary Parsons, pages 14/15; © Paul Simpson, page 11. B & U International Picture Service/© Werner Otto, pages 23, 25, 29, 65; © Loek Polders, pages 37, 47, 61, 64, 123 (left); © Herman Scholten, pages 28, 63 (top), 93. © Richard Berenholtz, pages 59 (right and left), 88/89, 135, 158. Black Star/© P. F. Bentley, 1985, page 77; © Rick Friedman, 1991, page 2; © Kenneth Hayden, 1991, page 122. © Hedrich Blessing, page 57. © The Brick Development Association, pages 71, 148, 156. © The Brick Institute of America, pages 154, 160. © Martin Charles, pages 50, 51. © Edifice, pages 18, 26, 32, 35, 42, 44, 53, 54 (left and right), 55, 67, 70, 72/73, 75, 78, 80 (top and bottom), 81 (top and bottom), 83, 84, 85, 86, 87, 90, 91, 92, 102, 106, 111, 113, 118, 119, 123 (right), 127, 129, 130, 131, 133, 134, 137, 139, 140, 141, 142, 143, 147, 150, 151, 159. Esto/© Peter Aaron, page 68. © Michael Freeman, pages 12, 13, 31, 38, 39, 40/41, 79, 99, 109, 115, 124, 152. © Hedgerow Publishing, page 136. © Angelo Hornak, pages 30, 52, 108. © Hughes-Gilbey, pages 24, 107. © Ibstock Building Products Ltd, page 117. © The Natural History Museum, London, page 157. © Redland Bricks Company, pages 103, 120/121. © Jo Reid and John Peck, page 95. © Walter Ritchie, page 153. © Royal Scottish Academy of Music and Drama, page 101. The Russia and Republics Photo Library/© Mark Wadlow, page 29.